Brian Melchut
204- 7055 Wu
Burnaby BC V.
521- 9119

D0517516

FIJI
ISLANDS
HANDBOOK

FIJI
ISLANDS
HANDBOOK

DAVID STANLEY

PUBLICATIONS, INC.

FIJI ISLANDS HANDBOOK, 2ND ED.
(Formerly Finding Fiji)

Please send all comments, corrections, additions, amendments, and critiques to:

DAVID STANLEY
c/o MOON PUBLICATIONS, INC.
722 WALL STREET
CHICO CA 95928, USA

Published by
Moon Publications, Inc.
722 Wall Street
Chico, California 95928, USA

Printing History
1st edition —May 1985
reprinted —July 1986
2nd edition —March 1990

Printed by
Colorcraft Ltd.

Library of Congress Cataloging in Publication Data

Stanley, David.
 Fiji Islands Handbook / David Stanley—2nd ed.
 p.198 cm.
 Rev., expanded ed. of: Finding Fiji. c 1985.
 Includes Bibliographical references.
 ISBN 0-918373-45-X : $8.95
 1. Fiji—Description and travel—Guide-books. I. Stanley, David
 Finding Fiji. II. Title.
 DU600.S73   1990   89-13656
 919.611'04—dc20   CIP

Printed in Hong Kong

cover photograph by David Stanley

CONTENTS

LIST OF MAPS

LIST OF CHARTS

SPELLING AND PRONUNCIATION

When 19th-century English missionaries created a written form of Fijian they rendered "mb" as "b," "nd" as "d," "ng" as "g," "ngg" as "q," and "th" as "c." For the convenience of travelers in this book we use the phonetic form, spelling "Ba" as Mba, "Nadi" as Nandi, "Sigatoka" as Singatoka, "Qamea" as Nggamea, and "Cicia" as Thithia. Most official Fiji government maps also use phonetic spelling. We feel that in a practical travel guide it's better to risk upsetting purists than have visitors going around mispronouncing place names and words. (The surnames of individuals are written in the Fijian manner, however.) Always keep this factor in mind as most local signs use the indigenous Fijian spelling.

ABBREVIATIONS

A$—Australian dollars
a/c—air conditioned
BBQ—barbecue
C—Centigrade
C.—century
d—double occupancy
DMA—Defense
   Mapping Agency
EEZ—Exclusive
   Economic Zone
F$—Fiji dollars
I.—Island
Is.—Islands
km—kilometer

kph—kilometers per hour
LMS—London Mission
   ary Society
MV—motor vessel
no.—number
N.Z.—New Zealand
OW—one way
PNG—Papua New Guinea
pp—per person
P.W.D.—Public Works
   Dept.
Rep.—Republic
RR—railroad
RT—roundtrip

s—single occupancy
SDA—Seventh-day
   Adventist
SPF—South Pacific
   Forum
t—triple occupancy
tel.—telephone
US$—U.S. dollars
WW II—World War Two
YHA—Youth Hostel
   Association
YWCA—Young
   Women's Christian
   Association

PHOTO AND ILLUSTRATION CREDITS

Illustrations: Salvatore Casa—pages 11, 81, 103, 123, 131, 139, 145, 155, 165, 171, 179; Louise Foote—pages 54, 65, 75, 92, 132, 137, 154; Diana Lasich—pages 18. 53. 122. 164. 169. 177; **Photos:** David Stanley—pages 39, 48, 49, 52, 95, 102, 106, 132, 134; *The Fiji Times*—pages 41, 119, 147, 148, 153, 166; Ministry of Information Government of Fiji—pages 34, 42, 44, 107; Caines Jannif LTD., Suva—pages 23, 38; Special Collection, Meriam Library, California State University, Chico—pages 27, 69; Richard Goodman—page 85; Bob Halstead—page 73; Doug Hankin—page 84; McKee/Rapport—page 26; Fiji Visitors Bureau—page 113; Field Museum of Natural History, Chicago—page 45.

ACKNOWLEDGEMENTS

Thanks to all the people at Moon Publications who worked on this book, especially editors Deke Castleman and Taran March. If the book reads smoothly, thank them. The maps were drawn by Alexandra Foote, Louise Foote, and Robert Race. Todd Clark and David Hurst designed, layed out, and pasted up the book . Christa Jorgensen proofread the set galleys and checked the hyphenation. Bette, Bill, Cindy, Donna, Lucinda, Magnus, Mark, Michelle, Rick, Robert K., and Virginia all contributed in their own ways.

I'm grateful to Sven Rosen for the tale of Count Felix von Luckner, to Peter Goodman for a very amusing nine-page letter, to D.B. Costello of Islands in the Sun and Wame Waqanisanini of the Fiji Visitors Bureau for color photos, and to Phil Esmonde of the South Pacific Peoples Foundation of Canada for a big box of resouces.

Many thanks to the following readers who sent in updating information since publication of the first edition of this book in 1985: Catherine Ammon, A.D. Anderson, Morgan Armstrong, Lucy Barefoot, John Birch, Angie Borden, David Bowden, Andrew Boyle, Robert Budin, Ric Cammick, Mark Chaffey, Rhoda Chaloff, Lal Chand, Julie A. Chesterman, Jack L. Cooper, Mary T. Crowley, S.J. Diston, George Duane, P. Erbsleben, Hedy Fischer, Edward Fox, Daniel S. Galanis, Mark Gallini, Michael Ghent, Katia Giscombe, Diane Goodwillie, Delia Gorey, Al Grobmeier, Valentine Guinness, Jack Haden, Doug Hankin, Marth M. Hassall, Josje Hebbes, Andrea Hemmann, Alan Jenkins, Dale Keeling, Robert Kennington, Sanford Kent, David K. King, Stacy Kunz-Ciulik, Richard S. Lowe, David MacDonald, Mario Maffi, John Maidment, John Malakkey, Lawrence Manson, Mike Mason, Frederick H. Matteson, James L. McKenna, Chris McLowerty, Dr. E. Morent, Glenn and Rhonda Mulligan, Don Mundell, Ruth O'Connor, Marcus Oliver, Mrs. E.A. Penn, Gerry Phillips, Richard Phinney, V.R. Ralogaivau, Juergen Rammelt, Dr. Van Richards, Theresa Rietberg, Sven Rosen, Peter Rumsitt, Brian Rutherford, Beatrice Schnidrig, Katja Schwarmann, Jamey Sorensen, Kevin Stanway, Boguslaw Szemioth, Mary Ellen Timmons, Carla Timpone, Kik Velt, Gisela E. Walther, Dave Weber, Leon Werdinger, Marge Williams, Nancy Winfrey, Corrie Wright, Juliet Yee, and Andy Zender. Thank you all.

IS THIS BOOK OUT OF DATE?

Travel writing is like trying to take a picture out the side of a bus: time frustrates the best of intentions. Because it takes over a year to research and write a new edition some things are bound to have changed. So if something is out of date, please let us hear about it. Did anything lead you astray or inconvenience you? In retrospect, what sort of information would have made your trip easier? If you're an island entrepreneur with a service or product to offer travelers, do bring it to our attention. When writing please be as precise and accurate as you can. Notes made on the scene are far better than later recollections. Make notes in your copy of *Fiji Islands Handbook* as you go along, then send us a summary when you get home. If this book helped you, please help us make it even better. Address your letters to:

David Stanley,
c/o Moon Publications,
722 Wall St.,
Chico, CA 95928 USA

INTRODUCTION

Once notorious as the "Cannibal Isles," Fiji is now the crossroads of the Pacific. Of the 322 islands that make up the Fiji Group, over 100 are inhabited by a rich mixture of vibrant, exuberant Melanesians, East Indians, Polynesians, Micronesians, Chinese, and Europeans, each with a cuisine and culture of their own. Here Melanesia mixes with Polynesia, ancient India with the Pacific, tradition with the modern world, in a unique blend. There's a diversity of landforms and seascapes, and a fascinating human history. Prices are affordable with a wide range of accommodations and travel options. Whatever your budget Fiji gives you good value for your money and plenty of ways to spend it.

Fiji preserves an amazing variety of traditional customs and crafts such as kava drinking, the presentation of whales' teeth, firewalking, fish driving, turtle calling, tapa beating, and pottery-making. Fiji offers posh resorts, good food and accommodations, night life, historic sights, outer-island living, hiking, camping, surfing, snorkeling, skin diving, and river running, plus travel by small plane, inter-island ferry, copra boat, outboard canoe, open-sided bus, or air-conditioned coach. Fiji's sun-drenched beaches, blue lagoons, panoramic open hillsides, lush rainforests, and dazzling reefs are truly magnificent. You'll barely scratch the surface of all there is to see and do.

In 1987 the backers of Fijian feudalism staged two bloodless military coups against the democratically elected government, shattering Fiji's delicate racial balance and throwing the country's political development back six decades. Since then things seem to have quieted down, but Fiji will never be the same again. For visitors there's only the slight inconvenience of having everything beyond the hotel doors closed on Sunday; both indigenous Fijians and Fiji Indians remain as friendly and welcoming as ever. The struggles of the peoples of the South Pacific for land rights, equality, social justice, and freedom from imperialism seem to have come together in Fiji and have torn the heart of this captivating, enchanting land.

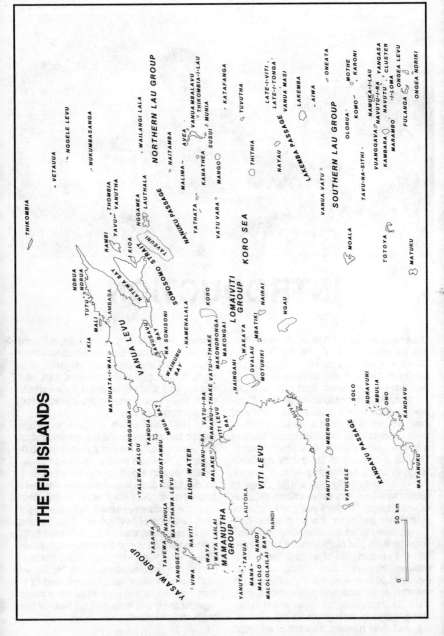

THE FIJI ISLANDS

THE PHYSICAL SETTING

THE LAND

Fiji sits in the middle of the main air route between North America and Australia, 4,450 km southwest of Hawaii and 2,730 km northeast of Sydney. Nandi is the hub of Pacific air routes, while Suva is a regional shipping center. The 180th meridian cuts through Fiji, but the International Dateline swings east so the entire group can share the same day. Together the Fiji Islands are scattered over 1,290,000 square km of the South Pacific Ocean.

The name Fiji is a Tongan corruption of the indigenous name "Viti." The Fiji Islands are arrayed in a horseshoe configuration with Viti Levu ("Great Fiji") and adjacent islands on the west, Vanua Levu ("Great Land") and Taveuni to the north, and the Lau Group on the east. This upside-down U-shaped archipelago encloses the Koro Sea, which is relatively shallow and sprinkled with more islands.

If every single island were counted the isles of the Fiji archipelago would number in the thousands. A mere 322 are judged large enough for human habitation however and of these only 106 are inhabited. That leaves 216 uninhabited islands, most of them prohibitively isolated or lacking the fresh water necessary for life.

Most of the Fiji Islands are volcanic, remnants of a sunken continent which stretched through Australia. This origin accounts for the mineral deposits on the main islands. The two largest islands, Viti Levu and Vanua Levu, together account for 87% of Fiji's 18,376 square km of land. Viti Levu has 50% of the land area and three-quarters of the people, while Vanua Levu with 30% of the land has 18% of the population. Viti Levu alone is bigger than all five archipelagos of Tahiti-Polynesia; in fact Fiji has more land and people than all of Polynesia combined.

The 1,000-meter-high Nandrau Plateau in central Viti Levu is cradled between Tomanivi (1,323 meters) on the north and Monavatu (1,131 meters) on the south. On different sides of this elevated divide are the Tholo-

FIJI AT A GLANCE

ISLAND	AREA (sq. km)	HIGHEST POINT (meters)	POPULATION (mid-1988 est.)	PERCENT FIJIAN*
Viti Levu	10,429	1,323	508,777	40.5
Vanua Levu	5,556	1,032	117,790	43.3
Taveuni	470	1,241	8,799	72.7
Kandavu	411	838	9,936	98.1
Ngau	140	747	3,054	99.4
Koro	104	522	3,654	98.5
Ovalau	101	626	6,660	88.3
Rambi	69	463	2,771	5.0
Rotuma	47	256	3,204	1.9
Mbengga	36	439	1,488	98.6

* Viti Levu, Vanua Levu, and Taveuni have sizable Fijian Indian populations, while Rambi is Micronesian and Rotuma is Polynesian.

East Plateau drained by the Rewa River, the Navosa Plateau drained by the Mba, the Tholo-West Plateau drained by the Singatoka, and the Navua Plateau drained by the Navua. Some 29 well-defined peaks rise above Viti Levu's interior; most of the people live in the river valleys or along the coast.

The Nandi River slices across the Nausori Highlands with the Mount Evans Range (1,195 meters) towering above Lautoka. Other highland areas are cut by great rivers like the Singatoka, Navua, Rewa, and Mba, navigable far inland by outboard canoe or kayak. Whitewater rafters shoot down the Navua and Mba, while the Singatoka flows through Fiji's market garden "salad bowl." Fiji's largest river, the Rewa, pours into the Pacific through a wide delta just below Nausori. After a hurricane the Rewa becomes a dark torrent worth going out of your way to see. Sharks have been known to enter both the Rewa and the Singatoka and swim far upstream.

Vanua Levu has a peculiar shape with two long peninsulas pointing northeast. A mountain range between Lambasa and Savusavu reaches 1,032 meters at Nasorolevu. Navotuvotu (842 meters), east of Mbua Bay, is Fiji's best example of a broad shield volcano with lava flows built up in layers. The mountains are closer to the southeast coast, and a broad lowland belt runs along the northwest. Of the rivers only the Ndreketi, flowing west across northern Vanua Levu, is large; navigation on the Lambasa is restricted to small boats. The interior of Vanua Levu is lower and drier than Viti Levu, yet scenically superb: the road from Lambasa to Savusavu is a visual delight.

Vanua Levu's bullet-shaped neighbor Taveuni soars to 1,241 meters, its rugged east coast battered by the southeast trades. Taveuni and Kandavu are known as the finest islands in Fiji for their scenic beauty and agricultural potential. Geologically the uplifted limestone islands of the Lau Group have more in common with Tonga than with the rest of Fiji.

Fringing reefs are common along most of the coastlines, and Fiji is outstanding for its many barrier reefs. The Great Sea Reef off the north coast of Vanua Levu is the fourth longest in the world, and the Astrolabe Reef north of Kandavu is one of the most colorful. Countless other unexplored barrier reefs are found off northern Viti Levu and elsewhere. The many cracks and crevices along Fiji's reefs are guaranteed to delight the scuba diver.

CORAL REEFS

To understand how a basalt volcano becomes a limestone atoll, it's necessary to know a little about the growth of coral. Coral reefs cover some 200,000 square km worldwide, between 35 degrees north and 32 degrees south latitude. A reef is created by the accumulation of millions of tiny calcareous skeletons left by myriad generations of tiny coral polyps. Though the skeleton is usually white, the living polyps are of many different colors. They thrive in clear salty water where the temperature never drops below 20 degrees centigrade. They must also have a base not over 25 meters from the surface on which to form.

The coral colony grows slowly upward on the consolidated skeletons of its ancestors until it reaches the low-tide mark, after which development extends outward on the edges of the reef. Sunlight is critical for coral growth. Colonies grow quickly on the ocean side due to clearer water and a greater abundance of food. A strong healthy reef can grow four to five cm a year. Fresh or cloudy water inhibits coral growth, which is why villages and ports all across the Pacific are located at the reef-free mouths of rivers.

Polyps extract calcium carbonate from the water and deposit it in their skeletons. All reef-building corals also contain limy encrustations of microscopic algae within their cells. The algae, like all green plants, obtain their energy from the sun and contribute this energy to the growth of the reef's skeleton. As a result, corals behave (and look) more like plants than animals, competing for sunlight just as terrestrial plants do. Some polyps are

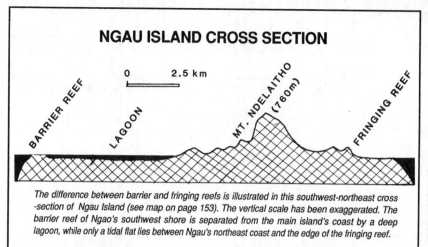

NGAU ISLAND CROSS SECTION

0   2.5 km

BARRIER REEF

LAGOON

MT. NDELAITHO (760m)

FRINGING REEF

The difference between barrier and fringing reefs is illustrated in this southwest-northeast cross -section of Ngau Island (see map on page 153). The vertical scale has been exaggerated. The barrier reef of Ngao's southwest shore is separated from the main island's coast by a deep lagoon, while only a tidal flat lies between Ngau's northeast coast and the edge of the fringing reef.

also carnivorous; with minute stinging tentacles they supplement their energy by capturing small planktonic animals at night. A small piece of coral is a colony composed of large numbers of polyps.

Exploring A Reef

Until you've explored a good coral reef, you haven't experienced one of the greatest joys of nature. Dive shops throughout Fiji rent scuba and snorkeling gear, so do get into the clear, warm waters around you. Be careful, however, and know the dangers. Practice snorkeling in the shallow water; don't head into deep water until you're sure you've got the hang of it. Breathe easily; don't hyperventilate.

When snorkeling on a fringing reef, beware of deadly currents and undertows in channels which drain tidal flows. Observe the direction the water is flowing before you swim into it. If you feel yourself being dragged out to sea through a reef passage, try swimming across the current rather than against it. If you can't resist the pull at all, it may be better to let yourself be carried out. Wait till the current diminishes, then swim along the outer reef face until you find somewhere to come back

in. Or use your energy to attract the attention of someone on shore. Most beach drownings occur in such situations, so try not to panic.

Snorkeling on the outer edge or drop-off of a reef is thrilling for the variety of fish and corals, but only attempt it on a very calm day. Even then it's best to have someone on shore or standing on the edge of the reef (at low tide) to watch for occasional big waves which can take you by surprise and smash you into the rocks. Also beware of unperceived currents outside the reef—you may not get a second chance.

A far better idea is to limit your snorkeling to the protected inner reef and leave the open waters to the scuba diver. Many of the scuba operators listed in this book offer resort courses for beginning divers. They know their waters and will be able to show you the most amazing things in perfect safety. Diving is possible year-round, with marinelife most profuse from July to November. All scuba divers must have a medical report from their doctors indicating that they are in good physical condition. Divers should bring their certification card, buoyancy compensator, and regulator. The main constraint is financial: snorkeling is free, while scuba diving becomes expensive.

FIJI CLIMATE CHART

LOCATION		JAN.	FEB.	MAR.	APRIL	MAY	JUNE	JULY	AUG.	SEPT.	OCT.	NOV.	DEC.	ALL YEAR
Nandi airport, Viti Levu	C	27.0	26.9	26.7	26.2	25.0	24.0	23.3	23.8	24.5	25.2	25.9	26.6	25.4
	mm	294	291	373	195	99	78	51	62	88	73	137	181	1922
Yasawa Island	C	27.0	26.9	26.6	26.4	26.0	25.3	24.6	24.8	25.1	25.7	26.1	26.7	25.9
	mm	281	287	344	168	110	106	45	68	90	78	187	165	1929
Mba, Viti Levu	C	27.2	27.1	26.9	26.5	25.3	24.1	23.3	23.8	24.7	25.5	26.1	26.1	25.6
	mm	322	409	387	203	101	67	46	65	72	91	126	228	2117
Nandarivatu, Viti Levu	C	21.6	22.0	21.5	21.0	20.0	18.9	18.3	18.8	19.0	20.1	20.6	21.1	20.2
	mm	599	668	689	362	181	99	89	125	126	136	220	400	3694
Rakiraki, Viti Levu	C	27.6	27.6	27.3	26.8	25.9	24.9	24.2	24.6	25.1	25.9	26.6	27.1	26.2
	mm	307	371	372	236	122	66	47	68	74	83	140	221	2107
Suva, Viti Levu	C	26.8	26.9	26.8	26.1	24.8	23.9	23.1	23.2	23.7	24.4	25.3	26.2	25.1
	mm	314	299	386	343	280	177	148	200	212	218	268	313	3158
Vunisea, Kandavu I.	C	26.4	26.8	26.1	25.4	24.2	23.2	22.4	22.6	23.1	23.9	24.7	26.1	24.6
	mm	239	225	313	256	208	102	112	121	122	126	151	177	2152
Nambouwalu, Vanua Levu	C	26.9	27.1	26.7	26.3	25.5	24.7	23.9	24.0	24.4	25.2	25.4	26.3	25.6
	mm	328	354	352	275	198	130	96	114	139	164	208	279	2637
Lambasa, Vanua Levu	C	26.8	26.8	26.6	26.2	25.3	24.4	23.8	24.2	24.7	25.4	25.9	26.4	25.6
	mm	449	457	465	236	97	86	38	60	77	96	210	263	2534
Vunikondi, Vanua Levu	C	26.6	26.7	26.6	26.3	26.0	25.3	24.6	24.7	25.0	25.6	25.9	26.6	25.8
	mm	302	377	409	225	143	131	92	90	114	132	264	220	2499
Rotuma Island	C	27.4	27.3	27.2	27.4	27.2	26.8	26.4	26.5	26.7	26.8	27.0	27.2	27.0
	mm	358	390	430	278	262	244	207	230	277	283	327	331	3617
Matuku, Lau Group	C	26.8	27.0	26.8	26.3	25.1	24.1	23.1	23.6	24.2	25.0	25.7	26.4	25.3
	mm	231	230	265	192	151	116	114	78	110	97	139	152	1875
Ono-i-Lau, Lau Group	C	26.3	26.5	26.4	25.7	24.3	23.4	22.4	22.4	22.7	23.6	24.5	25.3	24.4
	mm	201	199	266	196	144	109	90	94	106	114	128	145	1792

CLIMATE

Along the coast the weather is warm and pleasant without great variations in temperature. The southeast trades prevail from June to Oct., the best months to visit. In Feb. and March the wind often comes directly out of the east. These winds dump 3,000 mm of annual rainfall on the humid southeast coasts of the big islands, increasing to 5,000 mm inland. The drier northwest coasts, in the lee,

SUVA'S CLIMATE

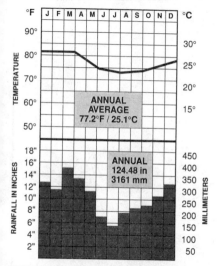

notes on the climate charts: The top figure indicates the average monthly temperatures in degrees and tenths centigrade, while the monthly rainfall average in millimeters (mm) is given below. The last column gives the annual temperature, and the total precipitation during the year. These figures have been averaged over a minimum of 10 years and, in most cases, much longer. Altitude is a factor at Nandarivatu (835 meters); all of the others are very near sea level. It will be seen that temperatures don't vary too much year-round, but there is a pronounced dry season mid-year. Note too that some areas of Fiji are far drier than others.

get only 1,500 to 2,000 mm. Yet even during the rainy months (Dec. to April) bright sun often follows the rains.

The official dry season (June to Oct.) is not always dry at Suva although most of the rain falls at night. In addition, Fiji's winter (May to Nov.) is cooler and less humid, the best months for mountain trekking. During the drier season the reef waters are clearest for the scuba diver. Summer (Dec. to April) is hurricane season, with Fiji, Samoa, and Tonga receiving up to five storms annually. But even in summer the refreshing tradewinds relieve the high humidity.

FLORA

The flora of Fiji originated in the Malaysian region; ecological niches are filled by similar plants in the two regions. There are over 3,000 species of plants in Fiji, a third of them endemic. Of the large islands Taveuni is known for its rare climbing *tangimauthia* flower. The absence of leaf-eating animals in Fiji allowed the vegetation to develop largely without the protective spines and thorns found elsewhere.

NANDI'S CLIMATE

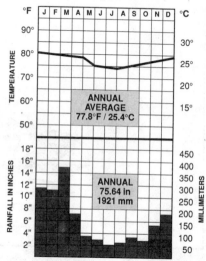

Patterns of rainfall are in large part responsible for the variety of scenery here. The wetter sides of the high islands are heavily forested, with occasional thickets of bamboo and scrub where the original vegetation has been destroyed by slash-and-burn agriculture. Coconut groves fill the coastal plains. On the drier sides open savannah or *talasinga* of coarse grasses predominates, with sugar cane cultivated in the lowlands. Caribbean pine has been planted in many dry hilly areas. The low islands of the Lau Group are restricted to a few hardy, drought-resistant species such as coconuts and pandanus.

Mangroves can occasionally be found in river deltas and along some high-island coastal lagoons. The cable roots of the saltwater-tolerant mangroves anchor in the shallow upper layer of oxygenated mud, avoiding the layers of hydrogen sulphide below. The tree provides shade for tiny organisms dwelling in the tidal mudflats—a place for birds to nest and fish or shellfish to feed and spawn. The mangroves also perform the same task as land-building coral colonies along the reefs. As sediments are trapped between the roots, the trees extend farther into the lagoon, creating a unique natural

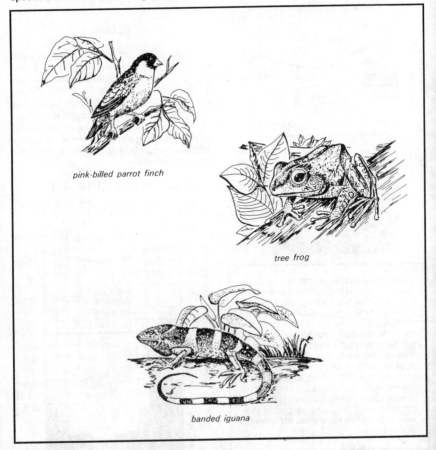

pink-billed parrot finch

tree frog

banded iguana

environment. The past decade has seen widespread destruction of the mangroves as land is reclaimed for agricultural use in north-west Viti Levu and around Lambasa.

Though only introduced to Fiji in the late 1860s, sugar cane probably originated in the South Pacific. On New Guinea the islanders have cultivated the plant for thousands of years, selecting vigorous varieties with the most colorful stems. The story goes that two Melanesian fishermen, To-Kabwana and To-Karavuvu, found a piece of sugar cane in their net one day. They threw it away, but after catching it again on the next two days, decided to keep it and painted the stalk a bright color. Eventually the cane burst and a woman came forth. She cooked food for the men but hid herself at night. Finally she was captured and became the wife of one of the men. From their union sprang the whole human race.

FAUNA

Of the 70 species of land birds, 22 are endemic including broadbills, cuckoos, doves, fantails, finches, flycatchers, fruitdoves, hawks, honeyeaters, kingfishers, lories, parrots, pigeons, rails, silktails, and warblers. The Fijian names of some of these birds, such as the *kaka* (parrot) and *kikau* (giant honeyeater), imitate their calls. Of the seabirds boobies, frigate birds, petrels, and tropicbirds are present. More in evidence is the introduced Indian mynah, with its yellow beak and legs, the bulbul, and the Malay turtle dove. The best time to observe forest birds is in the very early morning—they move around a lot less in the heat of the day.

The Indian mongoose was introduced by planters in the 1880s to combat rats which were damaging the plantations. Unfortunately, no one realized at the time that the mongoose hunts by day whereas the rats are nocturnal; thus, the two seldom meet. Today, the mongoose is the scourge of chickens, native ground birds, and other animals, though Taveuni is mongoose-free. In 1936 the giant toad was introduced from Hawaii to control beetles, slugs, and millepedes. When this food source is exhausted they tend to eat each other. At night gardens and lawns may be full of them.

The only native mammals are the fruit bat or flying fox, the insect-eating bat, and the Polynesian grey rat. Two species of snakes inhabit Fiji: the very rare, poisonous *bolo loa,* and the harmless Pacific boa, which can grow up to two meters long. Venomous sea snakes are common on some coasts, but docile and easily handled. The land- and tree-dwelling native frogs are noteworthy for the long suction discs on their fingers and toes. Because they live deep in the rainforests and feed at night, they are seldom seen. Some Fijian clans have totemic relationships with eels, prawns, turtles, and sharks and are able to summon these creatures with special chants.

One of the more unusual creatures found in Fiji and Tonga is the banded iguana, a lizard which lives in trees and can grow up to 70 cm long (two-thirds of which is tail). The iguanas are emerald green, and the male is easily distinguished from the female by his bluish-gray cross stripes. Banded iguanas change color to control their internal temperature, becoming darker when in the direct sun. Their nearest relatives are found in South America and Madagascar, and no lizards live farther east in the Pacific than these. In 1979 a new species, the crested iguana, was discovered on Yanduatambu, a small island off the west coast of Vanua Levu.

Four of the world's seven species of sea turtles nest in Fiji: the green, hawksbill, loggerhead, and leatherback. Nesting occurs from Nov. to Feb. at night when there is a full moon and a high tide. The female struggles up the beach and lays as many as 100 eggs in a hole which she digs and then covers with her hind flippers. The eggs are protected by law in Fiji, as are leatherback turtles, turtles with shells under 46 cm long, and all turtles during the nesting season. Persons who take eggs or turtles at this time are violating the Fisheries Act and face heavy fines.

HISTORY

The Pre-European Period

The first people to arrive in Fiji were of a broad-nosed, light-skinned Austronesian-speaking race, probably the Polynesians. They originated in insular Southeast Asia and gradually migrated east past the already occupied islands of Melanesia. Distinctive *lapita* pottery, decorated in horizontal geometric bands and dated from 1290 B.C., has been found in the sand dunes near Singatoka, indicating they had reached here by 1500 B.C. or earlier. Much later, about 500 B.C., Melanesian people arrived, bringing with them their distinct pottery traditions. From the fusion of these primordial peoples the Fijian race was born.

The hierarchical social structure of the early Fijians originated with the Polynesians. Status and descent passed through the male line and power was embodied in the *turanga* or chief. The hereditary chiefs possessed the *mana* of an ancestral spirit or *vu*. This feudal aristocracy combined in confederations or *vanua* and extended their influence through war. Treachery and cannibalism were an intrinsic part of these struggles; women were taken as prizes or traded to form alliances. Villages were fortified with ditches or built along ridges or terraced hillsides for defense.

The native aristocracy practiced customs which today seem barbarous and particularly cruel. The skull cap of a defeated enemy might be polished and used as a *yanggona* (kava) cup to humiliate the foe. Some chiefs even took delight in cooking and consuming bodily parts as their agonizing victims looked on. Men were buried alive to hold up the posts of new houses, war canoes were launched over the living bodies of young girls, and the widows of chiefs were strangled to keep their husbands company in the spirit world. The farewells of some of these women are remembered today in dances and songs known as *meke*.

These feudal islanders were, on the other hand, guardians of one of the highest material cultures of the Pacific. They built great oceangoing double canoes up to 30 meters long, constructed and adorned large solid thatched houses (*mbures*),

Fijian ndrua: These heavy, double-hulled canoes were sometimes more than 30 meters in length. William Lockerby, an early Pacific traveler describes one in which he was held prisoner in 1808. "The canoe I was held in," he wrote, "was one of the largest size of double canoe; it consisted of two single ones joined together by a platform, in the middle of which the mast was fixed. Round the sides of platform there was a strong breast work of bamboo, behind which they (the Fijians) stand in engaging the enemy. There was also a house on the platform which is erected and taken down as circumstances require. The number of men on board amounted to 200. Captain Cook's account of the sailing of these vessels is quite correct, however incredible it may appear to those who may not have seen them. With a moderate wind they will sail 20 miles an hour." Nineteenth-century Fijians showed great skill in handling these large catamaran canoes.

performed marvelous song-dances called *meke,* made tapa, pottery, and sinnit (coconut cordage), and skillfully plaited mats. Tongans had been coming to Fiji for centuries to obtain sandalwood for carving and great logs from which to make canoes.

European Exploration

In 1643 Abel Tasman became the European discoverer of Fiji when he sighted Taveuni, though he didn't land. Tasman was searching for *terra australis incognita,* a great southern continent believed to balance the continents of the north. He also hoped to find new markets and trade routes. Unlike earlier Spanish explorers, Tasman entered the Pacific from the west rather than the east. Apart from Fiji, he was the first European to see Tasmania, New Zealand, and Tonga. By sailing right around Australia from the Dutch East Indies he proved New Holland (Australia) was not attached to the elusive southern continent.

In 1779, Capt. Cook anchored off Vatoa (which he named Turtle Island) in Southern Lau. Like Tasman he failed to proceed farther or land and it was left to Capt. William Bligh to give Europeans an accurate picture of Fiji for the first time. After the *Bounty* mutiny in May 1789, Bligh and his companions were chased by canoe-loads of Fijian warriors just north of the Yasawa Islands as they rowed through on their escape route to Timor; some serious paddling, a timely squall, and a lucky gap in the Great Sea Reef saved the Englishmen from ending up as the main course at a cannibal feast. The section of sea where this happened is now known as Bligh Water. Bligh cut directly across the center of Fiji between the two main islands and his careful observations made him the first real European explorer of Fiji, albeit an unwilling one. Bligh returned to Fiji in 1792 but once again stayed aboard ship.

Beachcombers And Chiefs

All of these early explorers stressed the perilous nature of Fiji's reefs; this, combined with tales told by the Tongans of cannibalism and warlike Fijian natives, caused most travelers to shun the area. Then in 1804 a survivor from the shipwrecked American schooner *Argo* brought word that sandalwood grew abundantly along the Mbua coast of Vanua Levu. This precipitated a rush of traders and beachcombers to the islands. A cargo of sandalwood bought from the islanders for $50 worth of trinkets could be sold to the Chinese at Canton for $20,000. By 1814 the forests had been stripped to provide joss sticks and incense, and the trade collapsed.

During this period Fiji was divided among warring chieftains. The first Europeans to actually mix with the Fijians were escaped convicts from Australia, who instructed the natives in the use of European muskets and were thus well received. White beachcombers such as the Swedish adventurer Charles Savage acted as middlemen between traders and Fijians and took sides in local conflicts. In one skirmish Savage was separated from his fellows, captured, and eaten. With help from the likes of Savage, Naulivou, the cannibal chief of tiny Mbau Island just off eastern Viti Levu, and his brother Tanoa extended their influence over much of western Fiji.

In his book *Following the Equator* Mark Twain had this to say about the beachcombers:

They lived worthless lives of sin and luxury, and died without honor—in most cases by violence. Only one of them had any ambition; he was an Irishman named Connor. He tried to raise a family of fifty children and scored forty-eight. He died lamenting his failure. It was a foolish sort of avarice. Many a father would have been rich enough with forty.

From 1827 to 1850 European traders collected beche-de-mer, a sea slug which, when smoked and dried, also brought a good price in China. While the sandalwood traders only stayed long enough to take on a load, the beche de mer collectors set up shore facilities where the slugs were processed. Many traders such as David Whippy followed the example of the beachcombers and took local wives, establishing the Part Fijian community of today. By monopolizing the beche de mer trade and constantly warring, Chief Tanoa's son and successor, Ratu Seru Cakobau (pronounced Thakombau), became extremely powerful in the 1840s, proclaiming himself Tui Viti or king of Fiji.

The beginnings of organized trade brought a second wave of official explorers to Fiji. In 1838 Dumont d'Urville landed on Mbau Island and met Tanoa. The Frenchmen caused consternation and confusion by refusing to drink yanggona (kava) in preference to their own wine. The American Exploring Expedition of 1840 led by Commodore Charles Wilkes produced the first recognizable map of Fiji. When two Americans, including a nephew of Wilkes, were speared on a beach at Malolo Island in a misunderstanding, Wilkes ordered the offending fortified village stormed and 87 Fijians were killed. The survivors were made to water and provision Wilkes' ships as tribute. Capt. H.M. Denham of the HMS Herald prepared accurate navigational charts of the group in 1855-56, making regular commerce possible.

European And Tongan Penetration

As early as the 1830s an assortment of European and American beachcombers had formed a small settlement at Levuka on the east coast of Ovalau Island just northeast of Mbau, which whalers and traders used as a supply base. In 1846 John Brown Williams was appointed American commercial agent. On 4 July 1849 Williams' home on Nukulau Island near present Suva burned down. Though the conflagration was caused by the explosion of a cannon during Williams' own fervent celebration of his national holiday, he objected to the way Fijian onlookers carried off items they rescued from the flames. A shameless swindler, Williams had purchased Nululau for only $30 yet he blamed the Tui Viti for his losses and sent Cakobau a $5001.38 bill. American claims for damages eventually rose to $44,000 and in 1851 and 1855 American gunboats called and ordered Cakobau to pay up. This threat hung over Cakobau's head for many years, the 19th century equivalent of a 20th century Third World debt.

The early 1830s also saw the arrival from Tonga of the first missionaries. Though Tahitian pastors were sent by the London Missionary Society to Oneata in southern Lau as early as 1830, it was the Methodists based at Lakemba after 1835 who made the most lasting impression by rendering the Fijian language into writing. At first Christianity made little headway among these fierce, idolatrous people. Only after converting the powerful chiefs were the missionaries successful. Methodist missionaries Cargill and Cross were appalled by what they saw during a visit to Mbau in 1838. A white missionary, Rev. Thomas Baker, was clubbed and eaten in central Viti Levu as late as 1867.

In 1847 Enele Ma'afu, a member of the Tongan royal family, arrived in Lau and began building a personal empire under the pretense of defending Christianity. In 1853 King George of Tonga made Ma'afu governor of all Tongans resident in Lau. Meanwhile there was continuing resistance to Cakobau's dominance from the warlords of the Rewa River area. In addition the Europeans at Levuka suspected Cakobau of twice ordering their town set afire and were directing trade away from Mbau. With his power in decline Cakobau accepted Christianity in 1854 in exchange for an alliance with King George. With the help of 2,000 Tongans personally led by their king Cakobau put down the Rewa revolt in 1855. In the process, however, Ma'afu became the dominant force in Lau, Taveuni, and Vanua Levu.

During the 1860s, as Americans fought their Civil War, the world price of cotton soared, and large numbers of Europeans arrived in Fiji hoping to establish cotton plantations. In 1867 the USS Tuscarora called at Levuka and threatened to bombard the town unless the still-outstanding American debt was paid. The next year an enterprising Australian firm, the Polynesia Company, paid off the Americans in exchange for a grant of 80,000 hectares of choice land including the site of modern Suva from Cakobau. (The British government later refused to recognize this grant, though they refunded the money paid to the Americans and accepted the claims of settlers who had purchased land from the company.) The settlers soon numbered around 2,000 and Levuka boomed.

It was a lawless era and a need was felt for a central government. An attempt at national rule by a council of chiefs failed in 1867, then three regional governments were set up in Mbau (western), Lau (eastern), and Mbua (northern). These were only partly successful. With cotton prices collapsing as the American south resumed production, a national administration under Cakobau and planter John Thurston was established at Levuka in 1871. However Cakobau was never strong enough to impose his authority over the whole country, so with growing disorder in western Fiji, infighting between Europeans and Fijian chiefs, and a lack of cooperation from Ma'afu's rival confederation of chiefs in eastern Fiji, Cakobau decided he should cede his kingdom to Great Britain. The British had refused an invitation to annex Fiji in 1862 but this time they accepted rather than see the group fall into the hands of another power. On 10 Oct. 1874 Fiji became a British colony. In 1877 the Western Pacific High Commission was set up to protect British interests in the surrounding unclaimed island groups as well.

The Making Of A Nation

The first British governor, Sir Arthur Gordon, and his colonial secretary and successor, Sir John Thurston, created modern Fiji almost single-handedly. They realized that the easiest way to rule was indirectly through the existing Fijian chiefs. To protect the communal lands on which the chieftain system was based, they ordered that native land could not be sold, only leased. Not wishing to disturb native society Gordon and Thurston ruled that Fijians could not be required to work on European plantations. The blackbirding of Melanesian laborers from the Solomons and New Hebrides had also been restricted by the Polynesian Islanders Protection Act in 1872. By this time sugar had taken the place of cotton and there was a tremendous labor shortage on the plantations. Gordon, who had previously served in Trinidad and Mauritius, saw indentured Indian workers as a solution. The first arrived in 1879 and by 1916, when Indian immigration ended, there were 63,000 present. To come to Fiji the Indi-

Blackbirded Solomon Islanders, brought to work on European-owned plantations in Fiji, wait aboard ship off Levuka around the turn of the century. In 1910 the Melanesian labor trade was finally terminated by the British, but a few of the Solomon Islanders stayed on and small communities of their descendants exist on Ovalau and near Suva.

ans had to agree to cut sugar cane for their masters for five years. During the next five years they were allowed to lease small plots of their own from the Fijians and plant cane or raise livestock. Over half the Indians decided to remain in Fiji as free settlers after their 10-year contracts expired, and today their descendants form around half the population, many of them still working small leased plots.

Though these policies did help preserve traditional Fijian culture they also kept the Fijians backward—envious onlookers passed over by European and (later) Indian prosperity. The separate administration and special rights for indigenous Fijians installed by the British over a century ago continue in force today. In early 1875 Cakobau and two of his sons returned from a visit to Australia while infected with measles. Though they survived the resulting epidemic wiped out a third of the Fijian population. At the beginning of European colonization there were about 200,000 Fijians, approximately 114,748 in 1881, and just 84,000 by 1921.

The Colonial Period

In 1912 a Gujerati lawyer, D.M. Manilal, arrived in Fiji to fight for Indian rights just as his contemporary Mahatma Gandhi was doing in South Africa at the time. Indentured Indians continued to arrive in Fiji until 1916 but the protests led to the termination of the indenture system throughout the empire in 1920. Although Fiji was a political colony of Britain, it was always an economic colony of Australia; the big Australian trading companies Burns Philp and W.R. Carpenters dominated business. The ubiquitous Morris Hedstrom is a subsidiary of Carpenters. Most of the Indians were brought to Fiji to work for the Australian-owned Colonial Sugar Refining Company, which controlled the sugar industry from 1881 right up until 1973, when it was purchased by the Fiji government for $14 million.

No representative government existed in Fiji until 1904 when a Legislative Council was formed with six elected Europeans and two Fijians nominated by the Council of Chiefs. In 1916 the governor appointed an Indian member to the council. A 1929 reform granted five seats to each community: three elected and two appointed Europeans and Indians, and five nominated Fijians. The council was only an advisory body and the governor remained in complete control. The Europeans generally sided with the Fijians against any further demands for equality from the Indians—divide and rule.

Fijians were outstanding combat troops on the Allied side in the Solomon Islands campaign during WW II, and again from 1952-56 suppressing Malaya's national liberation struggle. So skilled were the Fijians at jungle warfare against the Japanese that it was never appropriate to list a Fijian as "missing in action" but to phrase it "not yet arrived." Until 1952, Suva, the present Fijian capital, was headquarters for the British Imperial Administration in the South Pacific.

In 1963 the Legislative Council was expanded but still divided along racial lines. Women and Fijians got the vote for the first time. Wishing to be rid of the British whom they blamed for their second-class position, the Indians pushed for independence. The Fijians had come to view the British as protectors and were somewhat reluctant. After much discusssion a constitution was finally adopted in 1970. Some legislature members were to be elected from a common roll (voting by all races) as the Indians desired and other seats remained ethnic (voting in racial constituencies) to protect the Fijians. On 10 Oct. 1970 Fiji became a fully independent nation. The first Fijian governor general was appointed in 1973—none other than Ratu Sir George Cakobau, great-grandson of the chief who had ceded Fiji to Queen Victoria 99 years previously.

Politics

In 1944 Ratu Sir Lala Sukuna, paramount chief of Lau, played a key role in the creation of a separate administration for indigenous Fijians. Native land (83% of Fiji) was to be under this administration's jurisdiction. In 1954 Ratu Sukuna formed the Fijian Association to support the British administration against Indian demands for equal representation. The Alliance Party was founded in 1966 as a coalition of the Fijian Association, the General Electors' Association (representing Europeans, Part Fijians, and Chinese), and the Fiji Indian Alliance (a minority Indian group). Alliance Party leader Ratu Sir Kamisese Mara became chief minister after the party won the 1966 legislative assembly elections. In 1970 Ratu Mara led Fiji into independence and in 1972 his party won Fiji's first post-independence elections. He served as prime minister almost continuously until the 1987 elections. The opposition National Federation Party (NFP) was formed in 1960 to represent Indian cane farmers. They called for equal rights for all.

In 1975 Mr. Sakeasi Butadroka, a member of parliament previously expelled from the Alliance Party, tabled a motion calling for all Indians to be repatriated to India at British expense. This was rejected but during the

April 1977 elections Butadroka's extremist Fijian Nationalist Party took enough votes away from Alliance to allow the predominantly Indian NFP to obtain a majority. After a few days' hesitation the governor general reappointed Ratu Mara as prime minister, but his minority Alliance government was soon defeated. Meanwhile Butadroka had been arrested for making racially inflammatory statements in violation of the Public Order Act. In new elections in September 1977 Alliance recovered its majority in parliament, due in part to a scission of the NFP into Hindu and Muslim factions.

In 1981 Ratu Osea Gavidi formed the Western United Front, a predominantly Fijian party which maintained that the interests of Fijians resident in western Viti Levu had been neglected by Alliance. During the July 1982 elections there were bitter allegations that Alliance had received backing from the American CIA through a U.S. consultancy firm, Business International, while the NFP was accused of accepting $1 million in Soviet funding. Alliance was reelected with a slim majority and in early 1984 a Royal Commission of Inquiry declared the charges on both sides unprovable.

The formation of the Fiji Labor Party headed by Dr. Timoci Bavadra in July 1985 dramatically altered the political landscape. Fiji's previously nonpolitical trade unions had finally come behind a party which campaigned on bread and butter issues rather than race. By cutting across racial and religious lines Labor challenged both Alliance and the NFP. A Nov. 1986 editorial in *Pacific Islands Monthly* stated prophetically: "If it can survive the next election intact—and current signs are that it can—the Fiji Labor Party will almost certainly represent the most significant political development in the South Pacific since the beginnings of independence. Its philosophy is well capable of export to nearby nations where trade unions have so far adopted mainly passive political roles."

Late in 1986 Labor and the NFP formed a coalition with the aim of defeating Alliance in the next election. Dr. Bavadra, a former director of Primary and Preventive Health Services and president of the Fiji Public Service Association, was choosen as Coalition leader. In the 12 April 1987 elections Coalition won 28 of 52 House of Representatives seats; 19 of the 28 elected Coalition members were Indians. What swung the election away from Alliance was not a change in Indian voting patterns but support for Labor from urban Fijians and Part Fijians which cost Alliance four previously "safe" seats around Suva.

Coalition had a broad base of public support and all cabinet positions of vital Fijian interest (Lands, Fijian Affairs, Labor and Immigration, Education, Agriculture and Rural Development) went to indigenous Fijian legislators. Coalition's progressive policies were quite a change from the conservatism of Alliance. Medical care was expanded, an Institute for Fijian Language and Culture was created, and Fijians were given greater access to loans (which had been going mostly to foreign corporations) by the Fiji Development Bank. The government also announced that nuclear warships would be banned from a nonaligned Fiji. Foreign Minister Krishna Datt said he would join Vanuatu and New Zealand in pressing for a nuclear-free Pacific at the 24 May 1987 meeting of the South Pacific Forum. Alleged corruption in the previous administration was to be investigated. Ratu Mara himself had allegedly accumulated a personal fortune of $4-6 million on his annual salary of $100,000. Given time Coalition might also have required the high chiefs to share the rental monies received from Indians for leased lands more fairly with ordinary Fijians. Most significant of all, Coalition would have transformed Fiji from a plural society where only indigenous Melanesian Fijians were called Fijians to a truly multi-racial society where all citizens would be Fijians.

The First Coup

After the election the extremist Fiji-for-Fijians Taukei (landowners) movement launched a destabilization campaign by throwing barricades across highways, organizing protest rallies and marches, and carrying out firebombings. On 24 April 1987 Senator Inoke Tabua and former Alliance cabinet minister Apisai Tora organized a march of 5,000

Dr. Timoci Bavadra, deposed prime minister of Fjii

Fijians through Suva to protest "Indian domination" of the new government. Mr. Tora told a preparatory meeting for the demonstration that Prime Minister Bavadra (an indigenous Fijian) was only a figurehead for NFP guru Mr. Jai Ram Reddy. Mr. Tabua said that Fijians must "act now" to avoid ending up as "deprived as Australia's aborigines." (In fact, under the 1970 constitution the Coalition government would have had no way of changing Fiji's land laws without indigenous Fijian consent.) In the following weeks five gasoline bombs were thrown against government offices though no one was injured. On 13 Sept. 1987 Alliance Senator Jona Qio was arrested for arson.

At 1000 on Thurs. 14 May 1987 Lieutenant Colonel Sitiveni Rabuka, third ranking officer in the Fijian Army, and 10 heavily armed soldiers dressed in fatigues, their faces covered by gas masks, entered the House of Representatives in Suva. Rabuka strode up to the speaker's dais and ordered Dr. Bavadra and the Coalition members to follow a soldier out of the building. When Dr. Bavadra hesitated the soldiers raised their guns. The legislators were loaded into army trucks and taken to Royal Fiji Military Forces headquarters. There was no bloodshed, though Rabuka later confirmed that his troops would have opened fire had there been any resistance. At a press conference five hours after the coup Rabuka claimed he had acted to prevent violence and had no political ambitions of his own.

Most Pacific governments denounced the region's first military coup. Governor General Ratu Sir Penaia Ganilau attempted to reverse the situation by declaring a state of emergency and ordering the mutineers to return to their barracks. They refused to obey. The next day the *Fiji Sun* ran a black-bordered editorial which declared, "Democracy died in Fiji yesterday. What right has a third-ranking officer to attack the sacred institutions of Parliament? What right has he to presume he knows best how this country shall be governed? The answer is none." Soon after, Rabuka's troops arrived at both daily papers and ordered publication suspended. Journalists were evicted from the buildings.

Later that day Rabuka named a 15-member Council of Ministers chaired by himself to govern Fiji, with former Alliance prime minister Ratu Mara as foreign minister. Significantly, Rabuka was the only military officer on the council; most of the others were members of Ratu Mara's defeated administration. Rabuka claimed that he had acted to "safeguard the Fijian land issue and the Fijian way of life."

On 19 May Dr. Bavadra and the other kidnapped members of his government were released after the governor general announced a deal negotiated with Rabuka. Within hours an ugly race riot broke out in Suva, forcing Dr. Bavadra and the others into hiding. Meanwhile the Great Council of Chiefs appointed Ratu Ganilau head of a 19-member caretaker Advisory Council until new elections could take place. Rabuka was put in charge of Home Affairs and the security forces. Only two seats were offered to Dr. Bavadra's government and they were refused. With this the possibility of foreign intervention subsided. Queen Elizabeth II refused to see Dr. Bavadra, who traveled to London especially for the purpose. Fiji had been abandoned to its fate.

Ratu Mara was seen playing golf with Rabuka at Pacific Harbor the Sunday before the coup. At the time of the coup he was at a Coral Coast hotel chairing a meeting of the Pacific Democratic Union, a U.S.-sponsored grouping of ultra-right politicians from Australia, New Zealand, and elsewhere. Though Ratu Mara expressed "shock" at the coup he accepted a position on Rabuka's Council of Ministers the next day, prompting New Zealand Prime Minister David Lange to accuse him of treachery under Fiji's constitution by acquiescing to military rule. Lange said Ratu Mara had pledged allegiance to the Queen but had brought about a rebellion in one of her countries. Ratu Ganilau was also strongly criticized for legitimizing a traitor by accepting Rabuka on his Advisory Council.

Behind The Coup

American interest in the South Pacific picked up in 1982 when U.S. ambassador to Fiji William Bodde Jr. told a luncheon at the Kahala Hilton in Hawaii: "The most potentially disruptive development to U.S. relations with the region...a nuclear-free zone would be unacceptable to the United States given our strategic needs. I am convinced that the United States must do everything possible to counter this movement. It will not be an easy task, but it is one that we cannot afford to neglect." In 1983 Ratu Mara lifted a ban on visits to Fiji by U.S. nuclear warships and Fiji soon became the first South Pacific country to receive American aid.

In Oct. 1984 Ratu Mara made a state visit to Washington at the invitation of President Reagan. In recognition of Fiji's new willingness to allow port visits by U.S. nuclear warships, Ratu Mara was promised increased bilateral aid. Although no agreement was reached on the question of Fiji's sugar quota, landing or fishing rights, Washington offered an immediate grant of US$300,000 to the Fiji army for "weapons standardization." Reagan praised Fiji as a "model of democracy and freedom" and promised that in the future the U.S. would work more closely with the coun-

try to achieve "prosperity and peace." From 1984 to 1986 U.S. aid to Fiji tripled. France also increased aid to Fiji as a means of dampening criticism of French nuclear testing at Moruroa Atoll in Tahiti-Polynesia.

Immediately after the coup there were accusations that the U.S. government was involved (see *Wellington Confidential,* issue 36, June 1987; *Pacific Islands Monthly,* Oct. 1987; *Wellington Pacific Report,* Nov. and Dec. 1987; *Covert Action Information Bulletin,* number 29, Winter, 1988). On 16 June 1987 at a press conference at the National Press Club in Washington, D.C., Dr. Bavadra publicly accused William Paupe, director of the South Pacific regional office of U.S. AID, of channeling US$200,000 to right-winger Apisai Tora of the Taukei movement for destabilization purposes. Later Dr. Bavadra dropped the charge, which Paupe and Tora emphatically denied.

From 29 April to 1 May 1987 Gen. Vernon A. Walters, U.S. ambassador to the United Nations and a former CIA deputy director, visited Fiji. At a long meeting with Foreign Minister Datt, Walters tried to persuade the new government to give up its anti-nuclear stance. Walters told the Fiji press that the U.S. "has a duty to protect its South Pacific interests." Walters is believed to have been involved in previous coups in Iran (1953) and Brazil (1964), and during his stay in Fiji he also met with Rabuka and William Paupe. Though there is no evidence that Walters was involved in preparations for the Fiji coup he did spread a bogus Libyan scare during his 10-country Pacific trip, diverting attention from what was about to happen.

On 22 Oct. 1987 the U.S. Information Service in New Zealand revealed that the amphibious assault ship USS *Belleau Wood* was just west of Fiji immediately after the coup, supported by three C-130 Hercules transport planes which staged through Nandi Airport from 20-22 June. The same release mentioned four other C-130s at Nandi that month to support the gigantic hospital ship USNS *Mercy,* which was at Suva from 23-27 June—an unprecedented level of military activity. By chance or design the U.S. would have been ready to intervene militarily within hours had anything gone wrong.

Yet the evidence of American involvement in the coup is circumstantial and inconclusive. Certainly an illegitimate, increasingly repressive government in Fiji is not in the American interest and the U.S. has had to distance itself from the Rabuka regime. In an article published in the *Sydney Morning Herald* on 16 Nov. 1987 the U.S. ambassador to Australia, William Lane, categorically denied the U.S. was behind the coup. In *No Other Way,* a biography of Rabuka by Eddie Dean, Rabuka is quoted as saying: "Everyone involved in my coup of 14 May were people I personally picked and trained...no foreigners came into the country to help."

Until the coup the most important mission of the Royal Fiji Defense Force was service in South Lebanon and the Sinai with peacekeeping operations. Half of the 2,600-member Fijian army was on rotating duty there, the Sinai force financed by the U.S., the troops in Lebanon by the United Nations. Since 1983 the U.S. has spent US$125,000 a year putting Fijian officers through military training programs. Service in the strife-torn Middle East gave the Fiji military a unique preparation for its present role in Fiji itself. (During WW II Fiji Indians refused to join the army unless they received the same pay as European recruits; indigenous Fijians had no such reservations and the force has been 95% Fijian ever since.)

The coup caught the Australian and New Zealand intelligence services totally by surprise, indicating that few knew of Rabuka's plans in advance. Rabuka may have acted on his own initiative or in collusion with members of the defeated Alliance Party in power from 1967-87. According to Dr. Tupeni Baba, minister of education in the Coalition government, "the main reason for the coup was basically the fear of Ratu Mara and his colleagues that we would explore the corruptive practices of the Alliance Party and their business colleagues."

In their Oct. 1987 issue *Pacific Islands Monthly* published this comment by noted author Brij V. Lal of the University of Hawaii:

More than anything else, the coup was about power. The emergence in an incipient form of a class-minded multi-racial politics, symbolised by the Labor Party and made possible by the support of many urban Fijians, posed a grave threat to the politics of race and racial compartmentalization preached by the Alliance and thus had to be nipped in the bud. The ascent of Dr. Bavadra, a chief from the long-neglected western Viti Levu, to the highest office in the land posed an unprecedented challenge to the traditional dominance of eastern chiefs, especially from Lau and Thakaundrove.

Anthony D. van Fossen of Griffith University, Queensland, Australia, summed it up this way in the *Bulletin of Concerned Asian Scholars* (Vol. 19, No. 4, 1987):

Although the first coup has been most often seen in terms of ethnic tensions between indigenous Fijians and Fijian Indians, it may be more accurately seen as the result of tensions between aristocratic indigenous Fijians and their commoner allies defending feudalism, on the one hand, and the cause of social democracy, small-scale capitalism, and multiethnic nationalism represented by middleclass indigenous Fijian commoners and Hindus on the other.

Constitutional Reform

Prior to 14 May 1987 the Fijian Parliament was composed of two houses. The House of Representatives had 52 members, 12 elected by the indigenous Fijian community, 12 by the Indian community, and three by "general electors" (Europeans, Part Fijians, Chinese, etc.). Another 10 Fijians, 10 Indians, and five general electors were chosen by a "common roll" of all voters. The 22-member Senate included eight members appointed by the Great Council of Chiefs, seven by the prime minister, six by the leader of the opposition, and one by the Council of Rotuma. Although the House of Representatives was by far the more important body, changes to the constitution and many laws of special concern to indigenous Fijians (such as land laws) required a 75% majority vote in both houses.

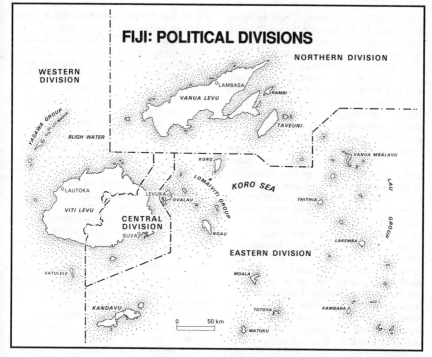

FIJI: POLITICAL DIVISIONS

A governor general represented the British Crown. He had the right to dissolve Parliament and order new elections.

The Great Council of Chiefs included the high chiefs of Fiji, the members of Parliament, and others appointed by the minister for Fijian Affairs. Government at the village *(koro)* level was led by a village herald *(turanga-ni-koro)* chosen by consensus. The villages were grouped into districts *(tikina)*, the districts into 14 provinces *(yasana)*, the provinces into four administrative divisions: central, eastern, northern, and western. The Micronesians of Rambi governed themselves through a council of their own. City and town councils also functioned.

In July and August 1987 a Constitutional Review Committee studied proposals for constitutional reform at the request of Governor General Ganilau. The Great Council of Chiefs (chaired by Ratu Mara) asked that a new 71-member unicameral Parliament be created with 40 seats reserved for indigenous Fijians (an increase of 18 over the 1970 constitution). Of these 40, 28 would be chosen by the Provincial Councils, eight by the Great Council of Chiefs, and four by the prime minister. Indigenous Fijians would not vote directly again. The other ethnic groups would have the same representation as previously: 22 Indians (four of them Muslims), eight general electors, and one Rotuman. The prime minister would be a Fijian elected by the Fijian members.

The Labor-NFP Coalition called for a return to the 1970 constitution which had served Fiji well up until the coup. They pointed out that with all the Fijian members chosen by traditional chiefs urban Fijians would be almost unrepresented and said the country "had been forced to review the constitution by a radical minority who had enlisted in the army to further their narrow interests." The Taukei extremists called for a republic with a single parliament comprised exclusively of native Fijian members. Some 800 other submissions were received. The 16-member review committee included no Indians.

In Sept. the committee presented two reports. The Majority Report backed a solution very similar to the one suggested by the Great Council of Chiefs, while a Minority Report recommended retaining the 1970 constitution. Meanwhile a nonpartisan "Back to Early May" group collected 108,000 signatures on a petition in support of the 1970 constitution. On 4 Sept. talks between Alliance and Coalition leaders under the chairmanship of Ratu Ganilau began at Government House in Suva. With no hope of a consensus on a revised constitution the talks were aimed at establishing a Government of National Unity which could prepare for new elections.

Even as the leaders met, Taukei thugs dressed as tribal warriors and carrying spears attacked and badly beat Richard Naidu, a spokesperson for Dr. Bavadra, in the lounge of the nearby TraveLodge before horrified hotel guests. That evening soldiers fired shots in the air near Dr. Bavadra's home. Refusing to negotiate under duress Dr. Bavadra broke off the negotiations. After assurances from Ratu Ganilau the talks resumed on 11 September. On 13 Sept. Taukei arsonists burned six Indian shops in downtown Suva and committed other acts of violence.

The Second Coup

On Friday, 26 Sept. 1987 Rabuka struck again, just hours before the governor general was to announce a Government of National Unity to rule Fiji until new elections could be held. The plan, developed over four months and finally approved by veteran political leaders on all sides, would probably have resulted in Rabuka being sacked. Rabuka quickly threw out the 1970 constitution and pronounced himself "head of state." Some 300 prominent community leaders were arrested and Ratu Ganilau was confined to Government House. Newspapers were shut down, trade unions repressed, the judiciary suspended, the public service purged, the activi-

ties of political opponents restricted, a curfew imposed, and cases of torture reported.

At midnight on 7 Oct. 1987 Rabuka declared Fiji a republic. Rabuka's new Council of Ministers included Taukei extremists Apisai Tora and Filipe Bole, Fijian Nationalist Party leader Sakeasi Butadroka, and other marginal figures. Rabuka appeared to have backing in the Great Council of Chiefs, which wanted a return to the style of customary rule threatened by the Indian presence and Western democracy. Regime ideologists trumpeted traditional culture and religious fundamentalism. Rabuka said he wanted Christianity adopted as Fiji's official religion and henceforth all trading (except at tourist hotels), sports, and public transport would be banned on the Sabbath. Residents stopped smiling when the ban was extended to family picnics, diplomats jogging, children playing in their own backyards, and even family singalongs. Rabuka called for the conversion of Hindu and Moslem Indians to Christianity. (Rabuka himself is a notorious womanizer with many illegitimate children.)

On 16 Oct. Ratu Ganilau resigned as governor general and two days later Fiji was expelled from the British Commonwealth. Indian Prime Minister Rajiv Ghandi said the Fijian minority had "taken over the political and human rights" of the Indian majority. On 6 Nov. Rabuka allowed the *Fiji Times* to resume publication after it pledged self-censorship but the more independent *Fiji Sun* remained shut. Nobody accused the U.S. of having anything to do with Rabuka's second coming and even Ratu Mara seemed annoyed that Rabuka had destroyed an opportunity to reestablish the prestige of himself and Ratu Ganilau. Clearly Rabuka had become his own man.

The Republic Of Fiji

Finally realizing that Taukei/military rule was a recipe for disaster, on 5 Dec. 1987 Rabuka appointed Ratu Ganilau president and Ratu Mara prime minister of his new republic. The 21-member cabinet included 10 members of Rabuka's military regime, including four army officers. Rabuka himself (now a self-styled brigadier) was once again minister of Home Affairs. Among Rabuka's eight conditions for relinquishing power to the old oligarchs were guarantees that no member of Coalition be included in the cabinet, that the new constitution would be drafted by the army, and that regular consultations would take place between the army commanders and the president and prime minister. Ratu Ganilau and Ratu Mara denied they had agreed to such terms which they said were only "discussion points." The leaders set themselves a deadline of two years to frame a new constitution and return Fiji to freely elected representative government.

By mid-1988 the army had been expanded into a highly disciplined 6,000-member force fiercely loyal to Brigadier Rabuka. There was no doubt Rabuka would intervene a third time if his agenda was not followed. Also in mid-1988 the 200-member Great Council of Chiefs decided to reduce its own numbers to a more manageable 52. The new council would include 10 members from each of the three confederacies (Kumbuna, Mburembasanga, and Tovato), one member from each of the 14 provinces, three members appointed by the president of the republic, three by the Ministry of Fijian Affairs, and two from Rotuma. This was to be the body which would largely decide on Fiji's republican constitution.

In early 1988 the regime issued a series of decrees muzzling the press through a licensing system, granting an amnesty to Rabuka's troops for any offenses committed during the 1987 coups, and overhauling the legal system to ensure Fijian control. At the same time a blacklist of potential critics was drawn up and these were refused permission to leave Fiji. An attempt was made to prevent Robert Keith-Reid, respected publisher of *Islands Business,* from boarding a flight at Nandi on a business trip though Mr. Keith-Reid was finally allowed to go after a heated argument with officials. Former Coalition ministers were not allowed to travel. Foreign journalists wishing to visit Fiji would henceforth need advance clearance from the Information Ministry in Suva. The government said it was anxious for life to return to normal so the tourists, investors, aid donors, trade, and international moneylenders would return.

The coups devastated the Fijian economy. In 1987 Fiji experienced 11% negative growth in the gross domestic product. To prevent a massive flight of capital the Fiji dollar was devalued 17.75% on 30 June 1987 and 15.25% on 7 October. Inflation which had been around 2% before the coups was up to 11.9% by the end of 1988. At the same time the public service (half the work force) had to accept a 25% wage cut as government spending was slashed. Food prices skyrocketed, causing serious problems for many families. At the end of 1987 the per capita average income was 11% *below* what it had been in 1980. By early 1989 some 12,000 Indian professionals—accountants, administrators, dentists, doctors, lawyers, nurses, teachers—had left for Australia, Canada, New Zealand, and the U.S.

On 14 May 1988 nine men and nine women joined hands in Suva's Sukuna Park in a peaceful protest to mark the first anniversary of the Rabuka coup. The "Democracy 18" were arrested for unlawful assembly and that evening as the women sang protest songs in their cells a large police van pulled up in front and pumped carbon monoxide fumes inside, forcing the women to lie on the floor to avoid being overcome. In an editorial in the Aug. 1988 issue of Tonga's Catholic newspaper *Taumau Lelei* Bishop Patelisio Finau SM of Tonga wrote: "Three Columban priests are among the 18 women and men who will appear before the court.... It was good that priests were with those who suffer. It was a Christlike thing to do. Those who have no experience of unjust suffering will not understand...We do not have to import militaristic and police state systems to our Pacific." On 31 Jan. 1989 the 18 anti-coup protesters were granted an absolute discharge though Father Tom Rouse was later expelled from Fiji. On the day of his expulsion Father Rouse's parishioners ran an ad in the *Fiji Times* mourning the loss of a "true Christian."

Internal Security

On 31 May 1988 Australian customs officials at Sydney discovered a mysterious 12-tonne arms shipment bound for Lautoka, Fiji. In the container which had arrived from North Yemen were Czech-made weapons including AK47 rifles, rocket launchers, antitank mines, and explosives. Australian officials implicated Mohammed Rafiq Kahan, an ex-resident of Fiji with a long criminal background, as responsible for the shipment. Kahan, who fled Australia when the arms were uncovered, was apprehended in London, England. Two other Fiji Indians were arrested in Sydney (charges against them were later dropped for lack of evidence).

For whom the arms were actually intended is uncertain and the Fiji police were unable to establish any link to Coalition. From the start Dr. Bavadra consistently advocated nonviolence. Kahan himself had been photographed wearing a military uniform in the Queen Elizabeth Barracks, Suva, just two months previously. On the same visit to Fiji Kahan developed contacts with key Alliance ministers Apisai Tora, Taniela Veitata, and Ahmed Ali. In March 1989 a London court considering Kahan's extradition to Fiji was told that the defendant had mentioned Alliance supporter Motibhai Patel, owner of the duty-free emporium at Nandi Airport, and Ratu Mara himself in connection with the arms shipment. Kahan was released on grounds that the case was political. Evidentally a second container had slipped into Fiji in April 1988 and by 8 June raids by security forces in western Fiji had netted over 100 rifles and other weapons, with 22 arrests. The shipments seemed to have been either in preparation for a counter-coup against Rabuka by disgruntled Alliance elements or the pretense for a crackdown on the political opposition within Fiji by the security forces.

On 17 June 1988 the government issued an 86-section Internal Security Decree giving the police and military unlimited powers to arrest and hold anyone up to two years without charge, to impose curfews, to shoot to kill within declared security areas, to search vehicles or premises without a warrant, to seize land and buildings, and to cancel passports. No inquests would be held into any killings under decree powers and the penalty for possession of firearms or explosives was life imprisonment. The decree also made it illegal to publish anything "prejudicial to the national interest and security of Fiji." The decree was modeled on similar laws in Malaysia and Singapore which have led to widespread human rights violations. On 17 Nov. 1988 the decree was suspended but not repealed.

On 22 June 1988 10 people were arrested in Suva, including the secretary of the Fiji Law Society who had merely called a meeting to discuss the new security decree and two lawyers who had defended persons charged with arms offenses. Several prominent Muslim businessmen suspected of financing the arms shipment were also held. Despite a one-month amnesty to surrender arms declared by Rabuka on 23 June the arrests continued, with families fearing their relatives had "disappeared." Most were held incommunicado about a week then released. Many reported being beaten in confinement.

The most notorious of the 22 June arrests (later mentioned in Amnesty International report ASA 18/01/88, Aug. 1988) was that of Som Prakash, a lecturer in English at the University of the South Pacific who wrote a critical review of Rabuka's biography. The review castigated the brigadier's "Messiah syndrome" and his intolerance of races and religions other than his own and questioned Rabuka's claim that he had acted to prevent "bloodshed," suggesting that political considerations were paramount. Mr. Prakash was held in solitary confinement without legal advice or access to his family until 6 July when he was released on the condition that he not speak to the news media. It was reported he had been beaten during his detention. Amnesty International called Mr. Prakash a "prisoner of conscience."

On 7 July 1988 Rabuka was refused admission to Australia to promote his biography after protests that the self-styled general would be allowed to use the free press of Australia to promote the book, while Som Prakash faced an uncertain fate in Fiji for daring to criticize it. This may have inspired a particularly vicious response. On 8 July an Australian tourist, Stephen Lock, was arrested for "looking suspicious" as he passed an army barracks in Suva. Over the weekend of 9-10 July he was so badly beaten he had no trouble displaying his battered face to press photographers on his return to Australia a week later. Lock reported that he had seen other prisoners, including a West German national and alleged "mercenary" named Peter Ritovsky, assaulted and beaten with broom handles. Lock was forced by his captors to sign a false confession to having photographed the barracks even though he didn't have a camera. Around the same time Rabuka also recommended that Australian banks be expelled from Fiji.

The Future

On 19 July 1988 a draft for a republican constitution similar to that proposed by the Great Council of Chiefs in mid-1987 was offered. Of the 71 members of Parliament 28 would be Fijians, 22 Indians, eight general electors, and one Rotuman. The other 12 would consist of eight appointed by the president and four by the prime minister. The army commander would automatically be minister of defense and a member of Parliament regardless of the party in power. All coup participants would be immune to prosecution. Under this system Coalition would need 70% of the votes to win, Alliance only 30%. Dr. Bavadra threatened to boycott the elections if this constitution were implemented. Also in early 1989 a rebel fundamentalist pastor, Rev. Manasa Lasaro, staged a mini-coup within the Methodist Church, ousting the legally elected church head. A more intolerant, blatantly racist church has resulted.

What does the future hold for Fiji? The grip of the feudal ruling class will continue to be challenged by both Coalition and, increasingly, Fijian nationalists. Ironically the most extreme Taukei leaders are mostly commoners or lesser chiefs who were dismayed when Rabuka returned power to the old aristocratic politicians after the second coup. Western Fijian chiefs have always been dissatisfied with rule by the easterners. The proposed constitution is so one-sided that Indians and educated Fijians will be alienated from the political mainstream. Ordinary indigenous Fijians have experienced the economic hardships of military rule as much as anyone. If enough of them come to realize that in the long term multi-racial democracy is the only hope for a peaceful, stable Fiji, then Coalition has a good chance of eventually returning to office through the ballot box.

That leaves the army, which still supports Rabuka. Throughout the Third World military forces have resisted surrendering power after tasting it. Ratu Mara has announced that he intends to retire at the end of 1989, and it will be hard for his tainted Alliance colleagues to come up with a candidate able to replace him. General Rabuka himself may decide to run for prime minister under the new constitution. A Rabuka victory would mean a divided, increasingly repressive Fiji; a Rabuka defeat could mean a third coup and a full totalitarian state. There may be a struggle for power within the army itself, and to distract attention Rabuka might intervene militarily in a neighboring country such as Tonga or Vanuatu in support of some embattled faction. The forced expulsion of all Indians from Fiji, Idi Amin-style, is not impossible.

Economically Fiji may prosper, just as undemocratic states such as Taiwan and South Korea prosper. But behind the tax-free factories, swank hotels, and golf courses will be an economy increasingly controlled by outside interests exploiting the working people of Fiji for greater profits. A few will do well and the country may appear to be booming but ordinary people of both races will pay the price.

It would be reprehensible to pretend that nothing has happened in Fiji and that everything is business as usual. Travel writers and tourism promoters who do so illustrate the exploitive nature of international tourism in Third World countries, where the only things that matter are good facilities for affluent visitors and handsome profits for transnational corporations. To some the events in Fiji are purely academic. One travel writer even commented that the change of government was positive because it led to a devaluation of Fijian currency making things cheaper for tourists! These comments may not be popular in some quarters but we'd rather sell fewer books than sell out. (For more information on these matters see *Fiji—Shattered Coups* by Robertson and Tamanisau listed in the Booklist.

ECONOMY

Economic Development

While eastern Viti Levu and the Lau Group dominate the country politically, western Viti Levu is Fiji's economic powerhouse. Both major earners of foreign exchange, sugar and tourism, are centered here. About 40% of the work force has paid employment; the remainder is involved in subsistence agriculture. Manioc, taro, yams, sweet potato, and corn are the principal subsistence crops. Since WW II a series of five-year plans have guided public investment and resulted in the excellent modern infrastructure and advanced social services Fiji enjoys today.

Almost all of Fiji's sugar is produced by small independent Indian farmers on contract to the government-owned Fiji Sugar Corporation, which took over from the Australian-owned Colonial Sugar Refining Company in 1973. Some 21,000 farmers cultivate cane on holdings averaging 4.5 hectares leased from indigenous Fijians. The farmers are well paid for their production. The corporation owns 644 km of 0.610-meter narrow gauge railway which it uses to carry the cane to the mills at Lautoka, Mba, Rakiraki, and Lambasa.

Most of Fiji's copra is produced in Lau, Lomaiviti, Taveuni, and Vanua Levu, half by European or Part Fijian planters and the rest by indigenous Fijian villagers. Timber is becoming important as thousands of hectares planted in western Viti Levu and Vanua Levu by the Fiji Pine Commission and private landowners in the late '70s reach

Taro, which grows marvelously well in the rich soils of Fiji's bush gardens, is one of the staples of the Pacific and ensures a steady supply of nourishing food for the villagers.

HOW A SUGAR MILL WORKS

The sugarcane is fed through a shredder towards a row of huge rollers, which squeeze out the juice. The crushed fiber (bagasse) is burned to fuel the mill or is processed into paper. Lime is then added to the juice and the mixture is heated. Impurities settle in the clarifier and mill mud is filtered out to be used as fertilizer. The clear juice goes through a series of evaporators where it is boiled into steam under partial vacuum to remove water and create a syrup. The syrup is boiled again under greater pressure in a vacuum pan, and raw sugar crystals form. The mix then enters a centrifuge, which spins off the remaining syrup (molasses—used for distilling or cattle feed). The moist crystals are sent on to a rotating drum were they are tumble-dried using hot air. Raw sugar comes out in the end.

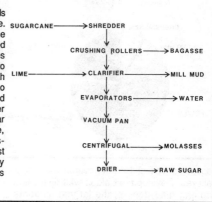

maturity. Mining activity still centers on gold at Vatukoula on Viti Levu, and extensive copper deposits at Namosi are now being considered for development. Commercial fishing is becoming increasingly important, and there is a major Japanese tuna cannery at Levuka. Fiji now grows almost half its own rice needs and is trying to become self-sufficient. Much of the rice is grown around Nausori and Navua.

Yet, in spite of all this potential, unemployment is turning into a major social problem as four times more young people leave school than there are jobs to take them. To stimulate industry, firms which export 95% of their production are offered duty-free status, 13-year tax holidays, and cheap electricity. The garment industry is growing, with female employees forced to work in sweat shop conditions for fifty cents an hour. The clothing is exported mostly to Australia where partial duty-free entry is allowed under the South Pacific Regional Trade and Economic Cooperation Agreement (SPARTECA). Food processors and furniture manufacturers are also prominent in the tax-free exporting sector and it's believed that within a decade manufacturing may overtake both sugar and tourism as the main source of income for the country.

Trade And Aid

Fiji is an important regional trading center. Although Fiji imports twice as much as it exports, much of this is later re-exported to smaller Pacific countries or sold to tourists who pay in foreign exchange. Sugar accounts for over half of the nation's export earnings, followed by gold, fish, molasses, coconut oil, ginger, and timber in that order. Huge trade imbalances exist with Australia, Japan, and New Zealand.

Fiji has long-term contracts to sell sugar to New Zealand, Singapore, Malaysia, Britain, and the European Community at fixed rates. These contracts cover over 300,000 tons annually, with the surplus sold on the world market. A distillery at Lautoka produces alcohol, including rum and other liquors.

Mineral fuels used to be Fiji's most expensive import item, but this declined as the Monasavu Hydroelectric Project and other self-sufficiency measures came on line. Manufactured goods, machinery, vehicles, and food account for most of the import bill.

Fiji is the least dependent Pacific nation (excluding Nauru). In 1982 overseas aid totaled only A$53 per capita (as compared to A$1104 per capita in Tahiti-Polynesia); it

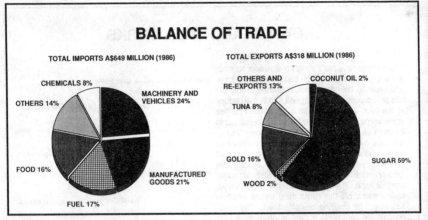

BALANCE OF TRADE

TOTAL IMPORTS A$649 MILLION (1986)

CHEMICALS 8%
OTHERS 14%
MACHINERY AND VEHICLES 24%
FOOD 16%
MANUFACTURED GOODS 21%
FUEL 17%

TOTAL EXPORTS A$318 MILLION (1986)

OTHERS AND RE-EXPORTS 13%
COCONUT OIL 2%
TUNA 8%
GOLD 16%
SUGAR 59%
WOOD 2%

accounts for just 10% of government expenditures. Development aid is well diversified among nine donors; the largest amounts come from the EEC, Britain, France, Australia, and New Zealand.

Tourism

Tourism is becoming a leading moneymaker, earning F$200 million a year as over 200,000 visitors reach Fiji. This is twice as many as Tahiti gets and ten times as many as Tonga. Things appear in better perspective, however, when Fiji is compared to Hawaii, which is about the same size in surface area. Hawaii gets five million tourists, 25 times as many as Fiji. The main tourist resorts are centered along the south coast of Viti Levu and on the islands off Nandi/Lautoka. Gross receipts figures from tourism are often misleading as over half this income is repatriated overseas by foreign investors. In real terms sugar is far more profitable for Fiji.

The May 1987 military coup ended a decade of steady increases in tourism to Fiji. Fiji's image as a trouble-free Pacific paradise has been shattered. From Jan. to April 1987 arrivals increased 10%; from May to Dec. they dropped 42%. Visitor arrivals peaked at 257,824 in 1986, dropped to 189,866 in 1987, and were back to 208,155 in 1988.

Continental Airlines severed service to Fiji after the 1987 coup and never returned.

About 40% of Fiji's tourists come from Australia, 20% from the U.S., 10% each from New Zealand and continental Europe, and 8% from Canada. The vast majority of visitors arrive in Fiji to or from Auckland, Sydney, and Honolulu. North Americans tend to view Fiji as a mere stopover on the way down under and spend far less time in the country than Australians or New Zealanders: over half of Australians stay longer than a week while a majority of Americans stay three days or less.

All the large resort hotels in Fiji are foreign-owned, and 80% of their purchases for food, beverages, linen, glassware, etc., are imported. Management is almost invariably European, with Fiji Indians filling technical positions such as maintenance, cooking, accounting, etc., and indigenous Fijians working the high profile positions, such as receptionists, waiters, guides, and housekeepers. The Fiji government has diverted large sums from its capital-improvements budget to provide infrastructure such as roads, airports, and other services to the foreign-owned resorts. Yet many of these same hotels have taken advantage of tax incentives and duty-free import allowances to escape paying any direct taxes back to the government.

THE PEOPLE

The Fijians

Fiji is a transitional zone between Polynesia and Melanesia. The Fijians bear a physical resemblance to the Melanesians, but like the Polynesians the Fijians have hereditary chiefs, patrilineal descent, a love of elaborate ceremonies, and a fairly homogeneous language and culture. Fijians have interbred with Polynesians to the extent that their skin color is lighter than that of other Melanesians. In the interior and west of Viti Levu where the contact was less the people tend to be somewhat darker than the easterners. Yet Fijians still have Melanesian frizzy hair, while most—but not all—Polynesians have straight hair.

The Fijians live in villages along the rivers or coast, anywhere from 50 to 400 people led by a hereditary chief. About 78% are Methodist, 8.5% Catholic. Away from the three largest islands the population is almost totally Fijian. The traditional thatched *mbure* is fast disappearing from Fiji as villagers rebuild (mostly following destructive cyclones) in tin and panel. Grass is not as accessible as cement, takes more time to repair, and is less permanent.

Fijians work communal land individually, not as a group. Each Fijian is assigned his piece of native land. They grow most of their own food in village gardens. Only a few staples such as tea, sugar, flour, etc., are imported from Suva and sold in local co-op stores. A visit to one of these stores will demonstrate just how little they import and how self-sufficient they are. Fishing, village maintenance work, and ceremonial presentations are done together. While village life provides a form of collective security, individuals are discouraged from rising above the group. Fijians who attempt to set up a business are often stifled by the demands of relatives and friends. This pattern makes it difficult for Fijians to compete with Indians for whom life has always been a struggle.

The Indians

Most of the Indians now in Fiji are descended from indentured laborers recruited in Bengal and Bihar a century ago. In the first year of the system (1879) some 450 Indians arrived in Fiji to work in the cane fields. By 1883 the total had risen to 2,300 and in 1916, when Indian immigration ended, 63,000 Indians

The descendants of late 19th-century arrivals, such as this characterful young woman, make up the majority of Fiji's population today. These indentured laborers faced many hardships and indignities, one of which stemmed from a British policy of allowing only 40 Indian women to be brought to the islands for every 100 men.

were present in the colony. In 1920 the indenture system was finally terminated, the cane fields were divided into four-hectare plots, and the Indian workers become tenant farmers on land owned by Fijians. In 1940 the Indian population stood at 98,000, still below the Fijian total of 105,000. But by the 1946 census Indians had outstripped Fijians 120,000 to 117,000—making Fijians a minority in their own home. In 1986 of Fiji's total population of 714,548, 46.2% were Fijian while 48.6% were Indian. The relative proportions are now changing as many Indians emigrate to North America and Australia in the wake of the coups, and by early 1989 indigenous Fijians once again outnumbered Fiji Indians.

Unlike the village-oriented Fijians, a majority of Indians are concentrated in the cane-growing areas and live in isolated farmhouses, small settlements, or towns. Many Indians also live in Suva, as do an increasing number of Fijians. Within the Fiji Indian community there are divisions between Hindu (80%) versus Muslim (20%), north Indian versus south Indian, and Gujerati versus the rest. The Sikhs and Gujeratis have always been somewhat of an elite as they immigrated freely to Fiji outside the indenture system.

The different groups have kept alive their ancient religious beliefs and rituals. Hindus tend to marry within their caste although the restrictions on behavior which characterize the caste system in India have disappeared. Indian marriages are often arranged by the parents, while Fijians generally choose their own partners. Rural Indians still associate most closely with other members of their extended patrilineal family group, and Hindu and Muslim religious beliefs still restrict Indian women to a position subservient to men.

It's often said that Indians concentrate on accumulation while Fijians emphasize distribution. Fiji's laws, which prevent Indians or anyone else from purchasing native communal land, have encouraged the Indians to invest their savings in business, which they now almost monopolize at the middle levels. (Big business is the domain of Europeans.) This has created envy on the part of the less business-oriented Fijians. If some Indians seem money-minded, keep in mind it's because they have been forced into that role. When one considers their position in a land where most have lived three generations and where they form about half the population, their industriousness and patience are admirable.

Land Rights

When Fiji became a British colony in 1874, the land was divided between white settlers who had bought plantations and the *taukei ni ngele,* the Fijian "owners of the soil." The government assumed title to the balance. Today the alienated (privately owned) plantation lands are known as "freehold" land—about 10% of the total. Another 7% is Crown land and the remaining 83% is inalienable Fijian communal land which can be leased (about 30% is) but may never be sold. Compare this 83% (much of it not arable) with only 3% Maori land in New Zealand and almost zero native Hawaiian land. Land ownership has provided the Fijian with a security which allows him to preserve his traditional culture, unlike most indigenous peoples in other countries.

Communal land is administered on behalf of some 6,600 clan groups *(matanggali)* by the Native Land Trust Board, a government agency established in 1940. In Nov. 1976 the Agricultural Landlords and Tenants Act increased the period for which native land can be leased from 10 to 30 years. Crown land may be assigned on a 99-year basis. Yet the difficulty in obtaining land has led to a serious squatter problem: people simply occupy unused areas without concerning themselves about who holds the title. Tenants too are less likely to develop land than owners, and so the system is an obstacle to development.

At the First Constitutional Conference in 1965, Indian rights were promulgated, and the 1970 independence constitution asserted that *everyone* born in Fiji would be a citizen with equal rights. But land laws, up to the present, have very much favored "Fiji for the Fijians." Fiji Indians have always accepted Fijian ownership of the land, provided they are granted satisfactory leases. Now there are fears among Indian farmers that the land may be reclaimed when the leases expire around the end of the century. Indians seem to effectively occupy most of the best land, while Fijian villages are often adjacent to land of little agricultural use. Radical Fijian nationalists backing Rabuka have already called for the Indians to be driven from the land.

Other Groups

The 5,000 Fiji-born Europeans or *Kai Viti* are descendants of Australians and New Zealanders who came to create cotton, sugar, or copra plantations in the 19th century. Many married Fijian women and the 13,000 Part Europeans of Fiji today often call themselves Part Fijians. Many other Europeans are present in Fiji on temporary contracts or as tourists. The 5,000 Chinese in Fiji are descended from free settlers who came to set up small businesses a century ago. Fiji Chinese tend to intermarry freely with the other racial groups. There is almost no intermarriage between Fijians and Fiji Indians.

The people of Rotuma, a majority of whom now live in Suva, are Polynesians. On neighboring islands off Vanua Levu are the Micronesians of Rambi (from Kiribati) and the Polynesians of Kioa (from Tuvalu). The descendants of Solomon Islanders blackbirded during the 19th century still live in communities near Suva, Levuka, and Lambasa. The Tongans in Lau and other Pacific islanders who have immigrated to Fiji make this an ethnic crossroads of the Pacific.

The three largest ethnic groups in Fiji are Indians, Fijians, and Polynesians.

Social Conditions

The partial breakdown in race relations after the Rabuka coups was a tragedy for Fiji, though racial antagonism has been exaggerated. Despite the rhetoric the different ethnic groups have always gotten along well together with remarkably little animosity. As important as race are the variations between rich and poor, urban and rural. About 9% of the population lives in absolute poverty. Avenues for future economic growth are limited and there's chronic unemployment. The population is growing at an annual rate of 2.1% (compared to 0.9% in the U.S.) and the subsistence economy simply can't absorb these numbers. The lack of work is reflected in the increasing crime rate.

Though literacy is high at 80% most schools are operated by religious groups and local communities. Tuition fees must be paid at all levels. The Fiji Institute of Technology was founded at Suva in 1963, followed by the University of the South Pacific in 1968. The university serves the 11 Pacific countries which contribute to its costs. Medical services in Fiji are heavily subsidized. The main hospitals are at Lambasa, Lautoka, and Suva, though smaller hospitals, health centers, and nursing stations are scattered around the country. The most common infectious diseases are influenza, gonorrhea, and syphilis.

Language

Fijian is a member of the Austronesian family of languages spoken from Easter Island to Madagascar. In 1835 two Wesleyan missionaries, David Cargill and William Cross, devised the form of written Fijian used in Fiji today. Since all consonants in Fijian are separated by vowels they spelled mb as b, nd as d, ng as g, ngg as q, and th as c. (For convenience this book employs phonetic spelling for place names and words, but Fijian spelling for the names of individuals.) Fijian vowels are pronounced as in Latin or Spanish, while the consonants are similar to English. Syllables end in a vowel and the next-to-last syllable is usually the emphasized. Where two vowels appear together they are sounded separately.

Though Cargill and Cross worked at Lakemba in the Lau Group, the political importance of tiny Mbau Island just off Viti Levu caused the Mbauan dialect of Fijian to be selected as the "official" version of the language and in 1850 a dictionary and grammar were published. When the Bible was translated into Mbauan that dialect's dominance was assured and it is today's spoken and written Fijian.

Hindustani or Hindi is the household tongue of most Fiji Indians. Fiji Hindi has diverged from that spoken in India with the adoption of many words from English and other Indian languages such as Urdu. Though a quarter of Fiji Indians are descended from immigrants from southern India where Tamil and Telegu are spoken, few use these languages today, even in the home. Fiji Muslims speak Hindi out of practical considerations, though they might consider Urdu their mother tongue. In their spoken form Hindi and Urdu are very similar. English is the second official language in Fiji and is understood by almost everyone. All schools teach exclusively in English after the fourth grade.

CUSTOMS

Fijians and Fiji Indians are very tradition-oriented people. Over the years they have retained a surprising number of their own ancestral customs despite the flood of conflicting influences which has swept the Pacific over the past century. Rather than becoming a melting pot where one group assimilated another, Fiji is a patchwork of varied traditions.

The obligations and responsibilities of Fijian village life include not only the erection and upkeep of certain buildings, but personal participation in the many ceremonies which give their lives meaning. Hindu Indians, on the other hand, practice firewalking and observe festivals such as Holi and Diwali, just as their forbears in India did for thousands of years.

Fijian Firewalking

In Fiji, both Fijians and Indians practice firewalking, with the difference that the Fijians walk on heated stones instead of hot embers. Legends tell how the ability to walk on fire was first given to a warrior named Tui-na-vinggalita from Mbengga Island, just off the south coast of Viti Levu, who had spared the life of a spirit god he caught while fishing for eels. The freed spirit gave to Tui-na-vinggalita the gift of immunity to fire. Today his descendants act as *mbete* (high priest) of the rite of *vilavilairevo* (jumping into the oven). Only members of his tribe, the Sawau, perform the ceremony. The Tui Sawau lives at Ndakuimbengga village on Mbengga, but firewalking is now only performed at the resort hotels on Viti Levu.

Fijian firewalkers (men only) are not permitted to have contact with women or to eat any coconut for two weeks prior to a performance. In a circular pit about four meters across, hundreds of large stones are first heated by a wood fire until they're white hot. If you throw a handkerchief on the stones, it will burst into flames. Much ceremony and chanting accompanies certain phases of the ritual, such as the moment when the wood is removed to leave just the red-hot embers. The men psych themselves up in a nearby hut, then emerge, enter the pit, and walk briskly once around it. Bundles of leaves and grass are then thrown on the stones and the men stand inside the steaming pit again to chant a final song. They seem to have complete immunity to pain and there's no trace of injury. The men appear to fortify themselves with the heat, to gain some psychic power from the ritual.

Indian Firewalking

By an extraordinary coincidence Fiji Indians brought with them the ancient practice of religious firewalking. In southern India, firewalking occurs in the pre-monsoon season as a call to the goddess Kali (Durga) for rain. Fiji Indian firewalking is an act of purification, or fulfillment of a vow to thank the god for help in a difficult situation.

Spikes piercing their cheeks, Fiji Indians walk over hot coals at a religious festival, to purify themselves or give thanks to Durga for assistance rendered.

Draped in croton leaves, the cupbearer offers a bowl of yanggona *to a visiting chief at a formal kava ceremony.*

In Fiji there is firewalking in most Hindu temples once a year, sometime between May and September. The actual event takes place on a Sun. at 1600 on the Suva side of Viti Levu, and at 0400 on the Nandi/Lautoka side. In Aug. there is firewalking at the Sangam Temple on Howell Road, Suva. During the 10 festival days preceding the walk, participants remain in isolation, eat only unspiced vegetarian food, and spiritually prepare themselves. There are prayers at the temple in the early morning and a group-singing of religious stories at about 1900 from Mon. to Thursday. The yellow-clad devotees, their faces painted bright yellow and red, often pierce their cheeks or other bodily parts with spikes as part of the purification rites. Their faith is so strong they feel no pain.

The event is extremely colorful; drumming and chanting accompany the visual spectacle. Visitors are welcome to observe the firewalking but since the exact date varies from temple to temple according to the phases of the moon (among other factors), you have to keep asking to find out where and when it will take place. To enter the temple you must remove your shoes and any leather clothing.

The *Yanggona* Ceremony

Yanggona (kava), a tranquilizing, nonalcoholic drink which numbs the tongue and lips, comes from the *waka* (dried root) of the pepper plant *(Macropiper methysticum)*. This ceremonial preparation is the most honored feature of the formal life of Fijians, Tongans,

and Samoans. It is performed with the utmost gravity according to a sacramental ritual to mark births, marriages, deaths, official visits, the installation of a new chief, etc.

New mats are first spread on the floor, on which is placed a handcarved *tanoa* (wooden bowl) nearly a meter wide. A long fiber cord decorated with cowrie shells and fastened to the bowl leads to the guests of honor. To step over this cord during the ceremony is forbidden. As many as 70 men take their places before the bowl. The officiants are adorned with tapa, fiber, and croton leaves, their torsos smeared with glistening coconut oil, their faces usually blackened.

The guests present a bundle of *waka* to the hosts along with a short speech explaining their visit, a custom known as *sevu sevu*. The *sevu sevu* is received by the hosts and acknowledged with a short speech of acceptance. The *waka* are then scraped clean and pounded in a *tambili* (mortar). Formerly they were chewed. Nowadays the pulp is put in a cloth sack and mixed with water in the *tanoa*. In the chiefly ceremony the *yanggona* is kneaded and strained through *vau* (hibiscus) fibers.

The mixer displays the strength of the grog (kava) to the *mata ni vanua* (master of ceremonies) by pouring out a cupful into the *tanoa*. If the *mata ni vanua* considers the mix too strong, he calls for "*wai*" ("water"), then says "*lose*" ("mix") and the mixer proceeds. Again he shows the consistency to the *mata ni vanua* by pouring out a cupful. If it appears right the *mata ni vanua* says "*lomba*" ("squeeze"). The mixer squeezes the remaining juice out of the pulp, puts it aside, and announces *"sa lose oti saka na yanggona, vaka turanga"* ("the kava is ready, my chief"). He runs both hands around the rim of the *tanoa* and claps three times.

The *mata ni vanua* then says *"talo"* ("serve"). The cupbearer squats in front of the *tanoa* with a *"mbilo"* ("half coconut shell") which the mixer fills. The cupbearer then presents the first cup to the guest of honor, who claps once, drains it, and everyone claps three times. The second cup goes to the guests' *mata ni vanua,* who claps once and drinks. The man sitting next to the mixer says *"aa"* and everyone answers *"matha"* ("empty"). The third cup is for the first local chief, who claps once before drinking and everyone claps three times after. Then the *mata ni vanua* of the first local chief claps once, drinks, and everyone says *"matha".* The same occurs for the second local chief and his *mata ni vanua.*

After these six men have finished their cups, the mixer announces *"sa matha saka tu na yanggona, vaka turanga"* ("the bowl is empty, my chief"), and the *mata ni vanua* says *"thombo"* ("clap"). The mixer then runs both hands around the rim of the *tanoa* and claps three times. This terminates the full ceremony, but then a second bowl is prepared and everyone drinks. During the first bowl complete silence must be maintained.

Social Kava Drinking

While the above describes one of several forms of the full *yanggona* ceremony which is performed only for high chiefs, abbreviated versions are put on for tourists at the hotels. However, the village people have simplified grog sessions almost daily. Kava drinking is an important form of Fijian entertainment and a way of structuring friendships and community relations. Even in government offices a bowl of grog is kept for the staff to take as a refreshment at *yanggona* breaks. Some say the Fijians have *yanggona* rather than blood in their veins.

Visitors to villages are invariably invited to participate in informal kava ceremonies, in which case it's customary to present 200 grams or more of kava roots to the group. Do this at the beginning, before anybody starts drinking, and make a short speech explaining the purpose of your visit (be it a desire to meet the people and learn about their way of life, an interest in seeing or doing something in particular on their island, or just a holiday from work). Don't hand the roots to anyone, just place them on the mat in the center of the circle. The bigger the bundle of roots, the bigger the smiles. (The roots are easily purchased at any town market for about F$5 a half kilo. Kava doesn't grow well in dry, cane-growing areas or in the Yasawas, so carry a good supply with you when traveling there, as it can be hard to buy more. Kava is prohibited entry into the U.S., so don't consider bringing home any leftovers.)

Clap once when the cupbearer offers you the *mbilo,* take it in both hands and say *"mbula"* just before the cup meets your lips. Clap three times after you drink. Remember, you're a participant not an onlooking tourist so don't take photos if the ceremony is rather formal. Even though you may not like the appearance or taste of the drink, do try to finish at least the first cup. Tip the cup to show you're done.

It's considered extremely bad manners to turn your back on a chief during a kava ceremony, to walk in front of the circle of people when entering or leaving, or to step over the long cord attached to the *tanoa.* At the other end of the cord is a white cowry which symbolizes a link to ancestral spirits.

Presentation Of The *Tambua*

The *tambua* is a tooth of the sperm whale. It was once presented when chiefs exchanged delegates at confederacy meetings and before conferences on peace or war. In recent times, the *tambua* is presented during chiefly *yanggona* ceremonies as a symbolic welcome for a respected visitor or guest or as a prelude to public business or modern-day official functions. On the village level, *tambuas* are still commonly presented to arrange marriages, to show sympathy at funerals, to request favors, to settle disputes, or simply to show respect.

Old *tambuas* are highly polished from continuous handling. The larger the tooth, the greater its ceremonial value. *Tambuas* are prized cultural property and may not be exported from Fiji. The Endangered Species Act prohibits their entry into the United States, Australia, and many other countries.

Fijian Dancing *(Meke)*

The term *meke* describes the combination of dance, song, and theater performed at feasts and on special occasions. Brandishing spears, their faces painted with charcoal, the men wear frangipani leis and skirts of shredded leaves. The war club dance reenacts heroic events of the past. Both men and women perform the *vakamalolo,* a sitting dance, while the *seasea* is danced by women flourishing fans. The *taralala,* in which visitors may be asked to join, is a simple two-step shuffle danced side-by-side. As elsewhere in the Pacific the dances tell a story, though the music now is strongly influenced by Christian hymns and contemporary pop. Fijian *meke* are often part of a *mangiti* or feast performed at hotels. The Dance Theater of Fiji at Pacific Harbor is well regarded.

Stingray-spearing And Fish Drives

Stingrays are lethal-looking creatures with caudal spines up to 18 cm long. To catch them, eight or nine punts are drawn up in a line about a kilometer long beside the reef. As soon as a stingray is sighted, a punt is paddled forward with great speed until close enough to hurl a spear.

Another time-honored sport and source of food is the fish drive. An entire village participates. Around the flat surface of a reef at rising tide, sometimes as many as 70 men and women group themselves in a circle a kilometer or more in circumference. All grip a ring of connected liana vines with leaves attached. While shouting, singing, and beating long poles on the seabed, the group slowly contracts the ring as the tide comes in. The shadow of the ring alone is enough to keep the fish within the circle. The fish are finally directed landward into a net or stone fish trap.

The Rising Of The *Mbalolo*

Among all the Pacific Island groups, this event takes place only in Samoa and Fiji. The *mbalolo (Eunice viridis)* is a segmented worm of the Coelomate order, considered a culinary delicacy throughout these islands. It's about 45 cm long and lives deep in the fissures of coral reefs, rising to the surface only twice a year to propagate and then die. This natural almanac keeps both lunar and solar times, and has a fixed day of appearance—even if a hurricane is raging—one night in the third quarter of the moon in Oct., and the corresponding night in November. It has never

closing the ring during a Mbengga fish drive

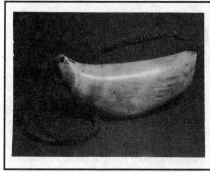

tambua: *Yanggona* (or kava) the Fijians share with the Polynesians, but the *tambua*, or whale's tooth, is significant only in Fiji. The *tambuas* obtained from the sperm whale have always played an important part in Fijian ceremonies. During great festivals they were hung around the necks of warriors and chiefs in the 19th century, and even today they are presented to distinguished guests and are exchanged at weddings, births, deaths, reconciliations, and also when personal or communal contracts or agreements are entered into. *Tambuas*, contrary to popular belief, have never been used as currency and cannot purchase goods or services. To be presented with a *tambua* is a great honor.

failed to appear on time for over 100 years now. You can even check your calendar by it.

Because this thin, jointed worm appears with such mathematical certainty, Fijians are waiting in their boats to scoop the millions of writhing, reddish-brown (male) and moss-green (female) spawn from the water when they rise to the surface just before dawn. Within an hour after the rising the sacs burst and the fertile milt spawns the next generation of *mbalolo*. This is one of the most bizarre curiosities in the natural history of the South Pacific and the southeast coast of Ovalau is a good place to observe it.

CRAFTS

The traditional art of Fiji is closely related to that of Tonga. Fijian canoes, too, were patterned after the more advanced Polynesian type although the Fijians were timid sailors. War clubs, food bowls, *tanoas* (kava bowls), eating utensils, clay pots, and tapa cloth *(masi)* are considered Fiji's finest artifacts. The Government Handicraft Center behind Ratu Sukuna House in Suva has the most authentic designs.

There are two kinds of woodcarvings: the ones made from *nawanawa (Cordia subcordata)* wood are superior to those of the lighter, highly breakable *vau (Hibiscus tiliaceus)*. In times past it often took years to make a Fijian war club as the carving was done in the living tree and left to grow into the desired shape. The best *tanoas* are carved in the Lau Group.

Though many crafts are alive and well some Fijians have taken to carving mock New Guinea masks painted with black shoe polish to look like ebony for sale to tourists. Also avoid crafts made from endangered species such as sea turtles (tortoise shell) and marine mammals (whales' teeth, etc.). Prohibited entry into most countries, they will be confiscated by Customs if found.

Pottery-making

Fijian pottery-making is unique in that it is a Melanesian artform. The Polynesians forgot how to make pottery thousands of years ago. Today the main center for pottery-making in Fiji is the Singatoka Valley on Viti Levu. Here, the women shape clay using a wooden paddle outside against a rounded stone held inside the future pot. The potter's wheel was unknown in the Pacific.

A saucer-like section forms the bottom; the sides are built up using slabs of clay, or coils and strips. These are welded and battered to shape. When the form is ready the pot is dried inside the house for a few days, then heated over an open fire for about an hour. Resin from the gum of the *dakua* (kauri) tree is rubbed on the outside while the pot is still hot. This adds a varnish which brings out the color of the clay and improves the pot's water-holding ability.

This pottery is extremely fragile, which accounts for the quantity of potsherds found on ancient village sites. Smaller, less-breakable pottery products such as ashtrays are now made for sale to visitors.

Fijian pottery-making has changed very little since this 1845 Sherman and Smith engraving.

Fijian masi *(tapa)*

Tapa Cloth

This is Fiji's most characteristic traditional product. Tapa is light, portable, and inexpensive, and a piece makes an excellent souvenir to brighten up a room back home. It's made by women on Vatulele Island off Viti Levu and on certain islands of the Lau Group.

To make tapa, the inner, water-soaked bark of the paper mulberry *(Broussonetia papyrifera)* is stripped from the tree and steeped in water. Then it's scraped with shells and pounded into a thin sheet with wooden mallets. Four of these sheets are applied one over another and pounded together, then left to dry in the sun.

While Tongan tapa is decorated by holding a relief pattern under the tapa and overpainting the lines, Fijian tapa *(masi kesa)* is distinctive for its rhythmic geometric designs applied with stencils made from green pandanus and banana leaves. The stain is rubbed on in the same manner one makes temple rubbings from a stone inscription.

The only colors used are red, from red clay, and a black pigment obtained by burning candlenuts. Both powders are mixed with boiled gums made from scraped roots. Sunlight deepens and sets the colors. Each island group had its characteristic colors and patterns, ranging from plant-like paintings to geometric designs. Sheets of tapa feel like felt when finished.

HOLIDAYS AND EVENTS

Public holidays in Fiji include New Year's Day (1 Jan.), Good Friday and Easter Monday (March/April), Queen Elizabeth's Birthday (a Mon. around June 14), Bank Holiday (first Mon. in Aug.), Fiji Day (a Mon. around 10 Oct.), Diwali (Oct. or Nov.), Prince Charles's Birthday (a Mon. around Nov. 14), Prophet Mohammed's Birthday (Nov. or Dec.), and Christmas Days (25 and 26 Dec.). Some dates vary from year to year.

Check with the Fiji Visitors Bureau to see if any festivals are scheduled during your visit. The best known are the Mbula Festival in Nandi (July), the Hibiscus Festival in Suva (Aug.), the Bougainvillea Festival in Mba (Sept.), and the Sugar Festival in Lautoka (Sept. or Oct.). Before Diwali, the Hindu festival of lights, Hindus clean their homes then light lamps or candles to mark the arrival of spring. Fruit and sweets are offered to Lakshmi, goddess of wealth. Holi is an Indian spring festival in Feb. or March.

The soccer season in Fiji is Feb. to Nov., while rugby is played from April to September. Rugby is played only by Fijians, while soccer teams are predominantly Indian. Cricket is played from Nov. to March, mostly in rural areas. Lawn bowling is also popular. Sports of any kind are forbidden on Sunday.

CONDUCT

It's a Fijian custom to smile when you meet a stranger and say something like "good morning" or at least "hello." Of course you needn't do this in the large towns, but you should almost everywhere else. If you meet someone you know, stop for a moment to exchange a few words. Fijian villages are private property and it's important to get permission before entering one. Of course it's okay to continue along a road that passes through a village but do ask before leaving the road. It's good manners to take off your hat while walking through a village, where only the chief is permitted to wear a hat. Some villagers also object to sunglasses. Don't point at people in villages. If you wish to surf off a village or picnic on their beach, you should also ask permission. If you approach the Fijians with respect you're sure to be so treated in return.

Shorts are not proper dress for women in villages, so carry a *sulu* to cover up. Topless sunbathing by women is not allowed in Fiji. Men should always wear a shirt in town and women should forgo halter tops, see-through dresses, and short shorts. Scanty dress in public shows a lack of respect. Notice how the locals are dressed.

Take off your shoes before entering a *mbure* and stoop as you walk around inside. Men should sit cross-legged, women with their legs to the side. Sitting with your legs stretched out in front is insulting. Fijian villagers consider it offensive to walk in front of a person seated on the floor (pass behind) or to fail to say "*tilou*" (excuse me) as you go by. Never place your hand on another's head and don't sit in doorways. Do you notice how

Fijians rarely shout? Keep your voice down. Don't stand up during a *sevu sevu* to village elders. When you give a gift hold it out with both hands, not one hand.

Fijian children are very wellbehaved. There's no running or shouting when you arrive in a village and they leave you alone if you wish. Also, Fijians love children, so don't hesitate to bring your own. You'll never have to worry about finding a babysitter.

Clad in a sulu, *the all-purpose garment of the Pacific, a Fijian poses before a traditional* mbure.

ACCOMMODATIONS

Accommodations

An 8% hotel tax is added to all accommodations. Standard big-city hotels are found in Nandi and Suva. Most of the beach resorts are on small islands off Lautoka, along the Coral Coast on Viti Levu's south side, or near Savusavu on Vanua Levu. The island resorts are secluded with fan-cooled *mbure* accommodations, while at the Coral Coast hotels you often get an a/c room in a main building. The Coral Coast has more to offer in the way of land tours, shopping, and entertainment/eating options, while the offshore resorts are preferable if you want a rest or are into water sports. Most guests at the deluxe hotels in both areas are on package tours. For economy and flexibility avoid prepaying hotel accommodations from home.

Many hotels offer dormitory beds as well as individual rooms. Most of the dorms are mixed. Women can sometimes request a women-only dorm when things are slow, but it's not usually guaranteed. The New Zealand Youth Hostel Association (Y.H.A.) has arranged a 20% discount for members in dormitories at selected tourist hotels on Viti Levu. They would do better to encourage the development of real youth hostels in the South Pacific, but evidently this is too much trouble for them.

Budget accommodations are spread out, with concentrations in Nandi, Suva, Lautoka, Levuka, and Savusavu. All are listed in this book. A few of the cheapies double as whorehouses, making them cheap in both senses of the word. Some Suva hotels lock their front doors at 1100 so ask first if you're planning a night on the town. Government resthouses exist in out-of-the-way places like Nandarivatu, Nambouwalu, and Lakemba. Some islands, such as Koro, Moala, Ngau, Rambi, Rotuma, and Thithia with air service from Nausori, have no facilities whatever for visitors so it really helps to know someone before heading that way.

Camping facilities (own tent) are found near Momi Bay south of Nandi, on Nukulau Island off Suva, and on Kandavu, Ovalau, and Taveuni islands. Elsewhere, get permission before pitching your tent as all land is owned by someone and land rights is a sensitive issue in Fiji. Some freelance campers on beaches such as Natandola near Nandi have been robbed, so take care. Don't ask a Fijian friend for permission to camp beside his house in the village itself. Although he

Campers, Kandavu Island. Where hotels don't exist, your tent is your home away from home.

may feel obligated to grant the request of a guest, you'll be proclaiming to everyone that his home isn't completely to your liking. Of course in places like Tavewa Island which receive visitors regularly this isn't a problem; elsewhere if all you really want is to camp make this clear from the start and get permission to do so on a beach or by a river, but *not* in the village. A *sevu sevu* should always be presented in this case. Never camp directly under a coconut tree: falling coconuts are lethal.

Staying In Villages

A great way to meet the people and learn a little about their culture is to stay in a village for a few nights. Since the Fiji Visitors Bureau hasn't set up a regular homestay program yet, you'll have to arrange this for yourself. If you befriend someone from a remote island ask them to write you a letter of introduction to their relatives back in the village. Mail a copy of it ahead with a polite letter introducing yourself, then start heading slowly that way.

In places off the beaten tourist track, you could just show up in a village and ask permission of the *turanga-ni-koro* to spend the night. Rarely will you be refused. Similarly, both Fiji Indians and native Fijians will spontaneously invite you in. The Fijians' innate dignity and kindness should not be taken for granted, however.

All across the Pacific it's customary to reciprocate when someone gives you a gift—if not now, then sometime in the future. Visitors who accept gifts (such as meals and accommodations) from islanders and do not reciprocate are undermining traditional culture, often without realizing it. It is sometimes hard to know how to pay for hospitality, but Fijian culture has a solution: the *sevu sevu*. This can be money, but it's usually a 500-gram bundle of *kava* roots *(waka)*, which can be easily purchased at any Fijian market. *Sevu sevus* are more often performed between families or couples about to be married, or at births or christenings, but the custom is certainly a perfect way for visitors to show their appreciation.

The Fiji Rucksack Club recommends that its members donate F$10 pp per night to village hosts. The *waka* is additional and anyone traveling in remote areas of Fiji should pack some (take whole roots, not powdered kava). If you give the money up front with the *waka* as a *sevu sevu* you'll get better treatment. On the overland trekking routes through villages which get scores of overnight visitors a year, it is absolutely essential to contribute.

The *sevu sevu* should be placed before (but not handed to) the *turanga-ni-koro* or village chief so he can accept or refuse. If he accepts (by touching the package) your welcome is confirmed and you may spend the night in the village. It is also possible to give some money to the lady of the house upon departure with your thanks. Just say it's your goodbye *sevu sevu* and watch the smile. A Fijian may refuse the money, but will not be offended by the offer. You could also take some gifts along such as lengths of material, T-shirts, accoustic guitar strings, or a big jar of instant coffee. Keep in mind however that Seventh-day Adventists are forbidden to have coffee, cigarettes, or kava, so you might ask if there are any SDAs around to avoid embarrassment. One thing *not* to take is alcohol which is always sure to offend somebody.

When choosing your traveling companions for a trip which involves staying in Fijian villages, make sure you agree on this before you set out. Otherwise you could end up subsidizing somebody else's trip, or worse, have to stand by and watch the Fijian villagers subsidize it. Never arrive in a village on a Sunday and don't overstay your welcome.

A final note from Josje Hebbes of the Netherlands:

If people only meet Indians on the street or in tourist centers they will get a totally wrong idea of Indian culture. To appreciate their hospitality and friendliness one should also try to spend some time in Indian settlements. If you go on a day hike you might be invited for lunch. First they will serve you something sweet like juice or tea. That's their way. Make sure you don't leave Fiji with a mistaken impression of Fiji Indians!

Village Life

Staying in a village is definitely not for everyone. Most houses contain no electricity, running water, toilet, furniture, etc., and only native food will be offered. Water and your left hand serve as toilet paper. You should also expect to sacrifice most of your privacy, to stay up late drinking grog, and to sit in the house and socialize when you could be out exploring. On Sunday you'll have to stay put the whole day. The constant attention and lack of sanitary conditions may become tiresome, but it would be considered rude to attempt to be alone or refuse the food or grog. Remember that villagers are not paid performers to entertain tourists but humans like yourself living real lives, so put your heart in it or stay away.

When you enter a Fijian village people will want to be helpful and will direct or accompany you to the person or place you seek. If you show genuine interest in something and ask to see how it is done you will usually be treated with respect and asked if there is anything else you would like to know. Initially, Fijians may hesitate to welcome you into their homes because they fear you will not wish to sit on a mat and eat native foods with your fingers. Once you show them that this isn't true, you'll receive the full hospitality treatment.

Consider participating in the daily activities of the family such as weaving, cooking, gardening, and fishing. Your hosts will probably try to dissuade you from "working" but if you persist you'll become accepted. Staying in the villages of Fiji offers one of the most rewarding travel experiences in the South Pacific, and if everyone plays fair it will always be so.

FOOD AND ENTERTAINMENT

Unlike some other South Pacific nations, Fiji has many good, cheap eateries. Chinese restaurants are everywhere. On the western side of Viti Levu, Indian restaurants use the name "lodge." Indian dishes are spicy, often curries with rice and *dhal* (lentil) soup. Goat curry is a unique Indian dish. Instead of bread Indians eat *roti*, a flat tortilla-like pancake. All but the hotel restaurants are closed on Sun. and an 8% tax is added to the bill. Drinking alcoholic beverages on the street is prohibited. Fijians have their own pace and trying to make them do things more quickly is often counterproductive. Their charm and the friendly personal attention you receive more than make up for the occasionally slow service at restaurants.

Real Fijian dishes such as baked fish *(ika)* in coconut cream *(lolo)* with cassava *(tavioka)*, taro *(ndalo)*, breadfruit, and sweet potato *(kumala)* take a long time to prepare and must be served fresh, which makes it difficult to offer them in a restaurant. Try *nduruka,* a native vegetable tasting something like a cross between artichoke and asparagus.

Taro leaves are used to make *palusami* (with coconut cream) and *rourou* (the local spinach).

Raw fish *(kokonda)* is an appetizing dish. To prepare it, clean and skin the fish, then dice the fillet. Squeeze lemon or lime juice over it, and store in a cool place about 10 hours. When it's ready to serve, add chopped onions, garlic, green peppers, tomatoes, and coconut cream to the fish to taste. Local fishmongers know which species makes the best raw fish, but know what you're doing before you join them—island stomachs are probably stronger than yours. It's safer to eat well-cooked food and to peel your own fruit.

The sweet potato is something of an anomaly—it's the only Pacific food plant with a South American origin. How it got to the islands is not known, but it and tobacco seem to have been introduced into New Guinea about 1600, suggesting the possibility of an Hispanic connection. Taro is an elephant-eared plant cultivated in freshwater swamps. Although yams are considered a prestige food, they're not as nutritious as breadfruit and taro. Yams can grow up to three meters long and weigh hundreds of kilos. Papaya *(pawpaw)* is nourishing: a third of a cup contains as much vitamin C as 18 apples. To ripen a green papaya overnight, puncture it a few times with a knife. Don't overeat papaya—unless you *need* an effective laxative.

The ancient Pacific islanders, who stopped making pottery over a millennium ago, developed an ingenious way of cooking in an underground earth oven *(lovo)*. First a stack of dry coconut husks is burned in a pit. Once the fire is going well, stones are heaped on top. When most of the husks have burnt away the food is wrapped in banana leaves and placed on the hot stones, fish and meat below, vegetables above. A whole pig may be cleaned then stuffed with banana leaves and hot stones. This cooks the beast from inside out as well as outside in and the leaves create steam. The food is then covered with more leaves and stones, and in about 2$\frac{1}{2}$ hours everything will be cooked.

Breadfruit

The breadfruit is the plant most often associated with the South Pacific. The theme of a man turning himself into such a tree to save his family during famine often recurs in South Pacific legends. Ancient voyagers brought breadfruit shoots or seeds from Southeast

Asia. When baked in an underground oven or roasted over flames, the now seedless Polynesian variety resembles bread. Joseph Banks, botanist on Capt. Cook's first voyage, wrote: "If a man should in the course of his lifetime plant 10 trees, which if well done might take the labor of an hour or thereabouts, he would completely fulfill his duty to his own as well as future generations."

The breadfruit *(Artocarpus altilis),* a tall tree with broad green leaves, provides shade as well as food. A well-watered tree can produce as many as 1,000 pale green breadfruits a year. Robert Lee Eskridge described a breadfruit thus: "Its outer rind or skin, very hard, is covered with a golf-ball-like surface of small irregular pits or tiny hollows. An inner rind about a half-inch thick surrounds the fruit itself, which when baked tastes not unlike a doughy potato. Perhaps fresh bread, rolled up until it becomes a semi-firm mass, best describes the breadfruit when cooked." The starchy, easily digested fruit is rich in vitamin B. When consumed with a protein such as fish or meat it serves as an energy food. Like the coconut, the breadfruit tree itself had many uses, including the provision of wood for outrigger canoes.

The Coconut Palm

Human life would not be possible on most of the Pacific's far-flung atolls without this all

slicing breadfruit

Every part of the coconut tree (Cocos nucifera) can be used. The husk provides cord, mats, brushes, and fuel, the leaves thatch, baskets, and fans, and the trunk building material. Food and oil from the nuts are the greatest prize. A healthy tree will produce 50 nuts a year for over 60 years.

purpose tree. It reaches maturity in eight years then produces about 50 nuts a year for 60 years. Aside from its aesthetic value and usefulness in providing shade, the water of the green coconut provides a refreshing drink, and the white meat of the young nut is a delicious food. The harder meat of more mature nuts is grated and squeezed, giving rise to a coconut cream used alone or in cooking. The oldest nuts are cracked open, the hard meat removed, then dried to be sold as copra. Copra is pressed to extract the oil, which in turn is made into candles, cosmetics, and soap. Millionaire's salad is made by shredding the growth cut from the heart of the tree. For each salad, a fully mature tree must be sacrificed.

The nut's hard inner shell can be used as a cup and makes excellent firewood. Rope, cordage, brushes, and heavy matting are produced from the coir fiber of the husk. The smoke from burning husks is a most effective mosquito repellent. The leaves of the coconut tree are used to thatch the roofs of the islanders' cottages or are woven into baskets, mats, and fans. The trunk provides tim-

ber for building and furniture. Actually, these are only the common uses: there are many others besides.

Entertainment

Considering the strong Aussie presence and the temperature it's not surprising that Fiji has its share of colorful bars where bottled Fiji Bitter beer is consumed cold in amazing quantities. Some bars become discos after 2100. Respectable visitors are welcome at the ex-colonial "clubs," where the beer prices are generally lower and the clientele more sedate. Barefoot beachcombers in T-shirts and shorts may be refused entry. Don't overlook the resort bars where the swank surroundings cost only slightly more. Unlike Australia and New Zealand it's not customary to bring your own booze into restaurants.

The large hotels around Nandi or on the Coral Coast often stage a weekly *lovo,* usually accompanied by a Fijian *meke* or song and dance performance in which legends, love stories, and historical events are told in song and gesture. Alternatively firewalking may be presented. This is a good opportunity to taste the local food and see traditional dancing for about F$40 pp. If you can't afford the meal it's often possible to witness the spectacle from the bar for the price of a drink. These events are held weekly on certain days, so ask. Friday night is the time to let it all hang out; on Sat. many people are preparing for a family get-together or church; everything grinds to a halt Sat. at midnight and Sun. is *very quiet*—a good day to go hiking or to the beach.

In Fiji it's cheap to go to the movies, usually romance, horror, and adventure. As everywhere good psychological films are the exception. Video fever is the latest craze, and you often see throngs of locals crowded into someone's living room watching an inane tape rented from one of the ubiquitous video rental shops. Many guesthouses have video too, so make sure your room is well away from it.

SHOPPING

Shops in Fiji close at 1300 on Sat. except in Nausori town where they stay open all day Sat. but only half a day on Wednesday. The 1987 military coups placed Fiji firmly in the South Pacific Bible Belt, which also encompasses Tonga, Western Samoa, and Cook Islands, so no business may be conducted on Sunday. Fiji Indians dominate the duty-free trade. If you're buying from an Indian merchant always bargain hard. Fijians usually begin by asking a much lower price in which case bargaining isn't so important.

Fiji's duty-free shops are not really duty-free as all goods are subject to a 10% fiscal tax plus the 8% turnover tax. Bargaining is the order of the day, but only in Suva is the selection really good. To be frank, Americans can buy the kind of Japanese electrical merchandise sold "duty-free" in Fiji cheaper at any of the discount houses in downtown Los Angeles or through discount mail order at home and get more recent models. If you do buy something get an itemized receipt and guarantee, and watch they don't switch packages and unload a demo on you. Camera film is cheap, however, and the selection good—stock up. .

If you'd like to do some shopping in Fiji, locally made handicrafts such as tapa cloth, mats, kava bowls, war clubs, woodcarvings, etc., are a better investment (see "Crafts" above). The four-pronged cannibal forks available everywhere make unique souvenirs. The Government Handicraft Center in Suva is a good place to learn what's available and familiarize yourself with prices. If you're willing to spend serious money for top quality work visit the Fiji Museum beforehand. Try to purchase your souvenirs directly from the Fijian producers at street markets, etc.

Videos

It's becoming the thing to buy commercial travel video tapes of the places you visit. Keep in mind that there are three incompatible video systems loose in the world: NTSC

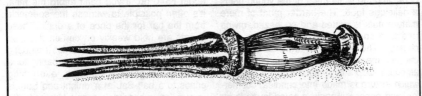

cannibal fork: It has been said that the Fijians were extremely hospitable to any strangers they did not wish to eat. Native voyagers who wrecked on their shores, who arrived "with salt water in their eyes," were liable to be killed and eaten, since all shipwrecked persons were believed to have been cursed and abandoned by the gods. Many European sailors from wrecked vessels shared the same fate. Cannibalism was a universal practice and prisoners taken in war, or even women seized while fishing, were invariably eaten. Most of the early European accounts of Fiji emphasized this trait to the exclusion of almost everything else; at one time the island group was even referred to as the "Cannibal Isles." By eating the flesh of the conquered enemy, one incorporated their mana or psychic power. One chief on Viti Levu is said to have consumed 872 people and to have made a pile of stones to record his achievement. The leaves of a certain vegetable (Solanum uporo) were wrapped around the human meat, and it was cooked in an earthen oven. Wooden forks such as the one pictured were employed at cannibal feasts by men who relied on their fingers for other food, but used these because it was considered improper to touch human flesh with fingers or lips. Presentday Fijians do not appreciate tourists who make jokes about cannibalism.

(used in North America), PAL (used in Britain, West Germany, Japan, and Australia), and SECAM (used in France and the USSR). Don't buy prerecorded tapes abroad unless they're of the system of your country.

VISAS

Everyone needs a passport valid at least six months beyond the date of entry. No visa is required of visitors from Europe, North America, or most Commonwealth countries for stays of 30 days or less although everyone needs a ticket to leave. You'll also need to have been vaccinated against yellow fever or cholera if you're arriving from an infected area, which is unlikely unless you happen to be arriving straight from the Amazon jungles or the banks of the Ganges River.

Extensions of stay are given out two months at a time up to a maximum of six months at no charge. Apply to the Immigration offices in Suva or Lautoka, and at Nandi Airport, or to the police stations in Singatoka, Mba, Tavua, Levuka, Lambasa, Savusavu, or Taveuni. You must apply before your current permit expires. Bring your passport, onward or return ticket, and proof of sufficient funds. The Immigration people can sometimes be unreasonably sticky, insisting on a ticket back to your home country no matter how much money you show. Avoid the Suva office. If you do extend up to six months you must then leave and aren't supposed to return until another six months have passed.

Fiji has three ports of entry for yachts: Suva, Lautoka, and Levuka. Levuka is by far the easiest place to check in or out as all of the officials have offices right on the main wharf. To visit the outer islands yachts require a letter of authorization from the commissioner (at Nausori, Lambasa, Lautoka, or Levuka) of the division they wish to visit or from the Secretary of Fijian Affairs in Suva. The army searches all arriving yachts for guns and charges a F$20 fee for the service.

Here's a list of Fiji's diplomatic offices around the world where you can inquire about the possibility of working in Fiji (special skill required) or just get information.

DIPLOMATIC OFFICES

Permanent Mission of Fiji to the United Nations
One U.N. Plaza, 26th Floor,
New York, NY 10017 USA

Embassy of Fiji
Suite 240, 2233 Wisconsin Ave. N.W.,
Washington, DC 20007 USA

Embassy of Fiji
9 Beagle St.,
Canberra, ACT 2600, Australia

Consulate General of Fiji
225 Clarence St.,
Sydney, NSW 2000, Australia

Embassy of Fiji
2nd Floor, Robert Jones House,
Jervois Quay, Wellington, New Zealand

Consulate General of Fiji
3rd Floor, Tower Block, 47 High St.,
Auckland, New Zealand

Embassy of Fiji
34 Hyde Park Gate,
London SW7 5BN, England

Embassy of Fiji
66 Ave. De Cortenberg,
1040 Brussels, Belgium

Embassy of Fiji
Noa Building (10th Floor),
3-5, Chome Azabudai, Minato-Ku,
Tokyo 106, Japan

MONEY AND COMMUNICATIONS

Money

The currency is the Fiji dollar, which is slightly lower than the U.S. dollar in value (about US$1 = F$1.30). It's based on a basket of currencies which means it doesn't fluctuate much. Always try to have lots of small bills handy and don't expect to change foreign currency outside the main towns. Tipping is only practiced in luxury hotels catering to packaged Americans. Ask the price of a room, meal, or service before accepting it. And don't forget the 8% turnover tax which is added to all hotel, restaurant, car rental, and duty-free shopping bills.

The bulk of your travel funds should be in traveler's cheques. Banking hours are Mon. to Thurs. 0930-1500, Fri. 0930-1600. The banks operating in Fiji are the ANZ Bank, Bank of Baroda, Bank of New Zealand, Hong Kong and Shanghai Bank, National Bank of Fiji, and Westpac Banking Corporation. There are banks in all the towns, but it's usually not possible to change traveler's cheques on the outer islands; credit cards are strictly for the cities and resorts. Avoid taking Fijian bank notes out of the country. Change whatever you have left over into the currency of the next country on your itinerary. Fijian dollars are difficult to change and heavily discounted outside Fiji.

Currency controls have spawned a small black market offering about 10% better than the official rate for cash dollars. Do the transaction in private as foreigners caught wheeling and dealing have been roughed up by the authorities. Also take care changing at hotels, which often give a much lower rate than the banks. If you need money sent, have your banker make a telegraphic transfer to any Westpac Bank branch in Fiji. If you're having money wired, have an odd amount (such as $501.35) sent. If there's an error a figure like this would be easier to trace in bank ledgers or computer printouts than a round figure like $500, which might be one of dozens of similar transactions.

Post And Telephone

Post offices are generally open weekdays 0800-1600. Always use airmail when posting letters from Fiji. Airmail takes two weeks to reach North America and Europe, surface mail takes up to five months. When writing to Fiji use the words "Fiji Islands" in the address, otherwise the letter might go to Fuji, Japan. Try to include the post office box number of the individual or business, since mail delivery is rare. If it's a remote island or small village you're writing to, the person's name will be sufficient. To send a picture postcard to an islander is a very nice way to say thank you. When collecting mail at poste restante (general delivery), be sure to check for the initials of your first and second names, plus any initial which is similar. Have your correspondents print and underline your last name.

Most post offices have public telephones which are often bright red. Lift the receiver, wait for a dial tone, then deposit a coin and dial. Over half the pay phones may be out of order, with long lines of people waiting to use the rest. Alternatively ask a shopkeeper if you may use his or her phone for a small fee. To make a long-distance call you'll have to call the operator at tel. 010. A better way to place a long-distance call is to go to the FINTEL (Fiji International Telecommunications) office on Victoria Parade, Suva, or any post office. International calls placed from hotel rooms are always much more expensive.

Fiji has direct dialing via satellite. If you want to place a call to Fiji from outside the region first dial the "international access code" (check your phone book), then the country code 679, then the number. Calling from the U.S. to Fiji is *much* cheaper than going in the other direction, so if you want to receive calls during your trip leave a list of dates and numbers where your friends or relatives can reach you.

Electric Currents

If you're taking along a plug-in razor, radio, or other electrical appliance, be aware that Fiji uses 240 AC voltage, 50 cycles. Most appliances require a converter to change from one voltage to another. You'll also need an adapter to cope with three-prong sockets with the two on top at angles. Pick both items up before you leave home as they're hard to find in Fiji. Keep voltages in mind if you buy duty-free appliances: dual voltage (110-220 V) items are best.

Time

The international date line generally follows 180 degrees longitude and creates a difference of 24 hours in time between the two sides. It swings east at Tuvalu to avoid slicing Fiji in two. Everything in the Eastern Hemisphere west of the dateline is a day later (or ahead), everything in the Western Hemisphere east of the line is a day earlier (or behind). Air travelers lose a day when they fly west across the dateline and gain it back when they return. Keep track of things by repeating to yourself, *if it's Sunday in Samoa, it's Monday in Melbourne.*

The islanders operate on "coconut time"—the coconut will fall when it's ripe. In the languid air of the South Seas punctuality takes on a new meaning. Appointments are approximate and the service relaxed. Even the seasons are fuzzy: sometimes wetter, sometimes drier but almost always hot. Slow down to the island pace and get in step with where you are. You may not get as much done but you'll enjoy life a lot more.

HEALTH

Fiji's climate is a healthy one and malaria is unknown. The sea and air are clear and usually pollution-free. The humidity nourishes the skin and the local fruit is brimming with vitamins. If you take a few precautions you'll never have a sick day. The information provided below is intended to make you knowledgeable, not fearful. Health care is good with an abundance of hospitals, health centers, and nursing stations scattered around the country. Attention at these is free or quite cheap but in the towns it's less time consuming to visit a private doctor. Their fees are also very reasonable. American-made medications may by unobtainable in Fiji, so bring a supply of whatever you think you'll need. Antibiotics should only be used to treat serious wounds and only after medical advice.

Don't go from winter weather into the steaming tropics without a rest before and after. Scuba diving on departure day can give you a severe case of the bends. Avoid jet lag by setting your watch to Fiji time as soon as you board the flight. Airplane cabins have low humidity, so drink lots of juice or water instead of carbonated drinks and don't overeat in-flight. It's also best to forego coffee as it will only keep you awake. Alcohol helps dehydrate you. If you start feeling seasick on board ship stare at the horizon, which is always steady, and stop thinking about it. Anti-motion-sickness pills are available.

Frequently the feeling of thirst is false and only due to mucous membrane dryness. Gargling or taking two or three gulps of warm water should be enough. Other means to keep moisture in the body are to have a hot drink like tea or black coffee, or any kind of slightly salted or sour drink in small quantities. Salt in fresh lime juice is remarkably refreshing.

The tap water in Fiji is usually drinkable except just after a cyclone or during droughts, when care should be taken. If in doubt, boil it or use purification pills. Tap water that is uncomfortably hot to touch is usually safe. Allow it to cool in a clean container. If the tap water is contaminated local ice will be also. Avoid brushing your teeth with water unfit to drink. If you're preparing your own meals wash your fruit and vegetables very carefully. Cooked food is less subject to contamination than raw.

Sunburn

Though you may think a tan will make you *look* healthier and more attractive, it's very damaging to the skin, which becomes dry, rigid, and prematurely old and wrinkled, especially on the face. And a burn from the sun greatly increases your risk of getting skin cancer. Begin with short exposures to the sun, perhaps half an hour, followed by an equal time in the shade. Drink plenty of liquids to keep your pores open. Avoid the sun from 1000 to 1400. Clouds and beach umbrellas will not protect you fully. Wear a T-shirt while snorkeling to protect your back. Beware of reflected sunlight. Sunbathing is the main cause of cataracts to the eyes, so wear sunglasses and a wide-brimmed hat.

Use a sunscreen lotion containing PABA rather than oil (don't forget your nose, lips, forehead, neck, hands, and feet). Sunscreens protect you from ultraviolet rays (a leading cause of cancer), while oils magnify the sun's effect. A 29- or 30-factor sunscreen such as Presun 29 or Sundown 30 will provide adequate protection. Apply the lotion *before* going to the beach to avoid being burned on the way, and re-apply periodically to replace sunscreen washed away by perspiration. After sunbathing take a tepid shower rather than a hot one, which would wash away your natural skin oils. Stay moist and use a vitamin E evening cream to preserve the youth of your skin. Calamine ointment soothes skin already burned, as does coconut oil. Pharmacists recommend Solarcaine to soothe burned skin. Rinsing off with a vinegar solution reduces peeling. Aspirin relieves some of the pain and irritation. Vitamin A and calcium counteract overdoses of vitamin D received from the sun. The fairer your skin the more essential it is to take care.

Ailments

Cuts and scratches infect easily in the tropics and take a long time to heal. Prevent infection from coral cuts by washing with soap and fresh water, then rubbing vinegar or alcohol (whisky will do) into the wounds—painful but effective. The locals usually dab coral cuts with lime juice. All cuts turn septic quickly in the tropics so try to keep them clean and covered. For bites, burns, and cuts, an antiseptic such as Solarcaine speeds healing and helps prevent infection. Bites by nono flies itch for days and can become infected.

Prickly heat, an intensely irritating rash, is caused by wearing heavy, inappropriate clothing. When the glands are blocked and the sweat is unable to evaporate, the skin becomes soggy and small red blisters appear. Synthetic fabrics like nylon are especially bad in this regard. Take a cold shower, apply calamine lotion, dust with talcum powder, and take off those clothes! Until things improve avoid alcohol, tea, coffee, and any physical activity which makes you sweat. If you're sweating profusely increase your intake of salt slightly to avoid fatigue, but not without concurrently drinking more water.

Use anti-diarrheal medications sparingly. Rather than take drugs to plug yourself up, drink plenty of unsweetened liquids like green coconuts or fresh fruit juice to help flush yourself out. Egg yolk mixed with nutmeg helps diarrhea, or have a rice and tea day. Avoid dairy products. Most cases of diarrhea are self-limiting and require only simple replacement of fluids and salts lost in diarrheal stools. If the diarrhea is persistent or you experience high fever, drowsiness, jaundice, or blood in the stool, stop traveling, rest, and consider attending a clinic. For constipation eat pineapple or any peeled fruit.

If you're sleeping in villages or with the locals, you may pick up head or body lice. Pharmacists and general stores usually have an emulsion which will eliminate the problem in minutes (pack a bottle with you if you're uptight). You'll know you're lousy when you start to scratch: pick out the little varmints and snap them between your thumb nails for fun. Intestinal parasites (worms) are also widespread. The hockworm bores its way through the soles of your feet, and if you go barefoot through gardens and plantations you're sure to pick up something.

AIDS is now present in the Pacific islands and sexually transmitted diseases (syphilis, gonorrhea, herpes) have reached almost epidemic proportions in urban areas in Fiji. Early in 1989 the first confirmed case of AIDS was diagnosed.

Toxic Fish

Over 400 species of tropical reef fish, including wrasses, snappers, groupers, barracudas, jacks, moray eels, surgeonfish, and shellfish, are known to cause seafood poisoning *(ciguatera).* There's no way to tell if a fish will cause *ciguatera:* a species can be poisonous on one side of the island but not on the other.

Several years ago scientists on Tahiti determined that a micro-algae called dinoflagellates was the cause. Normally these algae are found only in the ocean depths, but when a reef is disturbed by natural or human causes they can multiply dramatically in a lagoon. The toxins have no effect on the fish which feed on them but become concentrated in large predatory fish and enter the food chain.

There's no treatment except to relieve the symptoms (tingling, prickling, itching, nausea, vomiting, joint and muscle pains), which usually subside in a few days. Induce vomiting and take castor oil. Symptoms can recur for up to a year, and victims can be made allergic to all seafoods. Avoid biointoxication by cleaning fish as soon as they're caught, discarding the head and organs, and taking special care with oversized fish. Whether the fish is consumed cooked or raw has no bearing on this problem. Local residents often know from experience which species may be eaten.

Other Diseases

Infectious hepatitis A is a liver ailment transmitted person to person or through unboiled water, uncooked vegetables, or other foods contaminated during handling. The risk of infection is highest for those who eat village food. If you'll be spending much time in rural areas an immune globulin shot is recommended. You'll know you've got the hep when your eyeballs and urine turn yellow. Time and rest are the only cure. Viral hepatitus B is spread through sexual or blood contact.

There have been sporadic outbreaks of cholera in the Gilbert and Caroline islands (in Micronesia). Cholera is acquired via contaminated food or water, so avoid uncooked foods, peel your own fruit, and drink bottled drinks if you happen to arrive in an infected area. Horrible disfiguring diseases such as leprosy and elephantiasis are hard to catch, so it's unlikely you'll be visited by one of these nightmares of the flesh.

Dengue fever is a mosquito-transmitted disease endemic in the South Pacific. Signs are headaches, sore throat, pain in the joints, fever, nausea, and rash. It can last anywhere from five to 15 days; although you can relieve the symptoms somewhat, the only real cure is to stay in bed and wait it out. It's painful, but dengue fever usually only kills infants. No vaccine exists, so just avoid getting bitten.

Vaccinations

Officially, most visitors are not required to get any vaccinations at all before coming to Fiji. Since 1977 no naturally transmitted cases of smallpox have been recorded anywhere in the world, so forget that one. Tetanus, typhoid fever, polio, and diphtheria shots are not required, but they're a good idea if you're going off the beaten track. Tetanus and diphtheria are given together and a booster is required every 10 years. Typhoid fever is every three years, polio every five years.

The cholera vaccine is only 50% effective, valid just six months, and bad reactions are common, so forget it unless you're headed on for an infected area (such as Micronesia). Immune globulin (IG) isn't 100% effective against hepatitis A, but it does increase your general resistance to infections. IG prophylaxis must be repeated every five months. Hepatitus B vaccination involves three doses over a six-month period (duration of protection unknown). While yellow fever is confined to the jungles of South America and Africa, this vaccination is listed as a requirement if you're coming from those areas. Since the vaccination is valid 10 years, get one if you're an inveterate globetrotter.

THE
Fiji Times

INFORMATION

The **Fiji Visitors Bureau** (GPO Box 92, Suva, Fiji Islands) sends out free upon request a list of hotels with current prices and general brochures. In Fiji they have walk-in offices in Suva and at Nandi Airport. For a list of their overseas offices see the appendix in this book. Also browse the local booksellers, **Desai Bookshops** and the **Singatoka Book Depot**, both with stores all over Fiji.

The *Fiji Times,* "the first newspaper published in the world today," was founded at Levuka in 1869 but is now owned by right-wing publishing mogul Rupert Murdoch. The *Fiji Sun* was closed down right after the Rabuka coup but on-again, off-again negotiations may eventually reopen it under more manageable management. The press in Fiji is "self-censored" and upstart editors stand to

lose their license. The weekly *Fiji Post* is an official mouthpiece.

Fiji Voice, published by the Fiji Independent News Service (Box 106, Roseville, NSW 2069, Australia; US$40 a year to North America), is a monthly newsletter on political developments in Fiji. *Davui,* put out by the Movement for Democracy in Fiji (Box R500, Royal Exchange, NSW 2000, Australia; A$12 a year worldwide) is similar.

The free tabloid tourist newspapers, the weekly *Fiji Beach Press* (Box 2193, Government Buildings, Suva) and the monthly *Fiji "Fantastic"* (Box 12511, Suva), are useful to get an idea of what's on during your visit. Both regional news magazines, *Islands Business* and *Pacific Islands Monthly,* are published in Suva.

TOURIST OFFICES

Fiji Visitors Bureau
GPO Box 92
Suva, Fiji Islands

Fiji Visitors Bureau
Box 9217
Nandi Airport, Fiji Islands

Fiji Visitors Bureau
100 William St., Ste. 6, 7th Floor
Sydney, NSW 2011, Australia

Fiji Visitors Bureau
Box 1179
Auckland, New Zealand

Fiji Visitors Bureau
5777 West Century Blvd. Ste.220
Los Angeles, CA 90045 USA

Fiji Embassy
10th Floor, Noa Building
3-5, 2-Chome, Azabudai
Minato-Ku,
Tokyo 106, Japan

Marketing Services
Suite 433, High Holborn House,
52-54 High Holborn
London WDC1V 6RB, England

WHAT TO TAKE

Packing

Assemble everything you simply must take and cannot live without—then cut the pile in half. If you're still left with more than will fit into a medium-size backpack, continue eliminating. Now put it all into your pack. If the total (pack and contents) weighs over 16 kg, you'll sacrifice much of your mobility. If you can keep it down to 10 kg, you're traveling *light.* Categorize, separate, and pack all your things into plastic bags or stuff sacks for convenience and protection from moisture. In addition to your backpack you'll want a day-pack or flight bag. When checking in for flights carry anything which can't be replaced in your hand luggage.

Your Pack

A medium-sized backpack with a lightweight internal frame is best. Big external-frame packs are fine for mountain climbing, but are very inconvenient on public transport. Make sure your pack carries the weight on your hips, has a cushion for spine support, and doesn't pull backwards. The pack should strap snugly to your body but also allow ventilation to your back. It should be made of a water-resistant material such as nylon and have a Fastex buckle. Some packs have a zippered compartment in back where you can tuck in the straps and hip belt before turning your pack over to an airline.

Look for a pack with double, two-way zipper compartments and pockets which you can lock with miniature padlocks. They might not *stop* a thief, but could be deterrent enough to make him look for another mark. A 60-cm length of lightweight chain and another padlock will allow you to fasten your pack to something. Keep valuables locked in your bag, out of sight.

Camping Equipment And Clothing

A small nylon tent guarantees you a place to sleep every night. It *must* be mosquito- and waterproof. Get one with a tent fly. You'll seldom need a sleeping bag in the tropics. A youth hostel sleeping sheet is ideal—all YHA handbooks give instructions on how to make your own. You don't really need to carry a bulky foam pad as the ground is seldom cold.

For clothes take loose-fitting cotton washables, light in color and weight. Synthetic fabrics are hot and sticky in the tropics. The dress is casual with slacks and a sports shirt okay for men even at dinner parties. Local women wear long colorful dresses in the evening, but shorts are okay in daytime. If you're in doubt pack clothes which can be discarded and buy tropical garb here. Stick to clothes you can rinse in your room sink. In mid-winter (July, Aug.) it can be cool at night, so a warm piece of clothing may come in handy.

The lavalava or *sulu* is a bright two-meter piece of cloth both men and women wrap about themselves as an all-purpose garment. Any islander can show you how to wear it. Missionaries taught the South Sea island women to drape their attributes in long flowing gowns, called muu muus in Hawaii. In the South Pacific, for the muu muu-attired nursery rhyme character who "went to the cupboard to fetch her poor dog a bone," the dress is better known as a Mother Hubbard.

Take comfortable shoes that have been broken in. Running shoes and rubber thongs (zories) are very handy for day use, but will bar you from night spots with dress codes. Scuba divers' rubber booties are lightweight and perfect for both crossing rivers and reefwalking, though an old pair of sneakers may be just as good. Below we've provided a few checklists to help you assemble your gear. The listed items combined weigh well over 16 kg, so eliminate what doesn't suit you:

> pack with internal frame
> day pack or airline bag
> nylon tent and fly
> tent patching tape
> mosquito net
> synthetic sleeping bag
> YH sleeping sheet
> sun hat
> essential clothing only
> bathing suit

hiking boots
rubber thongs
rubber booties
mask and snorkel

Photography

Look at the ads in photographic magazines for the best deals on mail-order cameras and film, or buy at a discount shop in any large city. Run a roll of film through your camera to be sure it's in good working order. Register valuable cameras or electronic equipment with Customs before you leave home so there won't be any argument about where you bought the items when you return, or at least carry the original bill of sale.

The type of camera you choose could depend on the way you travel. If you'll be mostly staying in one place a heavy SLR with spare lenses and other equipment won't trouble you. If you'll be moving around a lot for a considerable length of time a 35mm compact camera may be better. The compacts are mostly useful for close-up shots; landscapes will seem spread out and far away. A wide-angle lens gives excellent depth of field but hold the camera upright to avoid converging verticals. A polarizing filter prevents reflections from glass windows. Avoid overexposure at midday by reducing the exposure half a stop; *do* overexpose when photographing dark-skinned islanders, however. High-speed film is required for shooting in dark rainforests. Ask permission before photographing people. If you're asked for money (extremely rare) you can always walk away—give your subjects the same choice. There is probably no country in the world where the photographer will have as interesting and willing subjects as in Fiji.

Keep your camera in a plastic bag during rain and while traveling in motorized canoes, etc. In the tropics the humidity can cause film to stick to itself; silica-gel crystals in the bag will protect film from humidity and mold growth. Protect camera and film from direct sunlight and load film in the shade. Whenever loading check that the takeup spool revolves when winding on. Never leave camera or film in a hot place like a car floor or glove compartment. When packing protect your camera against vibration. Remove the batteries from your camera when in storage at home for long periods.

Checked baggage is scanned by powerful airport X-ray monitors, so carry both camera and film aboard the plane in a clear plastic bag and ask security for a visual inspection. Some airports will refuse to do this. Otherwise use a lead-laminated pouch. The old high-dose X-ray units are the worst, but even low-dose inspection units can ruin fast film (400 ASA and above). Beware of the cumulative effect of X-ray machines.

Take double the amount of film and mailers you think you'll need. In the U.S. film can be purchased at big discounts through mail order companies which advertise in photography magazines. Whenever purchasing film in Fiji take care to check the expiration date. Don't plan on having any slides developed locally.

Accessories

A clip-on book light and extra batteries allows campers to read at night. If you're a serious scuba diver, write to the operators you'll be diving with (listed in the appendix) and ask about their equipment requirements. Serious scuba divers bring their own regulators and buoyancy-control devices. A mask and snorkel are essential equipment—you'll be missing half of Fiji's beauty without them.

Also take along postcards of your hometown, snapshots of your house, family, workplace, etc; islanders love to see these. Always keep a promise to mail the islanders photos you take of them. Think of some small souvenir of your country (such as a lapel pin bearing a kangaroo or maple leaf or Kennedy half dollars) which you can take along as gifts. Miniature compasses sold in camping stores also make good gifts.

Neutral gray eyeglasses protect your eyes from the sun and give the least color distortion. Take an extra pair (if you have them). If your eyesight is poor also take a magnifying glass to be able to read the maps in this book. The author has been urging Moon to use a larger typeface for years without success. Keep the laundry soap inside a couple of layers of plastic bags. To cook at campsites you'll often need a small stove: trying to keep rainforest wood burning will drive you to tears from smoke and frustration. Camping fuel cannot be carried on commercial airliners, however, so choose a common fuel like kerosene or gasoline.

Women should know that high humidity causes curly hair to swell and bush, straight hair to droop. If it's curly have it cut short or keep it long in a ponytail or bun. A good cut is essential with straight hair. Water-based make-up is best as the heat and humidity cause oil glands to work overtime. See "Health" above for more ideas.

camera and five rolls of film
compass
pocket flashlight
extra batteries
candle
pocket alarm/calculator
pocket watch
sunglasses
padlock and lightweight chain
collapsible umbrella
twine for clothes line
powdered laundry soap
sink plug (one that fits all)
mini-towel
sewing kit
mini-scissors
nail clippers
fishing line for sewing gear
plastic cup
can and bottle opener
cork screw
pen knife
spoon
water bottle
matches
tea bags
dried fruits
nuts
crackers
plastic bags
gifts

soap in plastic container
soft toothbrush
toothpaste
shampoo
comb and brush
skin creams
make-up
tampons or napkins
white toilet paper
multiple vitamins and minerals
Cutter's insect repellent
PABA sunscreen
Chap Stic
a motion sickness remedy
contraceptives
iodine
water purification pills
delousing powder
a diarrhea remedy
Tiger Balm
a cold remedy
Alka Selzer
aspirin
antihistamine
antifungal
Calmitol ointment
antibiotic ointment
antiseptic spray
disinfectant
simple dressing
Band-Aids

Toiletries And Medical Kit

Since everyone has his/her own medical requirements and brand names vary from country to country, there's no point going into detail here. Note, however, that even the basics (such as aspirin) are unavailable on some outer islands, so be prepared. Bring medicated powder for prickly heat rash. Charcoal tablets are useful for diarrhea and poisoning (absorbs the irritants). Bring an adequate supply of any personal medications, plus your prescriptions (in generic terminology).

Money And Documents

All post offices have passport applications. If you lose your passport you should report the matter to the local police at once, obtain a certificate or receipt, then proceed to your consulate (if any!) for a replacement. If you have your birth certificate with you it facilitiates things considerably.

Leave unneeded credit cards and jewelry at home. Traveler's cheques in U.S., Australian, or New Zealand dollars are recommended. In Fiji, American Express is by far the most efficient company as far as refunds for lost cheques go. Bring along a small supply of US$1 and US$5 bills to use if you don't manage to change money immediately upon arrival or if you run out of local currency and can't get to a bank.

Become a life member of the Youth Hostel Association if you feel the wanderlust in your veins. If you have a car at home, bring along the insurance receipt so you don't have to pay insurance every time you rent a car. Ask your agent about this. If you live outside the U.S. and want to obtain another Moon handbook consider ordering it direct by mail. Moon's foreign distributors charge a big markup, doubling retail prices.

Carry your valuables in a money belt worn around your waist or neck under your clothing; most camping stores have these. Make several photocopies of the information page of your passport, personal identification, driver's license, scuba certification card, credit cards, airline tickets, receipts for purchase of traveler's cheques, etc.—you should be able to get them all on one page. A brief medical history with your blood type, allergies, chronic or special health problems, eyeglass and medical prescriptions, etc. might also come in handy. Put these inside plastic bags to protect them from moisture. Carry the lists in different places, and leave one at home.

> passport
> vaccination certificates
> airline tickets
> scuba certification card
> driver's license
> traveler's cheques
> some U.S. cash
> photocopies of documents
> money belt
> address book
> notebook
> envelopes

preparing a *lovo* or underground oven at Korovou, central Viti Levu (D. Stanley)

1. a Fiji Indian family enjoying watermelon at Nandi (John Penisten);
2. pineapple vendor, Nandi Market (John Penisten)

1. guard at Government House, Suva (David Bowden); **2.** handicraft seller, Nandi (Doug Hankin);
3. market scene (Karl Partridge); **4.** along Numbukalou Creek, Suva (D. Stanley);
5. Suva market (D. Stanley)

1. Matuku I., Moala Group (Robert Kennington); 2. Mount Victoria, Viti Levu (D. Stanley); 3. road near Mbukuya, Viti Levu (Don Pitcher); 4. vegetation on the hike to Lovoni, Ovalau (Don Pitcher); 5. Rewa River near Vunindawa, Viti Levu (D. Stanley)

1. Waisomo Creek above Nasava, central Viti Levu (D. Stanley); 2. Maka Bay, Rotuma (Doug Hankin); 3. cane fields near Lautoka (D. Stanley); 4. cassava plantation, Mbukuya, Viti Levu (Don Pitcher); 5. female green iguana, Orchid Island, near Suva (Doug Hankin)

1. *mbure*, Viti Levu (Robert Kennington); **2.** house at Nasau, Koro I. (D. Stanley); **3.** pineapple fields, Viti Levu (D. Stanley); **4.** the chief's *mbure* at Nanggarawai on the Trans-Viti Levu Trek (D. Stanley); **5.** village on the Trans-Viti Levu Trek (D. Stanley)

GETTING THERE

Fiji's geographic position makes it the hub of transport for the whole South Pacific. Nandi Airport is the region's most important international airport, with long-haul services to points all around the Pacific Rim. Nine international airlines fly into Nandi: Air Calédonie International, Airline of the Marshall Islands, Air Nauru, Air New Zealand, Air Pacific, Canadian Airlines International, Polynesian Airlines, Qantas, and Solomon Islands Airlines. Air Pacific and three other carriers also use Suva's Nausori Airport, a regional distribution center with flights to many of the nearby Polynesian countries to the east.

From North America three airlines fly to Nandi: Air New Zealand (from Los Angeles via Honolulu), Canadian Airlines International (from Toronto and Vancouver via Honolulu), and Qantas (from Los Angeles via Tahiti). It's a five-hour flight from the West Coast to Hawaii, then another six hours from Hawaii to Fiji.

From Australia you can fly to Nandi on Air New Zealand (from Sydney), Canadian Airlines International (from Sydney), Air Pacific (from Brisbane, Melbourne, and Sydney), or Qantas (from Brisbane, Melbourne, or Sydney). From New Zealand to Nandi it's a choice of Air New Zealand (from Auckland and Christchurch), Canadian Airlines International (from Auckland), or Air Pacific (from Auckland). From Tokyo you'll fly Air New Zealand or Air Pacific.

Fiji's national airline, **Air Pacific**, was founded as Fiji Airways by Australian aviator Harold Gatty in 1951. Gatty flew around the world in eight days with American Willy Post to set a record in 1931. In 1972 the airline was reorganized as a regional carrier and the name changed to Air Pacific. Aside from the flights mentioned above they also arrive at Nandi from Apia, Honiara, Port Vila, and Tongatapu.

Other regional carriers landing in Nandi include Air Calédonie International (from Futuna, Noumea, and Wallis), Airline of the Marshall Islands (from Majuro and Tarawa), Air Nauru (from Nauru), Air New Zealand (from Rarotonga), Polynesian Airlines (from Apia), Qantas (from Papeete), and Solomon Islands Airlines (from Honiara).

Airlines offering direct flights to Suva include Air Pacific (from Apia and Tongatapu), Air Nauru (from Nauru), Fiji Air (from Funafuti), and Polynesian Airlines (from Apia). Some Air Pacific flights to Nandi from Auckland, Brisbane, Honiara, and Port Vila carry on to Suva.

Try to avoid arriving in Fiji on a Sunday.

AIR FARES

Tickets
Your plane ticket will be your biggest single expense, so spend some time considering the possibilities. Start by calling the airlines

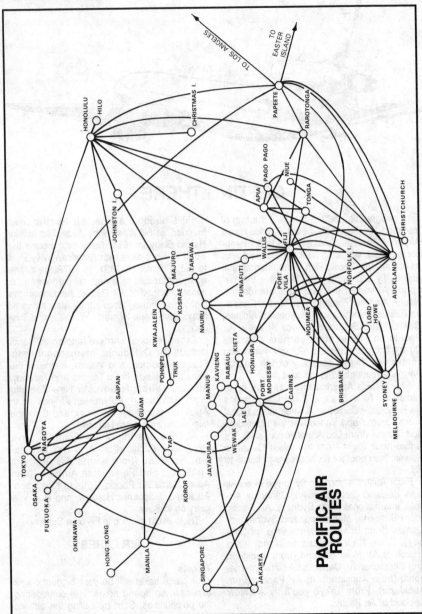

PACIFIC AIR ROUTES

directly over their toll-free 800 numbers to get current information on fares. In North America, to get the airline's toll-free number call (800)-555-1212 (all 800 numbers are free). Call all the carriers that fly to Fiji and say you want the *lowest possible fare*. Ask about restrictions. If you're not happy with the answers you get, call back later and try again. Many different agents take calls on these lines and some are more knowledgeable than others. The numbers are busy during business hours, so call at night or on the weekend. *Be persistent.*

Cheap Flights

Check the Sunday travel section in a newspaper like the *San Francisco Chronicle* or a major entertainment weekly. They often carry ads for "bucket shops," agencies which deal in bulk and sell seats for less than airline offices will. Most airlines have more seats than they can market through normal channels, so they sell their unused long-haul capacity on this "gray" market at discounts of 40-50% off the official IATA tariffs.

There are well-known centers around the world where globetrotters regularly pick up onward tickets (Amsterdam, Athens, Bangkok, Hong Kong, London, Penang, San Francisco, and Singapore are only a few—unfortunately Fiji isn't one). Rates are competitive so check a few agencies before deciding. Despite their shady appearance, most of the bucket shops are perfectly legitimate, and your ticket will probably be issued by the airline itself. Don't hand over the full price until you see it, though. Most discounted tickets look and are exactly the same as regular full-fare tickets. They're usually non-refundable.

Promotional Fares

The cheapest way to get to the South Pacific is on a special promotional fare from one of the major airlines. These fares often have limitations and restrictions, however—be sure to read the fine print. Some have an advance purchase deadline, so it's best to begin shopping early. There are low, shoulder, and peak seasons: inquiring far in advance could allow you to reschedule your vacation slightly to take advantage of a lower fare.

The APEX (advance purchase excursion) fare is nearly half the regular RT fare, but you must pay and be ticketed 14 days in advance. There's a minimum stay of five days and a six-month maximum, with a 35% penalty if you change your reservations or cancel the trip less than 14 days in advance, so be careful. You may change the return date for US$50 each time, but not less than 14 days in advance. If you decide to change the return on shorter notice, you'll be upgraded to full fare and the return portion of your ticket will be nearly worthless. Careful planning is required to ensure that you give yourself the right amount of time in the right places. APEX fares also limit where and how often you may stopover. "Super APEX" tickets allow no stopovers at all. Cheaper still are ITX (Independent Tour Excursion) fares available to passengers who prepay a land package worth at least US$150.

The most popular discount fare is the Roundtrip Excursion, called "Super Pass" by Air New Zealand. This one has no advance purchase requirement, reservations can be charged so long as your ticket doesn't have to be reissued, stopovers are allowed, and you have up to a year to finish your trip. There's a 35% penalty to refund the ticket and a US$50 charge if it has to be reissued. Seasonal pricing applies. Normal economy tickets carry no restrictions at all but cost almost double the excursion fares.

Travel Agents

Any travel agent worth his/her commission will probably want to sell you a package tour. Some vacation packages actually cost less than regular roundtrip airfare! If they'll let you extend your stay to give you some time to yourself this could be a good deal, especially with the hotel thrown in for "free." But check the restrictions.

Pick your agent carefully as many are pitifully ignorant about Fiji. They often know little about discounts, cheap flights, or alternative routes. With alarming frequency they give wrong or misleading information in an offhand manner. Ask an airline to suggest a travel agent. They won't *recommend* any, but they will give you the names of a few in your area that specialize in Pacific travel. Agencies belonging to ASTA (American Society of Travel Agents, Box 23992, Washington, D.C. 20012-3992 USA) or ACTA (Alliance of Canadian Travel Associations) must conform to a strict code of ethics. A travel agent's commission is paid by the airline, so you've nothing to lose.

Even if you decide to take advantage of the convenience of an agent, do call the airlines yourself beforehand so you'll know if you're getting a good deal. Airline tickets are often refundable only in the place of purchase, so ask about this before you invest in a ticket you may not use. There can be tremendous variations in what different passengers on the same flight have paid for their tickets. Allow yourself time to shop around; a few hours spent on the phone, asking questions, could save you hundreds of dollars.

AIR SERVICES

From North America
Air New Zealand, Canadian Airlines International, and Qantas are the carriers serving Fiji from North America. Their South Pacific fares vary according to seasons: low (May to Sept.), shoulder (April, Oct. to Nov.), and peak (Dec. to March). The airlines have made May to Sept., the best months in Fiji, their "low" season because that's winter in Australia and New Zealand. If you're only going to the islands and can make it at this time it certainly works to your advantage. You can usually get a free stopover in Honolulu on tickets to the South Pacific.

Air New Zealand offers a "Super Pass" from Los Angeles or San Francisco which allows a total of eight stops in the South Pacific, New Zealand, and Australia, including Tahiti, Rarotonga, Fiji, and Hawaii. Low-season prices begin at US$1245 RT to Auckland, US$1370 RT to Melbourne, including the stops. To go from San Francisco or Los Angeles to Hawaii, Fiji, Rarotonga, Tahiti, and back to California in the low season is US$950. You can stay up to a year and reservation changes can be made so long as you stick to your original routing. Their APEX fares are US$100 cheaper but you only get three stops (Tahiti not included), must book 14 days in advance, and face penalties if you change your reservations. There's a 35% cancellation fee on both tickets. For travel originating in the U.S., Air New Zealand guarantees your fare against subsequent price increases once you've been ticketed (provided you don't change your outbound reservation).

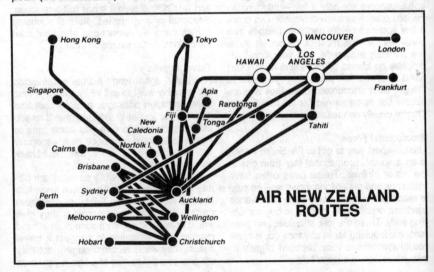

AIR NEW ZEALAND ROUTES

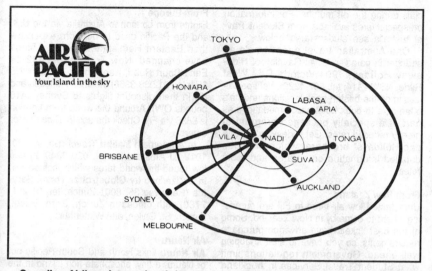

Canadian Airlines International departs Toronto and Vancouver for Honolulu, Nandi, Auckland, and Sydney. Travel agents in New York often sell Canadian Airlines International tickets to Fiji at deep discounts. Check the ads in the Sunday travel section of the *New York Times*. **Qantas** stops at Tahiti and Nandi on the way home to Australia. The main problem with all these carriers is their schedules, which are built around Auckland, Sydney, and Los Angeles: they'll drop you off in the middle of the night at Nandi.

Circle-Pacific Fares
Thanks to agreements between the carriers mentioned above and Asian or American companies such as Cathay Pacific, Japan Air Lines, Malaysian Airlines, Northwest Orient Airlines, Singapore Airlines, and United Airlines, you can get a Circle-Pacific fare which combines the South Pacific with Singapore, Bangkok, Hong Kong, Taipei, and Tokyo. These tickets must be purchased 30 days in advance, but they're valid up to a year and only the initial flight out of North America has to be booked 30 days ahead. The rest of the ticket can be left open-dated.

Prices run US$1870 RT from Los Angeles, CAN$2100 from Vancouver, or CAN$2566 from Toronto. You're allowed four free stopovers; additional stopovers are about US$50 apiece. Once again, Air New Zealand has the most to offer in the South Pacific, but the different carriers offer differing routes in Asia. Ask your travel agent to explain the alternatives to you. The Circle-Pacific fares, also available in New Zealand and Australia, are excellent value.

Overseas Tours (475 El Camino Real #206, Millbrae, CA 94030 USA; tel. 415-692-4892) offers Circle-Pacific fares on Air New Zealand and Malaysian Airlines routed Los Angeles-Tahiti-Rarotonga-Fiji-Auckland-Sydney-Melbourne-Singapore-Kuala Lumpur-Hong Kong-Tokyo-Los Angeles, all for US$1138 (Oct. and Nov.), US$1185 (April to Sept.), or US$1299 (Dec. to March). Other variations of this ticket throw in Honolulu, Perth, Bangkok, and Taipei.

From Australia
To help subsidize the state-owned carrier, Qantas, the Australian government keeps air fares out of Australia as high as they can; they also require foreign carriers to set high fares. The APEX and Circle-Pacific fares described above are available, however. See a travel agent. The carriers often offer spe-

cials during the off months. For information on special fares available from Student Travel Australia, see "student fares" below.

One Australian travel agent who's no stranger in paradise is Val Gavriloff of **Hideaway Holidays** (994 Victoria Rd., West Ryde, NSW 2114; tel. 807-4222). Val specializes in off-the-beaten-track locations and he's often able to book hotel accommodations as part of a specially packaged program at greatly reduced rates. Get Hideaway's "Polypac Holidays" brochure, which provides detailed information on airfares and room rates.

From New Zealand

Unrestricted low air fares to Fiji are surprisingly hard to come by in New Zealand. Some of the best tickets have advance purchase requirements, so you have to start shopping well ahead. Government regulations limit what Student Travel Services in Auckland and Wellington can offer, but they do have an Auckland-Fiji-Honolulu-Los Angeles student fare. Air New Zealand has 21-day, advance purchase EPIC fares to Fiji. Again, see your travel agent.

From Singapore And Bangkok

The bucket shops of Southeast Asia are famous for selling air tickets at enormous discounts. For example discount Air New Zealand tickets (Singapore-Auckland-Fiji-Rarotonga-Tahiti-Los Angeles) are available in Singapore and Penang for about US$750 OW. These are open tickets valid up to a year on any flight. To get the best deal shop around.

One recommended agency is **German Asian Travels Ltd.** (9 Battery Road, #14-03 Straits Trading Building, Singapore 0104; tel. 533-5466). Among the many variations available at German Asian are Singapore-Auckland-Nandi-Rarotonga-Papeete-Los Angeles (US$835) and Singapore-Sydney-Papeete-Los Angeles (US$645).

Similar tickets are available from **MAS Travel Center Ltd.** (19 Tanglin Road, #05-50 Tanglin Shopping Center, Singapore 1024; tel. 737-8877) and **K. Travel Service** (21/33 Soi Ngarmdupli, near Malaysia Hotel, Bangkok 10120, Thailand; tel. 286-1468). All of these companies have been operating for many years.

From Europe

Flights from London to Australia via the U.S. and the Pacific used to be more expensive than Eastern Hemisphere flights. Things have changed. Now **Trailfinders** (42-48 Earls Court Road, Kensington, London W8 6EJ; tel. 01-938-3366) includes Honolulu and Fiji in their discount flights to Sydney (418 pounds OW). Around the world from London is £835 via Fiji. Check the ads in *Time Out* for others.

In Amsterdam **Malibu Travel** (Damrak 30, 1012 LJ Amsterdam; tel. 020-234912) has low round-the-world fares which include Fiji. In Switzerland try **Globetrotter Travel Service** (Rennweg 35, 8001 Zurich; tel. 01-211-7780) with offices in Zurich, Bern, Basel, Luzern, St. Gallen, and Winterthur.

Air Nauru

Air Nauru links North and South Pacific out of Nauru, a tiny, phosphate-rich island in the Central Pacific. They have flights to many South Pacific islands from Auckland, Sydney, Melbourne, Guam, and a series of Asian cities such as Taipei, Hong Kong, and Manila. Air Nauru's fares are reasonable. Most are based on a journey via Nauru, so fit two of these one-way economy fares to Nauru together: Auckland (NZ$521), Guam (US$190), Hong Kong (A$450), Honiana (A$99), Manila (US$367), Melbourne (A$360), Nandi (F$148), Niue (NZ$300), Noumea (A$150), Port Vila (A$140), Suva (F$173), Sydney (A$310), Tarawa (A$75).

Though they have a reputation for cancelling flights on a moment's notice and bumping confirmed passengers to make room for local VIPs, Air Nauru flies modern jet aircraft and has a good safety record. One drawback is ground expenses on Nauru, which has only two higher-priced hotels. Another is the difficulty in obtaining reliable information—only the main offices are computerized. On many islands you'll end up going standby unless you book weeks ahead. Some flights are less than weekly and "operate only when scheduled." Others which *should* operate in fact don't, so take care. Also add to all fares the compulsory A$10 airport departure tax everyone (even through passengers continuing on the same aircraft) is charged at Nauru.

STUDENT FARES

If you're a student or recent graduate you can benefit from lower student fares by booking through a student travel office. There are two rival organizations of this kind: **Council Travel Services** (known as **Travel CUTS** in Canada) with offices in college towns right across North America, and **Student Travel Australia** (called the **Student Travel Network** in the U.S.). Both organizations require you to pay a nominal fee for an official student card and to get the cheapest fares you have to prove you're really a student. Slightly higher fares on the same routes are available to non-students, so check them out.

Student Travel Australia and their North American affiliate, the **Student Travel Network,** have been flying students across the Pacific for years. Basically, they will sell you the same APEX and Circle-Pacific tickets described above but at a lower price and without any restrictions whatsoever (although there are still low, shoulder, and peak season fare variations). The tickets are refundable with only a US$25 penalty. One-way tickets are about half the round-trip price. You can make your reservations over the phone a few days before you leave, pick up your ticket at their Los Angeles office (tel. 213-934-8722 or 800-777-0112 outside California) departure-day morning, and be on a flight to Hawaii or Tahiti that night. Reservations may be changed at will and the ticket is refundable.

Here's a partial list of STA/STN offices and affiliates:

North America

STN, 1208 Massachusetts Ave., Cambridge, MA 02138 tel. (617) 576-4623
STN, 273 Newbury St., Boston, MA 02116 tel. (617) 226-6014
STN, 82 Shattuck Sq., Berkeley, CA 94704 tel. (415) 841-1037
STN, 920 Westwood Blvd., Los Angeles, CA 90024 tel. (213) 824-1574
STN, 17 E. 45th St., New York, NY 10017 tel. (212) 986-9470
STN, 6447 El Cajon Blvd., San Diego,CA 92115 tel. (619) 286-1322

STN, 166 Geary St., #702, San Francisco, CA 94108 tel. (415) 391-8407
CUTS, 187 College St., Toronto, ON M5T 1P7, Canada tel. (416) 979-2406
CUTS has other offices in Calgary, Edmonton, Halifax, Montreal, Ottawa, Quebec City, Saskatoon, Vancouver, Victoria, and Winnipeg.

Australia/New Zealand

STA, 40 Creek St., Brisbane, QLD 4000 tel. 07-221-9629
STA, 220 Faraday St., Carlton, Melbourne 3053 tel. 03-347-6911
STA, 1a Lee St., Railway Square, Sydney, NSW 2000 tel. 02-212-1255
STA has other offices in Adelaide, Canberra, and Perth.
Student Travel, 64 High St., Auckland tel. 09-390458
Student Travel, 207 Cuba St., Wellington tel. 04-850560
Student Travel has other offices in Christchurch, Dunedin, and Hamilton

Europe/Asia

NBBS, Dam 17, Dam Square, Amsterdam, Netherland tel. 020-205071
ARTU, Hardenbergstr. 9, 1000 Berlin 12, West Germany tel. 030-310004-0
DIS, Skindergade 28, DK-1159 Copenhagen , Denmark tel. 01-110044
USIT, 7 Anglesea St., Dublin 2, Ireland tel. 01-778117
SSR, 3 rue Vignier, 1205 Geneva, Switzerland tel. 022-299733

Slightly different student fares are available from **Council Travel Services,** a division of the Council on International Educational Exchange. They're much stricter about making sure you're a "real" student: you must first obtain the widely recognized International Student Identity Card (US$8) to get a ticket at the student rate. Some fares are limited to students and youths under 26 years of age, but part-time students and teachers also qualify. Circle-Pacific and Around the World routings are available. Council Travel has special connecting flights to Los Angeles from other U.S. points. Seasonal pricing applies, so plan ahead.

Here are a few Council Travel offices:

2511 Channing Way, Berkeley, CA 94704,
    tel. (415) 848-8604
729 Boylston St., Boston, MA 02116,
    tel. (617) 266-1926
29 E. Delaware Pl., Chicago, IL 60611,
    tel. (312) 951-0585
1093 Broxton Ave., Los Angeles, CA 90024,
    tel. (213) 208-3551
205 E. 42nd St., New York, NY 10017,
    tel. (212) 661-1450
715 S.W. Morrison, Portland, OR 97205,
    tel. (503) 228-1900
24429 Cass St., San Diego, CA 92109,
    tel. (619) 270-6401
312 Sutter St., San Francisco, CA 94108,
    tel. (415) 421-3473
1314 N.E. 43rd St., Seattle, WA 98105,
    tel. (206) 632-2448

BAGGAGE

International airlines allow at least 20 kilos of baggage (many airlines permit two pieces of up to 30 kilos each within certain size limits). Small commuter aircraft restrict you to as little as 10 kilos, so pack according to the lowest common denominator. Bicycles, folding kayaks, and surfboards can usually be checked as baggage (sometimes for an additional US$50 charge), but sailboards may have to be shipped airfreight. If you do travel with a sailboard be sure to call it a surfboard at check-in.

Tag your bag with name, address, and phone number inside and out. If you'll be changing aircraft at a gateway city don't check your baggage straight through or it could be left behind. Collect it at the transfer point and check in again. Stow anything which could conceivably be considered a weapon (scissors, penknife, toy gun, mace, etc.) in your checked luggage. Incidentally, it can be considered a criminal offense to make jokes about bombings or hijackings in airports or aboard aircraft.

One reason for lost baggage is that people fail to remove used baggage tags after they claim their luggage. Get into the habit of tear-

ing off old baggage tags, unless you want your luggage to travel in the opposite direction! As you're checking in, look to see if the three-letter city code on your baggage tag and boarding pass are the same.

If your baggage is damaged or doesn't arrive at your destination, unless you inform the airline officials *immediately* and have them fill out a written report future claims for compensation will be compromised. Airlines will usually reimburse out-of-pocket expenses if your baggage is lost or delayed over 24 hours. The amount varies from US$25-50. Your chances of getting it are better if you're polite but firm. Keep receipts for any money you're forced to spend to replace missing articles.

Claims for lost luggage can take weeks to process. Keep in touch with the airline to show your concern; hang onto your baggage tag until the matter is resolved. If you feel you did not receive the attention you deserved, write the airline an objective letter outlining the case. Get the names of the employees you're dealing with so you can mention them in the letter. Of course, don't expect pocket money or compensation on a remote, outer island. Report the loss, then wait till you get back to their main office. Whatever happens, try to avoid getting angry. The people you're dealing with don't want the problem any more than you do.

ORGANIZED TOURS

Packaged Holidays
While this book is written for independent travelers rather than packaged tourists, greatly reduced group air fares and hotel rates make some tours worth considering. If there are two of you with limited time and a desire to stay at a first-class beach hotel, this is the cheapest way to go. Special-interest tours are very popular among sportspeople who want to be sure they'll get to participate in the various activities they enjoy. The main drawback to the tours is that you're on a fixed itinerary among other tourists out of touch with local life. Singles pay a healthy supplement.

Ted Cook's Islands in the Sun (760 West 16th St., Suite L, Costa Mesa, CA 92627

USA; tel. 714-645-8300), founded in 1965, was the first American travel company to specialize exclusively in the South Pacific (no connection with James or Thomas). Unlike the others Ted Cook usually includes air fare from Los Angeles to Fiji in the price, but most meals are extra. A 13-day package including a Coral Coast hotel, a resort off Nandi, and a three-day Blue Lagoon Cruise begins at US$1,875 pp (double occupancy). You have the option of selecting your own category of hotel. Ted Cook doesn't accept consumer inquiries, so you must work through a travel agent.

In Canada check with **WestCan Treks Adventure Travel** (#2, 10918-88 Ave., Edmonton, Alberta T6G 0Z1; tel. 800-661-7265) in Calgary, Edmonton, Toronto, and Vancouver for packages and plane tickets to Fiji. The very same trips are sold in the U.S. by the **Adventure Center** (5540 College Ave., Oakland, CA 94618, USA; tel. (415)-654-1879).

Scuba Tours
Facilities for divers are good in Fiji, but unless you've got unlimited time and are philosophical about disappointments, you'll probably want to go on an organized scuba tour. Prices aren't cheap, but the convenience of having all your arrangements made for you by a company able to pull weight with island suppliers is sometimes worth it. When booking ask if meals, regulator, pressure and depth gauges, mask, snorkel, fins, etc. are provided. In addition to the regular phone numbers given below, many companies have toll-free numbers which you can obtain by calling toll-free information at 1-800-555-1212. Of course, diver certification is mandatory.

Poseidon Venture Tours (359 San Miguel Dr., Newport Beach, CA 92660 USA; tel. (714)-644-5344; or 505 N. Belt, Suite 675, Houston, TX 77060 USA; tel. 713-820-3483) offers seven-night diving tours to Fiji's Mbengga Reef, Koro Sea, or Taveuni from US$1250. The price includes five days of two-tank diving, air fare from the U.S. West Coast, hotels, taxes, and transfers. Some packages include meals, others don't. The tours operate seven times a year.

feeding fish

Tropical Adventures (170 Denny Way, Seattle, WA 98109 USA; tel. 206-441-3483) sends divers to Fiji and Tonga for nine days for as little as US$1699, including air fare, accommodations, meals, diving, taxes, and more. They occasionally have specials which slice off $100 or more, so call up to compare prices. Call early as they only go every couple of months. Over 6,000 divers a year book through this company, which has been in business since 1973.

Aqua-Trek (110 Sutter St., Suite 608, San Francisco, CA 94104 USA; tel. 415-398-8990) is *the* Fiji specialist, with programs at six different resorts, beginning at US$980 a week double occupancy plus airfare. Aqua-Trek are the people to call if you want to stay at Mana Island or any of the resorts on or near Taveuni. They also work with two live-aboard dive boats which explore the Great Astrolabe Reef (from US$1500 pp a week plus air fare).

If you want a customized dive tour or simply an agent to pre-book your hotel rooms and flights try **Adventure Express** (185 Berry St., Suite 5503, San Francisco, CA 94107 USA; tel. 415-442-0799).

See & Sea Travel Service (50 Francisco St., Suite 205, San Francisco, CA 94133 USA; tel. 415-434-3400) is the specialist in live-aboard dive experiences. Their prices are higher than those mentioned above, but you're offered three or more dives a day plus the selected cream of diving facilities, and all meals are included! In Fiji they use the 35-meter dive boat *Pacific Nomad* based at Suva (US$1500 pp a week, air fare extra). This boat sleeps 20 divers in eight king-size cabins. By living aboard the boat you get in more diving, mostly on the Astrolabe Reef off Kandavu. Groups can charter the *Pacific Nomad* for explorations in remote areas such as the Lau Group, inaccessible to shore-based operations. See & Sea's president is the noted underwater photographer and author, Carl Roessler.

Alternatively you can make your arrangements directly with island dive shops. Information about these operators is included in the respective chapters of this book.

Tours For Active People

About the only North American company offering tours especially designed for cyclists is **Off the Deep End Travels** (Box 7511, Jackson, WY 83001 USA; tel. 307-733-8707). Once a year they take a two-week bicycle ride right around Fiji's Viti Levu (US$1125). The Fiji tour gets a "moderate challenge" rating. The price includes food, lodging, and bicycles, but air fares are extra.

Northern Lights Expeditions (5220 NE 180th, Seattle, WA 98155 USA; tel. 206-362-4506) offers two-week kayak tours to the south coast of Vanua Levu a couple of times a year. *Go Bananas* (740 Kapahulu Ave., Honolulu, HI 96816 USA; tel. 808-737-9514) extends their kayaking grounds from Vanua Levu to the wild east coast of Taveuni.

Sobek Expeditions (Angels Camp, CA 95222 USA; tel. 209-736-4524) runs a two-week trekking tour across Fiji's Viti Levu six times a year (US$892, air fare extra).

From May to Oct. **New Frontiers Trek Fiji**, a division of Rosie Travel Service (see below), runs adventuresome five-night hiking trips across the central highlands from Tavua to Nalawa. Horses carry trekkers' backpacks so it's quite accessible to almost anyone in good condition. The F$72 pp daily price includes transport to the trailhead, food and accommodations at a few of the 11 Fijian villages along the way, guides, and an outboard ride on the Wainimbuka River. Trekkers only hike about five hours a day, allowing lots of time to get to know the people. Outer-island treks are also arranged.

Yacht Tours

If you were planning to spend a substantial sum to stay at a luxury resort a cruise aboard a chartered yacht could be a more rewarding experience. **Emerald Yacht Charters Ltd.** (Box 15, Savusavu; telex FJ8281 NAMALE) has several skippered yachts at Savusavu, some equipped with tanks and compressor for scuba diving (beginning around F$340 daily). For information on other boats available in Fiji waters write: **Fiji Yacht Charter Assn.**, Box 2313, Suva, Fiji Islands (tel. 361-256).

Bareboat chartering is not available in Fiji due to the risks involved in navigating the poorly marked reefs. However **Rainbow Yacht Charters** arranges flotilla charters out of Nandi among the Mamanutha and Yasawa islands. You sail your own boat but follow a lead yacht which knows the way. If you don't know how to sail they'll teach you! A seven-day charter is US$1185 pp for four people, plus 8% tax. For more information contact the Pacific Insight Marketing, 2618 Newport Blvd., Newport Beach, CA 92663 USA; tel. 714-675-2250. In New Zealand it's Box 8327, Symonds St., Auckland (tel. 09-3089-419).

Ocean Voyages Inc. (1709 Bridgeway, Sausalito, CA 94965 USA; tel. 415-332-4681) organizes sailing tours on the 14-meter steel ketch *Seax of Legra* based at Taveuni. Skippers Dianne and Warwick Bain have 40 years sailing experience between them. A week sailing around the northeastern islands will run US$3600 for two persons or US$4250 for four, including accommodations and meals. Scuba diving (additional charge) can be arranged with Taveuni dive operators who rendezvous with *Seax* regularly. This is perfect if you're alone or two and can't afford to charter an entire yacht for yourself.

Mini-cruiseships

Blue Lagoon Cruises Ltd. (Box 54, Lautoka; tel. 61-268) has been offering mini-cruises of the Yasawa Islands from Lautoka since the 1950s. The three-night trips (from F$455) leave daily at 1900 while the six-night cruise (from F$875) is weekly. Prices are per person, double or triple occupancy, and include entertainment and shore excursions. Food is F$100 extra for three nights, F$200 extra for six nights. (Add 8% tax to all prices.) On the three-night cruises they use three-deck, 45-passenger vessels, while larger four-deck, 66-passenger mini-cruiseships are used on the six-night (and some of the three-night) voyages. The meals are often beach barbecue affairs with Fijians dancing. You'll have plenty of opportunities to snorkel in the calm crystal-clear waters (bring your own gear). Though expensive, these trips have a good reputation. There are daily departures but reservations are essential as they're usually booked solid months ahead—they're that popular.

Travel Agencies

The easy way to prebook a Blue Lagoon Cruise, a first class hotel room, airport transfers, sightseeing tours, or a rental car is through **United Touring International**, with overseas offices in the U.S. (1315 Walnut St., Suite 800, Philadelphia, PA 19107 USA; tel. 800-223-6486), Britain (71-75 Uxbridge Rd., Ealing Broadway, London, W5 5SL, England; tel. 01-566-1660), and Japan (Taiyo Building, 3F, 1-10 Wakaba, Shinjuku-ku, Tokyo 160; tel. 03-355-2391). They also have an office in the arrival concourse at Nandi Airport.

The Nandi Airport office of **Rosie Travel Service** (Box 9268, Nandi Airport; tel. 72-935) can also arrange hotels, transfers, cruises, tours, etc. for you upon arrival in Fiji. Rosie's bus tours from Nandi are much cheaper than other companies because lunch isn't included. Rosie's has the **Thrifty Car Rentals** franchise, with unlimited mileage rates beginning at F$65 a day, collision insurance and tax included. There's a 300-km limit on one-day rentals. The fourth and seventh days are free and after a week the daily rate drops to F$47 daily.

GETTING AROUND

By Air

While international flights are focused on Nandi, Fiji's domestic air service radiates from Suva. **Fiji Air** (Box 1259, Suva; tel. 22-666) is the main domestic carrier with flights a couple of times a week from Nausori Airport to such out-of-the-way islands as Kandavu (F$41), Koro (F$40), Lakemba (F$68), Moala (F$45), Ngau (F$32), Rambi (F$66), Rotuma (F$133), Thithia (F$68), and Vanua Mbalavu (F$75). More common destinations such as Levuka (F$20), Savusavu (F$41), and Taveuni (F$56) are served several times daily (all fares OW). Fiji Air also flies to Funafuti in Tuvalu (F$273 OW) three times a week.

Fiji Air's **Fiji Islands Pass** allows you to fly from Suva to Kandavu, Levuka, Savusavu, and Taveuni and back anytime within 30 days for F$100. Your initial flight is booked when you buy the ticket but subsequent reservations can be made no earlier than 24 hours in advance, so it's sort of like going standby. You must show your passport every time you use the pass. As flights to Kandavu are only twice a week, it's best to begin with that leg.

Also ask about regular standby fares, and if you're a full-time student aged 25 or under inquire about student fares. You'll need an International Student's Card. Always reconfirm your return flight immediately upon arrival at an outer island, as the reservation lists are sometimes not sent out from Suva. Fiji Air allows 15 kg of baggage. The service is reliable.

Air Pacific (tel. 313-511) has frequent daily service from Nandi to Suva (F$39) and Suva to Lambasa (F$43). **Sunflower Air-**

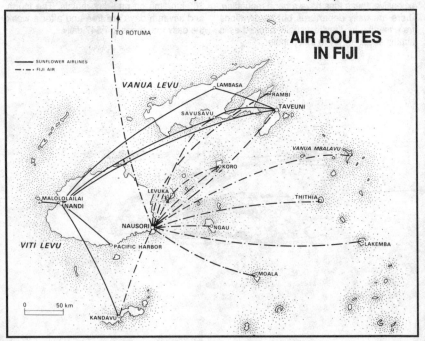

AIR ROUTES IN FIJI

— SUNFLOWER AIRLINES
—·—· FIJI AIR

TO ROTUMA

VANUA LEVU   LAMBASA
                              RAMBI
           SAVUSAVU   TAVEUNI

                          VANUA MBALAVU

                    KORO

         LEVUKA
                              THITHIA
MALOLOLAILAI
NANDI

     NAUSORI
                    NGAU
VITI LEVU   PACIFIC HARBOR
                              LAKEMBA

                    MOALA

0   50 km

KANDAVU

lines (Box 9452, Nandi Airport; tel. 73-016) bases their domestic network in Nandi, with daily flights to Lambasa (F$62), Malololailai (F$18), Pacific Harbor (F$34), Savusavu (F$68), and Taveuni (F$79). Nandi-Kandavu (F$44) is twice a week. The flight to Pacific Harbor includes a minibus into Suva, so it's actually more convenient than flying Nandi-Nausori on Air Pacific. From Taveuni Sunflower has flights to Savusavu (daily, F$31) and Lambasa (three a week, F$28). Flying in their four-engined, 18-seat Riley Herons or twin-engined, 10-seat Britten Norman Islanders is sort of fun. All flights are during daylight hours.

Sidetrips From Fiji

Air Pacific has two different triangle fares from Fiji, a good way to get around and experience the South Pacific's variety of cultures: Fiji-Noumea-Port Vila-Fiji and Nandi-Suva-Apia-Tonga-Fiji (F$495). Both are valid for one year, and can be purchased at any travel agency in Fiji or direct from the airline. Usually they're only good for journeys commencing in Fiji. These circular tickets combine perfectly with discount fares on Air New Zealand, bringing the whole South Pacific within reach.

A "Pacific Air Pass" allows 30 days travel from Fiji to Apia, Tonga, and Port Vila (US$399) or Apia, Port Vila, and Honiara (US$499). These tickets may be purchased only from Qantas Airways offices in North America. Air Pacific also has 28-day RT excursion fares from Fiji to Apia, Tonga, Port Vila, and Honiara at 25% off the regular fare. These can be bought in Fiji. Air Pacific has a U.S. office at 6151 West Century Blvd., Suite 524, Los Angeles, CA 90045 (tel. 213-417-2236).

By Bus

Since most shipping operates out of Suva, passenger services by sea both within Fiji and to neighboring countries are listed in the "Suva" section under "Transport."

Regular bus service is available all over Fiji and fares are low. The most important routes are between Lautoka and Suva, the biggest cities (about F$10 OW). If you follow the southern route via Singatoka you'll be on Queen's Road, the faster and smoother of the two. King's Road is longer and can be rough and dusty, but you get to see a little of the interior. If you're from the States you'll be amazed how accessible, inexpensive, and convenient the service is. Local people are always happy to supply information about buses and help you catch one.

Pacific Transport Ltd. has eight buses a day along Queen's Road (via Singatoka), with expresses (five hours) leaving Suva at 0645, 0930, 1210, and 1730. Local buses on Queen's Road take eight hours. To get around the bus service ban, on Sunday Pacific Transport has overnight buses in both directions between Suva and Lautoka, departing each end at 0100 Mon. morning, arriving 0540.

Sunbeam Transport Ltd. services the northern King's Road from Suva to Lautoka six times a day, with expresses (six hours) at 0645, 1330, and 1715. The Sunbeam express along King's Road is a comfortable way for those without a lot of time to see a little of the interior. Local buses take six hours on Queen's Road, nine hours on King's Road, Suva-Lautoka. **Reliance Transport** also services King's Road. The northern route is longer and rougher but far more scenic than the south road.

There are many other local buses, especially closer to Suva or Lautoka. The a/c expresses cost twice as much and are not as much fun as the ordinary expresses, whose big open windows with roll-down canvas covers give you a panoramic view of Viti Levu. Some expresses don't stop at the resorts along the Coral Coast. Check with the driver before you set out. Bus service on Vanua Levu and Taveuni is also good. Local buses often show up late but the long-distance buses are usually right on time. Bus stations are usually adjacent to local markets though local buses will usually stop anywhere along their routes. Fares average about F$1 for each hour of travel.

Passenger trucks serving as carriers charge set rates to and from interior villages. If you're hitching, be aware that truck drivers who give you a lift on the highway may expect the equivalent of bus fare; locals pay this without question. The excellent bus service makes bicycling rather redundant. No public transportation of any kind operates on Sunday.

Car Rentals

Car rental rates in Fiji are nearly double those charged in the U.S. and an 8% tax is added. All of the large chains are represented, including Avis, Budget, Hertz, National, and Thrifty. Local companies like A-Team Rentals, Khan's Rental Cars, Bula Rentals, Paul's Rentals, Roxy Rentals, and UTC Rent-A-Car are usually cheaper, but check around as prices vary. Many have offices in the concourse at Nandi Airport. Compare prices before you go by calling the large chains up on their toll-free numbers.

Both unlimited-mileage and per-kilometer rates are available, with full collision damage waiver insurance about F$10 per day extra. Third-party public liability insurance is compulsory for all vehicles and is included in the basic rate. The large companies allow you to drop the car off at one of their other branches at no extra charge, while at others you pay a delivery fee if you don't wish to return the car to the office where you rented it. **Budget** has a weekend rate which gives you three days for the price of two, while **Thrifty** has low unlimited mileage rates if you take the car for over three days. Ask about Thrifty's discount coupons which go with the car. **UTC Rent-A-Car** allows you to drop the car off at any of their six offices on Viti Levu at no additional charge.

Your home driver's license is valid. Most of the roads are atrocious (check the spare tire), with driving on the left-hand side. Queen's Road, which passes the Coral Coast resorts, is now completely paved from Lautoka to Suva. If you plan to use a rental car to explore rough country roads in Viti Levu's mountainous interior, think twice before announcing your plans to the agency as they may suddenly decline your business. Speed limits are 50 kilometers an hour in towns and 80 kilometers an hour on the highway. Unpaved roads can be very slippery, especially on inclines. Take care with local motorists, who sometimes stop in the middle of the road, pass on blind curves, and drive at high speeds. Driving at night can be a risky business.

Taxis

Taxis are common within towns and relatively cheap, about F$2 for a short trip. Meters are rare so ask the fare first. If in doubt, make sure it's understood the price is for the whole car, not per passenger although not many drivers are unscrupulous enough to try this trick. Unmarked vans cruising the market areas are often pirate taxis which will take you for a dollar or two less. They're not allowed to stop unless you wave them down. Taxis returning to their stand after a trip will pick up passengers at bus stops and charge the regular bus fare (ask if it's the "returning fare").

Don't tip your driver; tips are neither expected or necessary. Don't invite your driver for a drink or become overly familiar with him. He may abuse your trust. If you're a woman taking a cab in the Nandi area, don't let your driver think there is any "hope" for him or you'll be in trouble. Don't be intimidated by the taxi drivers waiting outside Nandi airport. They will do their jobs quite normally unless you give them cause to do otherwise.

OTHER TRAVEL OPTIONS

By Sailing Yacht

Hitch rides into the Pacific on yachts from California, New Zealand, and Australia, or around the yachting triangle Papeete-Suva-Honolulu. Check out the bulletin boards at yacht clubs and put up notices of your own. Meet people in the bars. Cruising yachts are recognizable by their foreign flags, wind-vane steering gear, sturdy appearance, and laundry hung out to dry. Rather than trying to find a yacht to the South Pacific it's much easier to fly down and look for a boat already in the islands. After months of cruising some of the original crew may have flown home or onward, opening a place for you.

The weather and seasons play a deciding role in any South Pacific trip by sailboat. You'll have to pull out of many beautiful places or be unable to stop there because of bad weather. Most important of all, be aware of the hurricane season: Nov. to March in the South Pacific. Few yachts will be cruising at this time. Also, know which way the winds are blowing; the prevailing tradewinds in the South Pacific are from the southeast.

Expense-sharing crew members pay US$50 a week or more per person. If you've never crewed before it's better to try for a short passage the first time. Once at sea there's no way they'll turn around to take a seasick crew member back to port. Good captains evaluate crew on personality and attitude more than experience, so don't lie. Be honest and open when interviewing with a skipper—a deception will soon become apparent. It's also good to know what a captain's *really* like before you commit yourself to an isolated month with her/him. Once you're on a boat and part of the yachtie community, things are easy. If you've had a good trip, ask the captain to write you a letter of recommendation; it'll help you hitch another ride. The **Seven Seas Cruising Association** (Box 1256, Stuart, FL 34995 USA; tel. 407-287-5615) is in touch with yachties all around the Pacific.

By Ocean Kayak

Ocean kayaking is experiencing a boom in Hawaii, but Fiji is still almost virgin territory. Almost every island group has sheltered lagoons ready-made for the excitement of kayak touring, but this effortless new transportation mode hasn't yet arrived. So you can be a real independent 20th-century explorer! Many airlines accept folding kayaks as checked baggage at no charge (ask).

Companies like **Long Beach Water Sports** (730 E. 4th St., Long Beach, CA 90802 USA; tel. 213-432-0187) sell inflatable one-person "Tradewind" sea kayaks for US$1395 (US$1545 for the two-person variety), fully equipped. LBWS runs four-hour sea kayaking classes ($40) every Sat. morning and all-day advanced classes ($70) about once a month. Part of the tuition is deductible from the price of any kayak you purchase from them. They also rent kayaks by the day or week.

For a better introduction to ocean kayaking than is possible here check your local public library for *Sea Kayaking: A Manual for Long-Distance Touring* by John Dowd (Seattle: University of Washington Press, 1981) or *Derek C. Hutchinson's Guide to Sea Kayaking* (Seattle: Basic Search Press, 1985).

AIRPORTS

Nandi International Airport

Nandi Airport (NAN) is between Lautoka and Nandi, 22 km south of the former and eight km north of the latter. There are frequent buses to these towns on the highway, just a short walk from the terminal. To catch a bus to Nandi cross the highway; those to Lautoka stop on the airport side. A taxi from the airport will be F$4 to downtown Nandi, F$12 to Lautoka. Most hotels around Nandi have their rates listed on a board inside the Customs area, so peruse the list while you're waiting for your baggage. The Fiji Visitors Bureau office is to the left as you come out of Customs. They open for all international arrivals and can advise you on accommodations. Pick up some brochures and the free tourist newspapers.

There's a 24-hour bank (50-cent commission) in the commercial arcade near the Visitors Bureau. Another bank is in the departure lounge. The airport restaurant serves good *kokonda*. Many travel agencies, car rental companies, and airline offices are also located in the arrivals arcade. The post office is across the road (ask). Coin lockers are over near the check-in counters, but half are broken and the other half taken. Most hotels around Nandi will store luggage. Check your change carefully if you buy anything at this airport as the clerks might try to pass Australian and N.Z. coins off on you. Tourists probably do the same to them.

The airport never closes so you can sleep on the benches on the departures side if you're leaving in the wee hours. There's a large duty-free store in the departure lounge with the usual range of insipid luxury items—don't wait to do your shopping here. A departure tax of F$10 is payable on all international flights but transit passengers connecting within 12 hours and children under the age of 16 are exempt.

Nausori Airport (SUV)

Nausori Airport is on the plain of the Rewa River delta, 23 km northeast of downtown Suva. The airport bus costs F$1 to the Air Pacific office in Suva. There's a local bus on the highway if you want to go to Nausori. A taxi will run about F$3 to Nausori, F$12 to Suva.

A lunch counter provides light snacks. The Bank of N.Z. counter opens Thurs. 1230-1400 only. There's the inevitable duty-free shop. The departure tax is F$10 on all international flights, but no tax is levied on domestic flights.

Fijian children pose for an early 20th-century photographer. Contrary to popular belief, perpetuated through the years by humorists, big black "cannibal" pots such as this were more likely used to boil sugar than shipwrecked sailors and missionaries.

SOUTHWEST VITI LEVU

NANDI

Nandi (population 15,179 in 1988), on the dry side of Fiji's largest island, offers a multitude of places to stay for incoming visitors landing at Nandi International Airport. A small airstrip existed at Nandi even before WW I,I and after Pearl Harbor the Royal New Zealand Air Force began converting it into a fighter strip. Before long the U.S. military was there building a major air base with paved runways for bombers and transport aircraft serving Australia and New Zealand. In the early 1960s Nandi Airport was expanded to take jet aircraft and today the largest jumbo jets can land here. This activity has made Nandi what it is today.

All around Nandi are cane fields worked by the predominantly Indian population. In the nearby Malolo Group a string of sun-drenched Robinson Crusoe resorts soak up vacationers in search of a place to relax. Nandi town has a kilometer of concrete duty-free tourist shops with high-pressure sales staff;

mass-produced souvenirs are sold at the stalls behind the post office. Yet there's also a surprisingly colorful market (best on Sat. morning). It's a rather touristy town, so if you're not that exhausted after your trans-Pacific flight you'd do better to head for Lautoka. Beware of the friendly handshake in Nandi for you may find yourself buying something you neither care for nor desire.

Budget Accommodations
Closer To The Airport
Most of the hotels offer free transport from the airport. As you leave Customs you'll be besieged by a group of Indian men holding small wooden signs bearing the names of the hotels they represent. If you know which one you want, call out the name: if their driver is there, you'll get a free ride. If not, the **Fiji Visitors Bureau** to the left will help you telephone them for a small fee. Don't be put off by the Indian hotel drivers at the airport, but

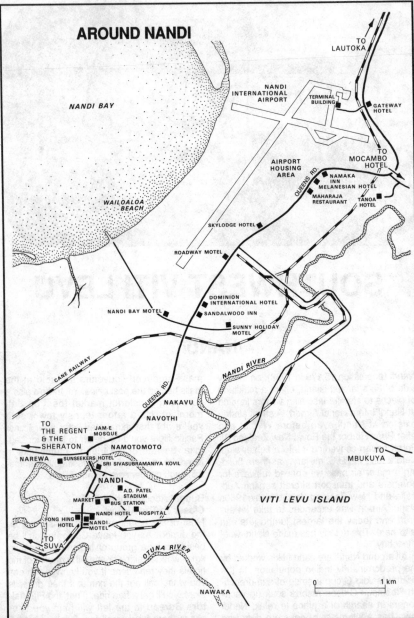

AROUND NANDI

NANDI BAY

TO LAUTOKA

NANDI INTERNATIONAL AIRPORT

TERMINAL BUILDING

GATEWAY HOTEL

TO MOCAMBO HOTEL

AIRPORT HOUSING AREA

QUEENS RD.

NAMAKA INN MELANESIAN HOTEL

MAHARAJA RESTAURANT

TANOA HOTEL

WAILOALOA BEACH

SKYLODGE HOTEL

ROADWAY MOTEL

DOMINION INTERNATIONAL HOTEL

NANDI BAY MOTEL

SANDALWOOD INN

SUNNY HOLIDAY MOTEL

CANE RAILWAY

NANDI RIVER

QUEENS RD.

NAKAVU

NAVOTHI

JAM-E MOSQUE

TO THE REGENT & THE SHERATON

NAMOTOMOTO

TO MBUKUYA

NAREWA

SUNSEEKERS HOTEL

SRI SIVASUBRAMANIYA KOVIL

NANDI

A.D. PATEL STADIUM

MARKET

BUS STATION

VITI LEVU ISLAND

FONG HING HOTEL

NANDI HOTEL

HOSPITAL

NANDI MOTEL

TO SUVA

OTUNA RIVER

NAWAKA

0   1 km

question them about the rates and facilities before you let them drive you to their place.

The closest budget hotel to the airport is **Johal's Motel** (Box 213, Nandi; tel. 72-192), set in cane fields, a 15-minute walk in from the main highway past the Mocambo Hotel. The 12 rooms go for F$14 s, F$19 d with private bath and fan, or camp by the pleasant swimming pool for only F$3.50. The motel lawns swarm with toads at night. Recommended, but avoid the noisy rooms near the active bar. It's rather run down.

The cheapest place to stay in Nandi is the **Namaka Inn** (tel. 72-276) near the Maharaja Restaurant, F$10 pp with breakfast or F$5 dorm (no breakfast). It's plain, noisy, and has little to recommend it except the low price. You might want to try a meal in the restaurant downstairs however.

Also very basic is the **Roadway Motel** (Box 9236, Nandi; tel. 72-520), F$12 s, F$16 d, or F$7 dorm (three persons maximum)—all with private facilities. Rooms with a/c are slightly more. The Roadway partly makes up for the lack of a pool and bar by offering cooking facilities, a washing machine (F$1), and luggage storage (20 cents a day).

The two-story **Sandalwood Inn** (John and Ann Birch, Box 445, Nandi; tel. 72-553) near the Roadway is F$20 s, F$26 d for one of the five standard rooms with shared bath in the old wing, or F$38 s, F$45 d for the 20 a/c rooms with fridge and private bath in the new wing. The cheaper rooms may be full. The layout is attractive with pool, bar, and restaurant. Video movies are shown nightly after dinner. The Inn has a very good reputation—recommended.

Close by and less expensive is the **Sunny Holiday Motel** (Box 9335, Nandi Airport; tel. 72-844), F$8.50 s, F$12.50 d, F$4.50 dorm (five beds), all with Continental breakfast included. **Camping** is F$3.50 but take care with your things. There's a pool table, games room, cooking facilities, and luggage storage. Show your Y.H.A. card for a discount.

A few hundred meters down Wailoaloa Beach Road off the main highway in the opposite direction from Sunny Holiday is **Nandi Bay Motel** (Box 1102, Nandi; tel. 73-319). All 22 rooms (F$20 s, F$28 d) have private bath, fan (a/c F$4 extra), and cooking

facilities but the roar of the jets on the adjacent runway can be jarring. Still, it's clean, comfortable, and good. Coin-operated washing machines are available.

Travellers Beach Resort (Box 700, Nandi; tel. 73-322) on Wailoaloa Beach (also known as Newtown Beach) three km from Nandi has eight rooms with cooking facilities at F$25 s, F$30 d, or F$10 pp in a dorm.

Budget Accommodations Closer To Town

On Narewa Road at the north edge of Nandi is **Sunseekers Hotel** (Box 100, Nandi; tel. 70-400). The 21 rooms here begin at F$20 s or d, F$6 dorm (F$1 extra if you want a sheet), all with Continental breakfast included (F$1 surcharge for one night). Show your Y.H.A. card for a possible discount. There's a tiny pool out back and a cafe. It's a good place to meet other travelers, but it can be noisy.

There are three choices in the downtown area. The **Fong Hing Private Hotel** (Box 143, Nandi; tel. 71-011) is a two-story Chinese commercial hotel on Vunavou St. offering 17 a/c rooms with private bath at F$18 s, F$24 d. Their restaurant is famous and not expensive. It's okay to go up and sit on the hotel roof.

The other two places have confusingly similar names and are located side-by-side but have separate managements. The **Nandi Town Motel** (Box 1326, Nandi; tel. 70-600) occupies the top floor of an office building opposite Khan's Service Station and looks rather basic at first glance but the rooms are okay with fridge and private bath. The price is F$12 s, F$15 d, F$18 t. Cooking facilities are about F$2 extra. Show your Y.H.A. card for a possible discount.

Rates at the two-story **Nandi Hotel** (Box 91, Nandi; tel. 70-000) begin at F$20 s, F$26 d, or F$10 pp in a dorm. The neat courtyard with a swimming pool out back and a variety of entertainment both at the hotel and nearby make this a pleasant, convenient place to stay. Nice people too.

Upmarket Airport Hotels

The two-story **Castaway Gateway Hotel** (Box 9246, Nandi Airport; tel. 72-444) is just across the highway from the airport (easy walking distance). Its 92 a/c rooms begin at F$74 s or d. Happy hour in the Flight Deck

handicraft seller, Nandi

Bar is from 1800-1900 (half-price drinks) and there's disco dancing in the hotel restaurant Thurs., Fri., and Sat. after 2200 (F$1 cover)—worth checking out if you're stuck in the terminal waiting for a flight.

Tanoa Hotel (Box 9211, Nandi Airport; tel. 72-300) one km from the airport is on a hilltop overlooking the runway and surrounding countryside. The 107 a/c rooms are priced from F$93 s, F$99 d. The hotel *meke* buffet (F$24) is accompanied by Fijian dances Sat. night. In 1988 a kitchen fire gutted the hotel but they should be back in operation by now.

A little inland from the Tanoa is the two-story **Nandi Airport TraveLodge** (Box 9203, Nandi Airport; tel. 72-277). The 114 a/c rooms in this Australian-owned establishment are F$103 s, F$110 d. Aside from the Indian curry buffet (F$24) offered Tues. and Sun., the restaurant menu includes Fijian specialties.

The **Fiji Mocambo Hotel** (Box 9195, Nandi Airport; tel. 72-000), a sprawling two-story hotel near the TraveLodge two km inland from the airport, is the finest of the airport hotels. The 124 a/c rooms with patio or balcony begin at F$111 s or d. Secretarial services are arranged for businesspeople, and there's a golf driving range. Their much-touted French restaurant is reported to be overrated so ask another guest about it before sitting down to a pricey meal. Alterna-

tively stick to the salads. Lots of in-house entertainment is laid on, including *mekes* four nights a week. The big event of the week is the Fijian firewalking Sat. at 1830 followed by a *lovo* feast and *meke* (F$31). A live band plays in the Vale Ni Marau Lounge every evening except Sunday.

There are two good middle-priced choices between the airport and Nandi. The first is the **Skylodge Hotel** (Box 9222, Nandi Airport; tel. 72-200), four km from the airport. The Skylodge was constructed as Nandi Airport was being expanded to take jet aircraft in the early 1960s. The 60 a/c units begin at F$48 s, F$58 d—good value. Be sure to get a room with cooking facilities in one of the four-unit clusters well-spaced among the greenery rather than a smaller room in the main building or near the busy highway.

The **Dominion International Hotel** (Box 9178, Nandi Airport; tel. 72-255), a three-story building facing a pool is near the Sandalwood Inn halfway between the airport and town. The 85 a/c rooms with rather loud bedspreads and curtains are F$61 s, F$68 d.

Deluxe Beach Hotels

Nandi's two big international hotels, The Regent and the Sheraton, are on Ndenarau Beach opposite Yakuilau Island seven km west of the bridge on the north side of Nandi town, a 15-minute drive from the airport.

These are Nandi's only up-market hotels right on the beach and the sunsets here are great. In mid-1988 the huge Japanese group Electrical Industrial Enterprises bought control of both The Regent and the Sheraton.

Rub elbows with Tokyo and Osaka nouveau riche at **The Regent of Fiji** (Box 441, Nandi; tel. 70-700), an a/c 294-room palace where prices begin at F$172 s or d. The spacious rooms are in parallel rows of two-story buildings. Facilities include an impressive lobby with shops to one side, a poolbar you can swim right up to, and 10 floodlit tennis courts. A special event is organized every night, notably the firewalking at the Wed. buffet (F$43) and a *meke* buffet on Mon. and Fri. (F$43). Yachties anchored offshore are not especially welcome at this hotel. Cruise boats to resorts on Castaway and Malololailai islands depart from here.

Nandi's other Hawaiian-style hotel and The Regent's neighbor is the **Sheraton-Fiji Resort** (Box 9761, Nandi Airport; tel. 71-777). This luxurious $60-million hotel complex complete with shopping arcade and an 800-seat convention center opened just as the 1987 military coups axed tourism to Fiji. The 300 a/c rooms begin at F$178 s or d. You can see firewalking here at the Thurs. barbecue (F$35), or a *meke* at the Tues. and Sat. *lovo* (F$35). If bigger is better the Sheraton is slightly bigger.

Grasping war clubs, Fijian men perform a meke.

Food And Entertainment

For Chinese and European food try **Poon's Restaurant** upstairs, across from the Mobil service station on the main street on the north side of town. **Mama's Pizza Inn** nearby has—surprise—pizza and spaghetti. The **Indian Curry House** at the north end of the main street serves reasonable shrimp curries.

Kwong's Refreshment Bar on the north side of the market is a good place to get a cheaper meal or a snack. The **Farmer's Restaurant** near the market is also good and cheap. For Chinese food it's the **Fong Hing Hotel**.

The **Maharaja Restaurant** (tel. 72-962) out near the Skylodge Hotel is popular among flight crews who come for the good Indian curries. The **Hacienda** is a huge pizza place on the airport road.

For night life ask about the barbecue and *meke* by the pool at the **Nandi Hotel**. The **Bamboo Palace Night Club** at the Nandi Hotel has a live band from 2100-0100 on Thurs., Fri., and Sat. nights (F$2.50 cover). Locals call it "the zoo." The **Farmer's Club** near Poon's is a good place for a drink with the boys. Out near the airport the Tanoa and Mocambo hotels usually have live music after 2100 Tues. to Saturday.

During the sports season (Feb. to Nov.), see rugby or soccer on Sat. afternoon at the A.D. Patel Stadium near the bus station. There are four movie houses in Nandi.

Transport And Tours

Many day cruises and bus tours which operate in the Nandi area are listed in the free tourist papers, the *Fiji Beach Press* and *Fiji "Fantastic"*. Rubber raft trips down the Mba River are also offered. Reservations can be made through hotel reception desks or the travel offices in the Nandi Airport arcade. Bus transfers to and from your hotel are included in the price. For information on Beachcomber Island day trips and scuba diving with Diver Services, see the "Lautoka" section. Both these trips also include free transfers from Nandi.

If you're headed for the offshore resorts on Malololailai, Malolo, Castaway, or Mana islands, the 300-passenger *Island Express* catamaran (tel. 70-144) departs Nandi's

Regent Hotel twice daily at 0900 and 1330 (about F$25 OW). Inter-island hops are F$15 each. A four-hour F$26 roundtrip cruise on this boat provides a fair glimpse of the lovely Malolo Group, or pay F$47 for a daytrip to Mana Island (lunch included). Be prepared to wade on and off the boat.

Turtle Airways (tel. 72-988) runs a quick seaplane shuttle to the offshore resorts for F$57 pp each way. A combined catamaran/seaplane roundtrip fare to the resorts is F$75 pp. Scenic flights with Turtle are F$26 pp for 10 minutes (minimum of three persons).

Horseback riding can be arranged with Inoke Derenalagi (tel. 70-443) at Nawaka village near Nandi (bus from the market or a taxi). Inoke has five horses in so-so shape, but they'll run if you insist. Prices begin at F$8 and go up according to how much you seem willing to spend. Three-day trips with accommodations in Fijian villages begin at F$35 pp and up. Inoke takes you out himself and makes stops to visit friends, so this is a great way to meet some local people.

Khan's Rental Cars (Box 299, Nandi; tel. 71-009) at the service station opposite the Nandi Motel has the lowest unlimited mileage rates in Nandi. With Khan's you must return the car to Nandi and cannot drop it off somewhere else. **Thrifty Car Rental** (Box 9268, Nandi Airport; tel. 72-935) also has low unlimited mileage rates, especially if you take the car for longer than three days.

You can bargain for fares with the collective taxis cruising the highway from the airport into Nandi. They'll usually take what you'd pay on a bus, but ask first. Pirate taxis also take passengers nonstop from Nandi to Suva in three hours for only a couple of dollars more than the bus. Nandi's bus station adjoining the market is an active place (except Sunday).

SOUTH OF NANDI

Momi Bay

On a hilltop overlooking Momi Bay 28 km from Nandi are two **British six-inch guns**, one named Queen Victoria (1900), the other Edward VIII (1901). Both were recycled from the Boer War and set up here in 1941 by the New Zealand army to defend the southern approach to Nandi Bay. Take a bus along the old highway to Momi, then walk three km west. The Nambilla village bus runs directly there from Nandi.

Just a stroll from the Momi historical gun site is **Trekkers Camping Resort** (Box 9839, Nandi Airport; tel. 72-253), Fiji's first backpackers' campground. Two people together pay F$8 per tent or it's F$14 pp in a Fijian dorm for those without tents. Vegetarian meals are served with some seafood, or use the barbecue to cook your own (firewood supplied). Their tropical breakfast is juice, muesli, toast, and coffee. It's spacious and in an unspoiled rural setting, but the beach isn't that great. Trekkers runs a three-day camping tour to a remote island for F$37 pp daily if four people go, including fresh fish and other food prepared by the guide. You'll need to have your own tent. It's great and your Sydneysider hosts Corrie and Paul Wright deserve credit for putting this place together.

Seashell Cove

Also on Momi Bay 37 km southwest of Nandi is **Seashell Cove Resort** (Box 9530, Nandi Airport; tel. 72-900). They have 14 duplex *mbures* with fans and cooking facilities at F$35 s, F$50 d, and a big 25-bed dormitory divided into six-bed compartments for F$10 pp, breakfast included (F$2 discount with a Y.H.A. card). Otherwise pitch your own tent for F$6 pp but beware of prancing ponies around the tents. Baggage storage is available free.

Seashell has a swimming pool, bar, and restaurant (expensive—bring groceries). There's a *meke* Sat. evening. The beach here isn't exciting, but they do their best to keep you occupied with day trips to Natandola Beach (F$10) and a deserted island (F$10), tennis, water skiing (F$5), and volleyball (free). If you're a **surfer** charter one of their boats to Namotu Island or Natandola Beach; otherwise consider the possibilities around Momi Bay lighthouse. A public bus direct to Seashell Cove leaves Nandi bus station at 1545 Mon. through Saturday. There's a good onward connection from the resort by public bus to Singatoka Mon. through Fri. at

0900. The resort will provide F$2 airport transfers if they know 24 hours in advance. Opinions about Seashell are mixed.

Natandola Beach
The long, white, unspoiled sandy beach here has become popular for surfing and camping. You can camp on the beach, but campers and sunbathers be aware that thefts by locals are a daily occurrence and the police make no effort to stop it. It might be better to stay at Sanasana village by the river at the far south end of the beach. There's a store on the hill just before your final descent to Natandola.

Get there on the bus to Sangasanga village, which leaves Nandi at 1630 (or catch one from Singatoka at 1130). You have to walk the last three km to the beach. Otherwise get off at the Maro School stop on the main highway and hitch 10 km to the beach. The sugar train passes close to Natandola, bringing day trippers from Yanutha Island.

THE MALOLO GROUP

The Malolo Group is a paradise of eye-popping reefs and sand-fringed isles shared by traditional Fijian villages and jet-age resorts. The white coral beaches and super snorkeling grounds attract visitors aplenty; boats and planes arrive constantly, bringing them in from nearby Nandi. These islands are in the lee of big Viti Levu, which means you'll get about as much sun here as anywhere in Fiji. Some of the South Pacific's best skin diving, surfing, game fishing, and yachting await you. Dive spots include The Pinnacles, Sunflower Reef, Wilkes Passage, and Land of the Giants. As yet only a few have noticed the potential for ocean kayaking in this area. Unpack your folding kayak on the beach a short taxi ride from the airport, and you'll be in for some real adventure. (For information on Beachcomber and Treasure islands see "Lautoka" below.)

Malololailai Island
Malololailai, 18 km west of Nandi, is the first of the Malolo Group. It's a fair-sized island eight km around (a nice walk). In 1860 an American sailor named Louis Armstrong bought Malololailai from the Fijians for one musket. In 1966 Dick Smith purchased it for many muskets. You can still be alone at the beaches on the far side of the island, but with two growing resorts, projects for a golf course and marina, and lots more time-share condominiums in the pipeline it's in danger of becoming overdeveloped. An airstrip across the island's waist separates its two resorts;

inland are rounded grassy hills. At low tide you can wade to nearby **Malolo Island**, which is much bigger and has two Fijian villages. One of them, Solevu, is known to tourists as "shell village" for what the locals offer for sale.

Plantation Island Resort (Box 9176, Nandi Airport; tel. 72-333) on the southwest side of Malololailai is one of the largest of the resorts off Nandi. The 98 rooms (beginning at F$145 s or d, meals extra) are divided between individual *mbures,* big group or family *mbures,* and a/c hotel rooms in a two-story building. In addition three 12-bed dormitories are F$45 pp including meals. Unlike better-known Beachcomber Island off Lautoka there are **separate dormitories for men, women, and couples**. Plantation's excellent night life makes it a good place for the young or young at heart. Snorkeling gear, row boats, and windsurfing are free, but boat trips cost extra.

Musket Cove Resort (Dick Smith, Private Mail Bag, Nandi Airport; tel. 62-215), formerly known as Dick's Place and also on Malololailai Island, offers 24 fully equipped *mbure* units with fans and hot water for F$88 s, F$108 d, F$118 t, F$128 for four, F$138 for five. Small kitchenettes allow you to cook and a well-stocked grocery store selling fresh fruit and vegetables is on the premises. There's also a bar and restaurant by the pool (meal package available). Entertainment is provided at the Thurs. night pig roast. Activities such as snorkeling, windsurfing, water skiing, line fishing, and boat trips are free for guests.

Scuba diving and deep-sea fishing are offered at an additional charge. Roundtrip airfare to Malololailai on **Island Air** (five flights daily, F$20 OW or F$25 same day return; tel. 72-521) from Nandi Airport is included for anyone who stays at least six nights.

Malololailai is a favorite stopover for **cruising yachts**. Membership in the Musket Cove Yacht Club (F$1 for skippers, F$5 pp for crew) gets you water, clean showers, and half price at the weekly Fijian feast. The marked anchorage is protected and 15 meters deep with good holding. Fuel and groceries are sold ashore. In mid-Sept. there's a yacht regatta at Musket Cove, culminating in a yacht race from Fiji to Port Vila. Among the unique rules is one which says that the first yacht to arrive at Vila is disqualified unless it can be proven that blatant cheating occurred.

The "race" is timed for the boats' annual departure east prior to the onset of the hurricane season. It costs F$30 pp to enter the regatta, but for that you get feasts, parties, prizes, groceries, exemption from harbor fees at Port Vila, and more. If you're on a boat in Fiji at this time, Musket Cove is *the* place to be.

Malololailai's grass-and-gravel airstrip is the only one in the Mamanutha Group and serves as a distribution point for the other resorts. You can fly to Malololailai from Nandi several times a day on **Sunflower Airlines** (F$18 OW) or take the twice-daily Island Express catamaran from Nandi's Regent Hotel for F$20 OW (tel. 70-103 for free pickup).

Malolo Island

Australian-owned **Club Naitasi** (Erol and Antoinette Fifer, Box 9147, Nandi Airport; tel.

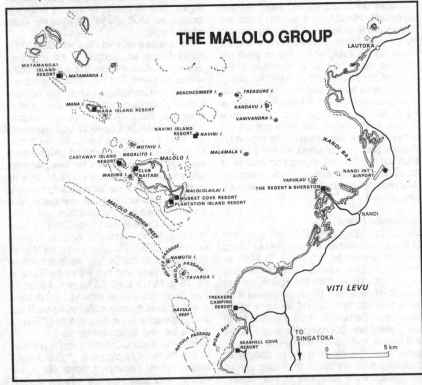

THE MALOLO GROUP

72-266) is at the western tip of Malolo Island, largest of the group. The 28 one-bedroom bungalows with fan go for F$111 s, F$127 d, the 10 two-bedroom family villas are F$185. Meals are extra and while some breakfast groceries are available in the hotel boutique it's best to bring your own food and make use of the full cooking facilities provided. The individual units are privately owned under a time-sharing scheme and each is decorated differently.

The compulsory F$25 pp club membership fee covers most non-motorized watersports activities; scuba diving with Aqua-Trek is extra. They'll teach you how to windsurf, and this is the only resort offering paraflying on a regular basis. Club Naitasi has a freshwater swimming pool. Get there on Sunflower Airlines from Nandi to Malololailai, then by speedboat to Club Naitasi (F$27 pp combined fare each way). Access may also be possible on the twice-daily Island Express tourist boat from The Regent Hotel, Nandi, for F$20.50 pp each way (ask). No day trippers are allowed at the club. Club Naitasi could be your choice if you're really into nautical activities.

Tavarua Island
Tavarua Island just south of Malololailai operates as a **surfing** base camp (Dave Clark and Scott Funk, Box 1419, Nandi; tel. 73-513). There are both lefts and rights in Malolo Passage at Tavarua although the emphasis is usually on the lefts. When the swell is high enough you'll have some of the best surfing anywhere. On the off days you can get in some deep-sea fishing, windsurfing, snorkeling, or scuba diving. Only 15 surfers are allowed on the island at a time and the F$100 pp a day charge includes meals, accommodations, transfers from Nandi, and activities (three-day minimum stay). Non-surfers are accommodated at half price and couples get preference.

Bookings must be made through Aquarius Tours, 18411 Crenshaw Blvd., #102, Torrance, CA 90504 USA (tel. 805-683-6696). They're usually sold out, especially in June, July, and August. You can always try calling upon arrival, and they'll probably take you if vacancies have materialized. If not or you simply can't afford those prices stay at Seashell Cove Resort south of Nandi and charter one of their boats out to Wilkes Pass or nearby Namotu Island. The Tavarua supply boat often calls at Seashell Cove.

Castaway Island
Castaway Island Resort (Bob and Tracy, Private Mail Bag, Nandi Airport; tel. 61-233) on Nggalito Island just west of Malolo and 15 km from Nandi was erected in 1961 as Fiji's first outer-island resort. A small Fijian village shares the 80-hectare island. The 66 thatched *mbures* with fan and fridge sleep four and run F$147 (meals extra). Some water sports are included. There's a daily boat from Nandi's Regent Hotel.

Mana Island
Japanese-owned **Mana Island Resort** (Wayne and Jeanette McKeague, Box 610, Lautoka; tel. 61-455), northwest of Castaway and 32 km west of Lautoka, is popular with scuba divers. It's by far the largest of the resorts off Nandi with 132 tin-roofed bungalows crowded together beneath the island's grassy rounded hilltops. The rates (F$135 s or d, F$150 t) don't include meals at the three restaurants on Mana and cooking facilities are not provided, so it's expensive.

The price does include most non-motorized water sports, though scuba diving is extra (F$45 one tank, F$70 two tanks). The five-day certification course is F$320. There are two boat dives a day and night diving two or three times a week. Lots of other activities are offered. Mana Island features beautiful white sandy beaches, crystal-clear waters, and a superb reef; topless and even nude sunbathing is said to be tolerated. The Island Express catamaran from Regent Hotel, Nandi, calls twice a day (F$22 OW).

Aqua-Trek (110 Sutter St., Ste. 608, San Francisco, CA 94104 USA; tel 415-339-2550) offers one-week packages to Mana Island from US$999 pp including accommodations (double occupancy), meals, and scuba diving (air fare extra)—cheaper than if you were to go individually. Aqua-Trek has full PADI training facilities located right at their base on Mana.

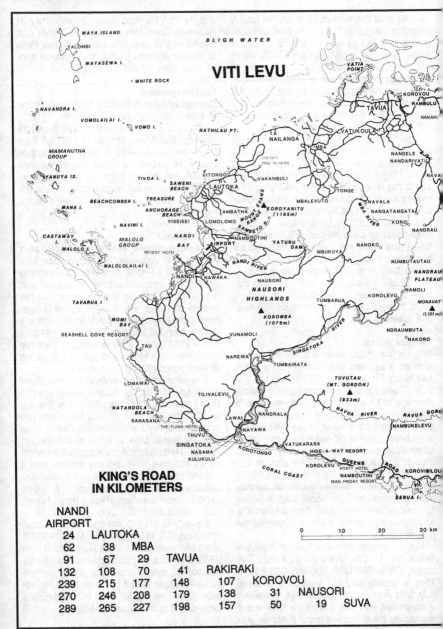

KING'S ROAD
IN KILOMETERS

NANDI AIRPORT							
24	LAUTOKA						
62	38	MBA					
91	67	29	TAVUA				
132	108	70	41	RAKIRAKI			
239	215	177	148	107	KOROVOU		
270	246	208	179	138	31	NAUSORI	
289	265	227	198	157	50	19	SUVA

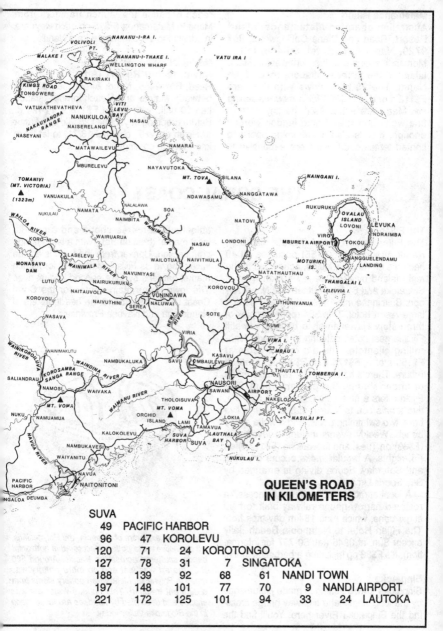

QUEEN'S ROAD IN KILOMETERS

SUVA							
49	PACIFIC HARBOR						
96	47	KOROLEVU					
120	71	24	KOROTONGO				
127	78	31	7	SINGATOKA			
188	139	92	68	61	NANDI TOWN		
197	148	101	77	70	9	NANDI AIRPORT	
221	172	125	101	94	33	24	LAUTOKA

Matamanoa Island

Australian-operated **Matamanoa Island Resort** (Road and Diane Collingwood, Box 9729, Nandi Airport; tel. 60-458) in the Mamanutha Group to the northwest of Mana Island is the farthest offshore resort from Nandi. The 26 bungalows with fanS are F$112 s or d, or F$224 for a *mbure* sleeping six. Meals are extra. As if the tiny island's fine white beach and blue lagoon weren't enough, there's also a swimming pool and lighted tennis court. It's more expensive to reach because the launch transfers from Mana to Matamanoa (F$15 pp each way) are in addition to the catamaran from Nandi.

Navini Island

Navini Island Resort (Arthur and Helen Reed, Box 9445, Nandi Airport; tel. 62-188) between Malolo and Beachcomber islands has 10 units with fan at F$110 s, F$124 d. Before dropping in yachties should call Arthur or Helen on VHF, channel 16/71, to let them know they're coming.

THE CORAL COAST

The Fijian

The Fijian Resort Hotel (Private Mail Bag, Nandi Airport; tel. 50-155) occupies all 40 hectares of Yanutha Island, connected to the main island by a causeway 10 km west of Singatoka and 61 km southeast of Nandi Airport. Built in the mid 1960s, this was Fiji's first large resort hotel. This 364-room complex of three-story Hawaiian-style buildings is still Fiji's largest hotel, catering to a trendy, high-rolling clientele. The a/c rooms begin at F$150 s or d, F$175 t, or F$360 for a beach *mbure*. There's no charge for two children 18 or under sharing the parents' room. The Fijian offers a nine-hole golf course (par 31), five tennis courts, four restaurants and five bars, two swimming pools, and a white sandy beach. Weekly events include a *lovo/meke* (F$39) on Tues. and firewalking (F$11.50) on Fri. nights. A regular *meke* occurs on Wed. and Saturday. Scuba diving is arranged by Sea Sports Limited.

A local attraction is the "Fijian Princess," a restored narrow-gauge railway built to haul sugar cane, which runs 16-km day trips from The Fijian Hotel to Natandola Beach daily except Sun. at 0945 (tel. 50-757 for information). It's F$38 pp including a barbecue lunch.

Singatoka

Singatoka town's setting is made picturesque by the long single-lane highway bridge crossing the Singatoka River here. You'll find the ubiquitous duty-free shops and a colorful local market (best on Sat.) with a large handicraft section. Upriver from the town is a wide valley known as Fiji's "salad bowl" for its rich market gardens by Fiji's second largest river. The town is the main center for the Coral Coast tourist district and the headquarters of Nandronga and Navosa Province.

The original explorers of Oceania, the Polynesians, left distinctive lapita pottery, decorated in horizontal bands, scattered across the Pacific. Around 500 B.C. the art was lost and no more pottery was made in Polynesia. Melanesian pottery stems from a different tradition. This antique water pot was shaped and decorated by hand, as are those made in the Singatoka Valley today.

Strangely, the traditional handmade **Fijian pottery**, for which Singatoka is famous, is not available here. Find it by asking in Nayawa (where the clay originates), Yavulo, and Nasama villages near Singatoka. Better yet, take the two-hour **boat cruise** (F\$12) up the river from Singatoka to Nakambuta and Lawai villages, where the pottery is displayed for sale.

The **Singatoka Hotel** (Box 35, Singatoka; tel. 50-011) is an older commercial establishment not far from the center of town. The 11 rooms range from F\$10-15 s, F\$15-21 d, but are often full. You can choose from among 116 Chinese dishes in the hotel restaurant.

Eat cheap but good Indian food at the **Singatoka Lodge** behind the market.

Kulukulu
Another favorite surfing beach is Kulukulu, five km south of Singatoka, where the Singatoka River breaks through Viti Levu's fringing reef. Incredibly high **sand dunes** separate the cane fields from the shore. Winds sometimes uncover human bones from old burials and potsherds lie scattered along the seashore—these fragments have been dated up to 2,000 years old. Giant sea turtles sometimes come ashore here to lay their eggs. Altogether a fascinating, evocative place.

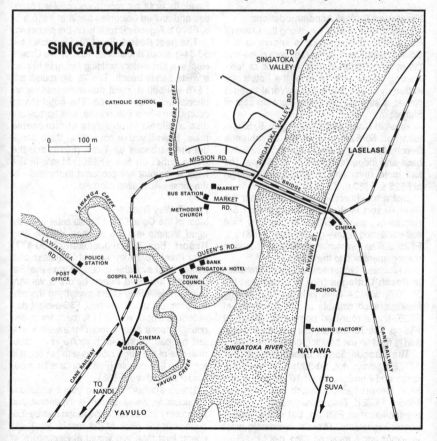

A group of American **surfers** have opened a base camp here called **Club Masa** (Marcus Oliver, Box 3338, Lami, Fiji Islands). So far there's a dormitory cabin (F$5 pp) and camping area F$3. There's plenty of firewood on the beach for evening bonfires. Surfing gear is for hire. The **windsurfing** in this area is fantastic as you can either sail "flat water" across the river mouth or do "wave jumping" in the sea (all-sand bottom and big rollers with high wind). Be prepared, however, as these waters are treacherous for novices. About four buses a day run from Singatoka to Kulukulu village (26 cents); the one at 1400 is the most reliable.

Korotongo Budget Accommodations

The south side of Viti Levu along the Queen's Road around Singatoka is known as the Coral Coast. The fringing reef here gives you the option of snorkeling at high tide or reef-walking at low tide. Most of the hotels are expensive, but there are several budget places to stay at Korotongo, eight km east of Singatoka.

Vakaviti Units and Cabins (Box 5, Singatoka; tel. 50-526) next to the Casablanca Beach Motel has a single dormitory with five beds and fridge (no cooking) at F$8 pp. The four motel units with cooking facilities begin at F$25 s, F$30 d. It's often full.

Just a few hundred meters east near the Reef Resort is **Waratah Lodge** (Box 86, Korotongo; tel. 50-278) with five very nice self-contained units—good value at F$16 s, F$25 d. The swimming pool and charming management add to the allure.

A kilometer farther east again is **Tumbakula Beach Cottages** (Box 2, Singatoka; tel. 50-097), with 24 units with fan and cooking facilities, each capable of sleeping three, at F$35, and a four-bed dorm with kitchen at F$6 pp. The Tumbakula has a swimming pool and is right on the beach (good snorkeling).

The **Tambua Sands Beach Resort** (Box 177, Singatoka; tel. 50-399) between Korotongo and Korolevu about 10 km east of the Reef Resort has 23 beach bungalows at F$65 s, F$72 d. Their "luxury dorm" (no cooking facilities) is F$8 pp, but call ahead to check availability. There's live music most evenings and a *meke* on Wed. night.

Korotongo Upmarket Accommodations

The Crow's Nest (Box 270, Singatoka; tel. 50-230) at Korotongo is run by Paddy Doyle, a pioneer of Fiji tourism who helped develop Nandi Airport and The Fijian Hotel in the 1960s. Doyle's 18 duplex units with cooking facilities are F$58 s, F$77 d. The nautical touches in the excellent moderately priced restaurant spill over into the rooms. Good views over the lagoon are obtained from The Crow's Nest's elevated perch.

The **Casablanca Beach Motel** (Box 164, Singatoka; tel. 50-766) next door to the Crow's Nest is a pleasant two-story building on a hillside on the inland side of Queen's Road. Its eight a/c rooms with cooking facilities and arched balconies begin at F$60 s or d, F$70 t. A good pizzeria is on the premises.

The Reef Resort (Box 173, Singatoka; tel. 50-044) about a kilometer east of the Crow's Nest is a three-story building facing right onto a white sandy beach. The 72 a/c rooms are F$75 s, F$80 d; most non-motorized recreational activities are free. The hotel tennis courts, nine-hole golf course, and horses are also available to outsiders at reasonable rates. Even if you're not staying there check out the barbecue on Tues. (F$13) and the *meke* buffet on Sat. (F$20). Meals in the hotel restaurant are prepared to the taste of the mostly Australian clientele.

Hide-A-Way Resort

Most of the Coral Coast hotels cater to packaged tourists and the affluent. **Hide-A-Way Resort** (Box 233, Singatoka; tel. 50-177) near Korolevu 20 km east of Singatoka also makes itself available to budget travelers. Set on a palm-fringed beach before a verdant valley, Hide-A-Way offers everything the others offer, but also eight-bed, F$9-a-night dormitories. Show your Y.H.A. card for a discount. There's always room for travelers who just happen to drop in. If you're in a group, take one of the large *mbures* with fan suitable for up to five people (F$85) or smaller *mbures* for up to three (F$66).

Here's the catch: cooking your own food is not possible, the restaurant is expensive, and no grocery stores are to be found nearby. But even with the price of the meals, you'll still spend less than you would at Beachcomber

Myriad snails crawl for the money at Hide-A-Way's weekly mollusk marathon.

Island. What Hide-A-Way does offer is free live entertainment nightly, including a real *meke* Tues. and Fri. at 2100 and an all-you-can-eat Fijian feast Sun. night. Day excursions to the hot spring and sliding falls depart the resort regularly, if you want to hang out a while. Don Spencer, the manager, is a bit of a cave freak and will arrange to take you through a few if you show any interest. Surfing is possible in the pass here. It's a good stop on the way to Suva.

Korolevu Upmarket Accommodations

Korolevu is the heart of the Coral Coast hotel area. The **Naviti Beach Resort** (Box 29, Korolevu; tel. 50-444) just west of Korolevu and 100 km from Nandi Airport has 144 a/c rooms at F$86 s or d. Firewalking (F$10) is performed Wed. and a *meke/lovo* (F$21) Friday. Scuba diving is arranged by Sea Sports Ltd. but the hotel beach is rather poor.

Hyatt Regency Fiji (Box 100, Korolevu; tel. 50-555) on the Queen's Road just east of Korolevu, 107 km from Nandi Airport, is the second largest hotel on the Coral Coast (after

the Fijian). The 249 a/c rooms in low-rise blocks begin at F$104 s or d. There's live music in the Hibiscus Lounge nightly until 0100, disco dancing Sundays. Weekly events include the *meke/lovo* (F$38) Mon. and Fri., firewalking (F$12) Mon. and Thurs., the Polynesian buffet (F$33) Thurs., and the seafood buffet with a Fijian fashion show (F$40) on Friday. This plush resort also offers a nine-hole golf course, a complete sports and fitness center, an excellent beach, an offshore artificial island, and scuba diving with Sea Sports Limited.

The **Man Friday Resort** (Box 20, Korolevu; tel. 50-185) right by the beach five km off Queen's Road at Namboutini is the most secluded place to stay on the Coral Coast. The 24 thatched *mbures,* each with fan and cooking facilities, are F$60 s, F$65 d. The footprint-shaped freshwater swimming pool alludes to Daniel Defoe's novel *Robinson Crusoe* which gave Man Friday its name.

Scuba Diving

Sea Sports Ltd. (Box 688, Singatoka; tel. 50-598) offers scuba diving daily at 0900 and 1400 from The Fijian, Hyatt Regency, Hide-A-Way, Reef, and Naviti Beach hotels. Night dives are possible. A one-tank boat dive with only tank and weightbelt is F$35; with full equipment it's F$67. Their ten-dive package is F$300 without equipment, F$450 with equipment. Rental of snorkeling gear is F$4. Sea Sports runs PADI openwater certification courses for F$395. Most dive sites are within 15 minutes of the resort jetties so you don't waste much time commuting.

Getting Around

The easy way to get between the Coral Coast resorts and Nandi/Lautoka is on the a/c **Hyatt Express** shuttle bus. Every morning except Sun. at 0630 the bus departs the Hyatt Regency calling at Paradise Point (0635), Naviti Resort (0640), Reef Hotel (0700), Fijian Hotel (0725), Nandi Hotel (0820), The Regent Hotel (0830), Nandi Airport (0850), and Lautoka Wharf (0915). In the afternoon the return trip leaves Lautoka Wharf at 1715, reaching the Hyatt at 2000. Fares range from F$4.50 to F$11.50.

In the other direction the a/c **Queen's**

Coach leaves The Fijian Hotel for Suva at 0910 (F$16), the Hyatt Regency and Naviti Beach at 1030 (F$14), and Pacific Harbor at 1115 (F$7). The return trip departs Suva around 1700. Any of the above hotels will know about these services. Many other non-a/c buses pass on the highway but make sure you're waiting somewhere they'll stop.

AROUND NAVUA

Deumba
The **Coral Coast Christian Camp** (Postal Agency, Pacific Harbor; tel. 45-178), 13 km west of Navua near Pacific Harbor, offers five-bed Kozy Korner dormitories with communal kitchen and cold showers at F$8 pp, or older dormitory cabins at F$6 pp. The adjoining motel units go for F$15 s, F$18 d complete with private bath, kitchen, fridge, and fan. No alcoholic beverages or dancing are permitted on the premises; on Wed. and Sun. at 1930 you're invited to the Fellowship Meeting in the manager's flat. Recommended.

Pacific Harbor
Pacific Harbor (Postal Agency, Pacific Harbor; tel. 45-022) is a misplaced Hawaiian condo development and tourist culture village, 152 km east of Nandi Airport. The place was developed by Charles Stinson, a former minister of Finance, and his son Peter, Ratu

a model of a fortified village at the Pacific Harbor Cultural Center

Mara's minister of Economic Development and an early supporter of the first Rabuka coup. Millions of dollars in loans to Stinson's firm from the Fiji National Bank were allegedly written off at government request. In July 1988 the Japanese corporation, South Pacific Development, purchased Pacific Harbor.

The 84 a/c hotel rooms at Pacific Harbor are F$90 s or d. Many of the 180 surrounding villas are owned by Australian or Hong Kong investors. On Thurs. night there's a *meke* buffet (F$22). The resort is best known for its 18-hole, par-72 championship **golf course**, designed by Robert Trent Jones Jr., and said to be the South Pacific's finest. Course records are 69 by Bobby Clampett of the U.S. (amateur) and 64 by Greg Norman of Australia (professional). Green fees including clubs are F$16. You'll find a restaurant and bar in the clubhouse.

Beqa Divers, a branch of Suva's Scubahire (tel. 361-088), is based at Pacific Harbor's marina and organizes diving in the nearby Mbengga Lagoon. Entry is free to the Waikiki-style **Marketplace** made up of mock-colonial boutiques and assorted historical displays.

Pacific Harbor's **Cultural Center** is on the regular tour bus circuit. This recreated Fijian village on a small "sacred island" behind the hotel is complete with natives attired in jungle garb and a 20-meter tall temple. Tourists see the island from an hourly double-hulled *ndrua* with a tour guide "warrior" carrying a spear. Crafts and village occupations such as canoe-making, weaving, tapa, and pottery are demonstrated for the seated, canoe-bound tourists at various stops. It's best to come with the buses in the early afternoon to be there at 1530 for a performance by the

the reef off Ovalau (Don Pitcher)

1. Beachcomber Island (Islands in the Sun); **2.** the tourist boat *Tui Tai* (islands in the Sun); **3.** camping at Natandola Beach, Viti Levu (D. Stanley); **4.** dormitory at Beachcomber Island (D. Stanley); **5.** *mbure* on Beachcomber Island (Islands in the Sun)

1. Yasawa boats at Lautoka, Viti Levu (D. Stanley); **2.** Prince's Wharf, Suva (D. Stanley);

1. Queen's Wharf, Levuka, Ovalau (D. Stanley);
2. unloading gear, Mbalea, central Viti Levu (D. Stanley)

1. Sri Krishna Kaliya Temple, Lautoka, Viti Levu (D. Stanley);
2. Renwick Road, Suva (John Penisten); **3.** Government House, Suva (D. Stanley);
4. Grand Pacific Hotel, Suva (D. Stanley); **5.** Sikh Temple, Lautoka, Viti Levu (D. Stanley)

1. boy at Tholo-i-Suva Forest Park near Suva (David Bowden); **2.** carver at Mbukuya, Viti Levu (Don Pitcher); **3.** washing clothes, Lovoni, Ovalau (Karl Partridge); **4.** planting kava, Ovalau (Karl Partridge); **5.** Lawaki Beach, Mbengga (D. Stanley)

The tortuous Navua River drains much of central Viti Levu.

Dance Theater of Fiji (Mon., Wed., Thurs., and Sat.) or Fijian firewalking (Tues. and Fri.). Admission is F$9 pp for the village alone (Mon. to Sat. 0930-1400) or F$16 for village and show. It may be packaged culture but it is informative.

The **Fiji Palms Beach Club Resort** (Box 6, Postal Agency, Pacific Harbor; tel. 45-050) at Pacific Harbor has 14 two-bedroom apartments with cooking facilities at F$90 s or d, F$105 t—a better deal than the hotel.

Navua

This untouristed river town is the center of a rice-growing delta area near the mouth of the Navua River and headquarters of Serua Province. The **Navua Hotel** (tel. 46-006) is set on a hilltop just upstream from the bridge. A pleasant terrace overlooks the river. The six rooms (F$14 s, F$20 d) are rarely full.

Village boats leave from the wharf beside Navua market for Mbengga Island (F$3) south of Viti Levu. Boats may leave any day but more depart on Saturday. Also ask at Navua for village outboards that cruise 25 km up the Navua River to **Namuamua** (F$3) on Thurs., Fri., and Sat. afternoons. The hour-long ride takes you between high canyon walls and over boiling rapids with waterfalls on each side.

Livai Fiji Ethnic Tours (GPO Box 13498, Suva; tel. 313-908) runs canoe tours down the Navua River for F$32 pp including minibus transfers from Suva and lunch. Above Namuamua is the fabulous **Navua Gorge**, accessible only to intrepid river-runners in rubber rafts who go in by helicopter. It's also possible to reach the river by road at Nambukelevu.

OFFSHORE ISLANDS

Vatulele Island

This small island, just south of Viti Levu, is famous for its tapa cloth. Vatulele reaches a height of only 34 meters on its north end; there are steep bluffs on the west coast, and gentle slopes on the east face a wide lagoon. Both passes into the lagoon are from its north end. Five different levels of erosion are visible on the cliffs as the uplifted limestone was undercut. There are rock paintings but no one knows when they were executed.

Another unique feature of Vatulele are the sacred **red prawns** which are found in a tidal pool in Korolamalama Cave near the island's rocky north coast. These scarlet prawns with remarkably long antennae are called *ura mbuta* or cooked prawns for their color. The red color probably comes from iron oxide in the limestone of their abode. It's strictly *tambu* to eat them or remove them from the pools. If one does, it will bring ill luck or even shipwreck. The story goes that a princess of yesteryear rejected a gift of cooked prawns from a suitor and threw them in the pools where the boiled-red creatures were restored to life. Villagers can call the prawns by repeating a chant.

Village boats leave for Vatulele from the Naviti Beach Resort at Korolevu on Tues., Thurs., and Sat. mornings if the weather is good (F$6 OW). The 43-meter three-masted schooner *Tui Tai* does a day trip to Vatulele every Mon. at 0900 from the Naviti Beach Hotel (F$43 pp including a barbecue lunch). This and other tourist boats stop at a fine sandy beach on the west side of the island, several hours' walk from the one village on the east side. As many as 300 passengers can board the *Tui Tai*.

Mbengga Island

Mbengga is the home of the famous Fijian **firewalkers**; Rukua, Natheva, and Ndakuimbengga are firewalking villages. Nowadays, however, they perform only in the hotels on Viti Levu. At low tide you can walk the 27 km around the island: the road only goes from Waisomo to Ndakuni. There are caves with ancient burials near Suliyanga, which can be reached on foot from Mbengga at low tide, but permission from the village chief is required to visit. Have your *sevu sevu* ready. Malumu Bay between the two branches of the island is thought to be a drowned crater. Climb Korolevu (439 meters), the highest peak, from Waisomo or Lalati.

Frigate Passage on the west side of the barrier reef is one of the best dive sites near Suva. There's a vigorous tidal flow in and out of the passage which attracts large schools of fish, and there are large coral heads. **Sulphur Passage** on the east side of Mbengga is equally good.

The best beach is **Lawaki** to the west of Natheva. Present the village chief of Natheva with a nice bundle of *waka* if you want to camp. The villagers could set up a great little resort here if they got it together. Kandavu Island is visible to the south of Mbengga.

KANDAVU ISLAND

This big, 50- by 13-km island 100 km south of Suva is the fourth largest in Fiji. A mountainous, varied island with waterfalls plummeting from the rounded hilltops, Kandavu is outstanding for its vistas and beaches. The three hilly sections of Kandavu are joined by two low isthmuses which bite so deeply into the island that on a map it resembles the shape of a wasp. Just northeast of the main island is the smaller Ono Island and the fabulous Astrolabe Reef stretching halfway to Suva. The reef is named for Dumont d'Urville's ship *Astrolabe* which passed this way in 1827. The famous red-and-green Kandavu parrots may be seen and heard.

In the 1870s steamers bound for New Zealand and Australia would call at the one-time whaling station at Ngaloa Harbor to pick up passengers and goods, and Kandavu was considered as a possible site for a new capital of Fiji. Instead Suva was chosen and Kandavu was left to lead its sleepy village life; only today is the outside world making a comeback with the arrival of roads, planes, and visitors.

Sights
The airstrip and wharf are each a 10-minute walk in different directions from the post office and hospital in the tiny government station of **Vunisea**. Vunisea is strategically located on a narrow, hilly isthmus where Ngaloa Harbor and Namalata Bay almost cut Kandavu in two.

The longest sandy beach on the island is at **Ndrue**, an hour's walk north from Vunisea. Another good beach is at **Muani** village, eight km south of Vunisea by road. Just two km south of the airstrip by road and a 10-minute hike inland is **Waikana Falls**. Cool spring water flows over a 10-meter-high rocky cliff between two deep pools, the perfect place for a refreshing swim on a hot day. A second falls six km east of Vunisea is even better.

The women of **Namuana** village just west of the airstrip can summon **giant turtles** up from the sea by singing traditional chants to

the *vu* (ancestral spirits) Raunindalithe and Tinandi Thambonga. On a bluff 60 meters above the sea, the garlanded women begin their song and in 15 minutes a large turtle will appear. This turtle, and sometimes its mates, will swim up and down slowly offshore just below the overhanging rocks. The calling of turtles can be performed for tour groups for a charge of F$400 (no photos allowed).

Hiking
Hike over the mountains from Namuana to **Tavuki** village, seat of the Tui Tavuki, paramount chief of Kandavu. A couple of hours beyond is the **Yawe** area where large pine tracts are being established. In the villages of Nalotu, Yakita, and Nanggalotu at Yawe, traditional Fijian **pottery** is still made. Without potter's wheel or kiln, the women shape the pots with a paddle and fire them in an open fire. Sap from the mangroves provides a glaze.

Carry on from Yawe to **Lomati** village, from where you begin the ascent of **Nambukelevu** (838 meters). There's no trail—you'll need a guide to help you hack a way. The abrupt cone of Nambukelevu (Mt. Washington) dominates the west end of Kandavu and renders hiking around the cape too arduous. Petrels nest in holes on the north side of the mountain.

There's **surfing** off Nambukelevuira village at the island's west point but you'll need a boat. Cut south from Lomati to **Ndavinggele** village, where another trail leads east along the coast to **Mburelevu**, end of the road from the airstrip. This whole loop can be done in three days without difficulty, but take food and be prepared to sleep rough.

The Great Astrolabe Reef
The Great Astrolabe Reef stretches unbroken for 30 km along the east side of the small islands north of Kandavu. One km wide, the reef is unbelievably rich in coral and marinelife; because it's so far from shore it still hasn't been fished out. The reef surrounds a lagoon containing 10 islands, the

largest of which is Ono. The reef was named by French explorer Dumont d'Urville who almost lost his ship, the *Astrolabe,* here in 1827.

There are frequent openings on the west side of the reef and the lagoon is never over 10 fathoms deep, which makes it a favorite of scuba divers and yachtspeople. The Astrolabe also features a vertical drop-off of 10 meters on the inside and 1,800 meters on the outside, with visibility of about 75 meters.

The configuration of the Astrolabe Reef confirms Darwin's Theory of Atoll Formation. The famous formulator of the theory of evolution surmised that atolls form as high volcanic islands subside into lagoons. The original island's fringing reef grows into a barrier reef as the volcanic portion sinks. When the last volcanic material finally disappears below sea level, the coral ring of the reef/atoll remains to indicate how big the island once was. Of course, this takes place over millions of years but deep down below any coral atoll is the old volcanic core. Darwin's theory is well illustrated here, where Ono and the small volcanic islands to the north remain inside the Astrolabe Reef. Return in a million years and all you'll find will be the reef itself.

Accommodations

Mosese and Louisa Sakuka have set up the **Nai Teitei e Delana Campground** at Vunisea,

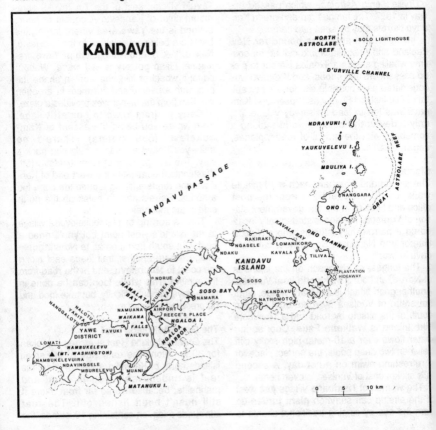

an early 19th century print of the southwest end of Kandavu Island

just a 10-minute walk from Kandavu's airstrip. There's no beach, but there are running water, cold showers, toilets, a campfire pit, a crude shelter in which to sit, and lots of space to erect your tent (F$3.50 pp). You can cook and the owners will sell you fresh fish, fruit, and vegetables for reasonable prices. Boat trips or visits to nearby villages can be arranged. You'll get a real taste of the Fijian countryside here.

Also ask for Orisi Qalomaiwasa who takes his launch to Vunisea fairly often. Orisi has built a couple of *mbures* called **Sealovers' Beach Resort** on the north side of Kandaveu for very adventuresome travelers. His prices are about the same as the two places mentioned below and campers are welcome. He'll take you snorkeling on some really gorgeous reefs.

Reece's Place (Box 6, Vunisea, Kandavu), just off the northwest corner of Kandavu on tiny Ngaloa Island, was the first to accommodate visitors to Kandavu. It's a one-km walk from the airstrip to the dock at Vunisea station; the launch ride costs F$6 pp each way. There are eight beds (F$10 pp) in four Fijian *mbures,* or pitch your tent for F$3.50 pp. At times it can get crowded. It's F$12 pp for all three meals. Unless you have a camp stove, cooking your own food is not possible. The electricity is on from 1800-2030 only, but everyone lingers around Joe Reece's kava bowl until much later.

Reece's Place is also a large, working, subsistence farm growing pawpaw and bananas. The view of Ngaloa Harbor is excellent. There's a long sandy beach a 10-minute walk away but the snorkeling is only fair. For F$10 pp Joe will arrange for someone to take you to the Ngaloa Barrier Reef where the snorkeling is vastly superior (better than at Taveuni). Scuba diving (F$35) and even PADI certification courses (F$295) are offered (bring two passport photos and a medical certificate stating that you are fit to dive).

Albert O'Connor's Plantation Hideaway (c/o Naletha P.O., Kandavu; tel. Naletha 42-090 and leave a message) at Langalevu at the east end of Kandavu is similar to Reece's Place but more remote (and far less crowded). Each of the 10 *mbures* has a double and a single bed, coconut mats on the floor, and a kerosene lamp for light. The dormitory *mbure* sleeps six. Accommodations are F$9 pp; camping is F$2 pp. The units share rustic flush toilets and cold showers with plenty of running water. Mosquito nets and coils are supplied.

Meals are another F$16 pp for all three, but the portions are huge so breakfast and dinner (F$10) should suffice. Unless you're planning to let Ruth O'Connor do the cooking, bring food as there are no stores nearby. Ruth's meals are exceptional, consisting of fish dishes with root vegetables. She bakes

Shoppers from outlying villages headed for Kandavu's market land on this beach near Vunisea. The hiking trails of Kandavu vie with untouched beaches as this one in "downtown" Vunisea.

her own bread daily. For F$15 minimum or F$4 pp (whichever is greater) their boat will take you out to the nearby Astrolabe Reef (fantastic 25-meter visibility). Scuba diving is F$30 pp.

You can get to Albert's on the weekly boat (F$20 OW) from Princes Wharf (ask for the *Princess Ashika, Sinikaloni, Adi Lau, Gurawa*, or *L. Tui*). In Suva call Mrs. Lumon (tel. 381-727), owner of the *Gurawa*, which stops right at Plantation Hideaway. The *Princess Ashika* leaves Suva at 1200 Fri. but only goes to Vunisea. Albert will pick you up at Vunisea Airport for F$45 each way for two persons, F$20 pp for three or more, a two-hour boat ride. Be sure to let him know you're coming by calling Manoa Kaiyanuyanu (tel. 312-600 or 301-895) in Suva. It's best to allow plenty of time coming and going, so plan to stay at Plantation Hideaway early in your visit to Fiji so you don't have to be in a big rush to leave. People rave about this place and it's highly recommended; just don't expect luxuries like electricity at those prices!

Practicalities

There are no restaurants at Vunisea, but a coffee shop at the airstrip opens mornings, and there are two general stores selling canned goods. A lady at the market serves tea and scones when the market is open, Tues. to Saturday. Buy *waka* at the Co-op store for formal presentations to village hosts. Occasional carriers ply the roads of Kandavu: F$1 pp to Wailevu.

Getting There

The easy way to come is on **Fiji Air** from Suva (F$41) on Mon. and Thursday. **Sunflower Airlines** flies Nandi-Kandavu twice a week (F$44 OW). Boats arrive at Vunisea from Suva (F$20 OW) about twice a week, calling at villages along the north coast.

SUVA

The pulsing heart of the South Pacific, Suva is the most cosmopolitan city in Oceania. The harbor is always jammed with ships bringing goods and passengers from far and wide. Busloads of commuters and enthusiastic visitors constantly stream into the busy market bus station nearby. In the business center are Indian women in saris, large sturdy chocolate-skinned Fijians, Australians and New Zealanders in shorts and knee socks, and wavy-haired Polynesians from Rotuma and Tonga.

Suva squats on a hilly peninsula between Lauthala Bay and Suva Harbor in the southeast corner of Viti Levu. The verdant mountains north and west catch the southeast trades, producing damp conditions year-round. Visitors sporting a sunburn from Fiji's western sunbelt resorts may appreciate Suva's warm tropical rains. In 1870 the Polynesia Company sent Australian settlers to camp along mosquito-infested Numbukalou Creek on land obtained from High Chief Cakobau. When efforts to grow sugar cane here failed, the company convinced the British to move their headquarters here and since 1882 Suva has been the capital of Fiji.

Today this exciting multi-racial city of 157,611 (1986)—a fifth of Fiji's population—is also about the only place in Fiji where you'll see a building taller than a palm tree. Highrise office buildings and hotels overlook the compact downtown area. The British left behind imposing colonial buildings, wide avenues, and manicured parks as evidence of their rule. The Fiji School of Medicine, the University of the South Pacific, the Fiji Institute of Technology, and the Pacific Theological College have all been established here. In addition the city offers some of the best night life between Kings Cross (Sydney) and North Beach (San Francisco) plus shopping, sightseeing, and many good-value places to stay and eat.

Keep in mind that on Sunday all but the hotel restaurants will be closed and no taxis or buses will be running. It's smart to clear out of Suva for the weekend. The lovely *Isa Lei*, a Fijian song of farewell, tells of a youth whose love sails off and leaves him alone in Suva, smitten with longing.

SIGHTS

South Suva

The most beautiful section of the city is the area around **Albert Park**. On 6 June 1928 aviator Charles Kingsford Smith landed his tri-motor Fokker VII-3M in the middle of this park after arriving from Hawaii on the first-ever flight from California to Australia. (The first commercial flight to Fiji was a Pan Am flying boat which landed in Suva Harbor in Oct. 1941.) To the north the stern and heavy lines of the **Government Buildings** (1939) reflect the tensions rampant in Europe at the time they were built. Statues of Chief Cakobau and Ratu Sir Lala Sukuna stand outside. It was here that Col. Sitiveni Rabuka carried out his raid on Parliament on 14 May 1987. To the west is the elegant, Edwardian-style **Grand Pacific Hotel** (1914), which dates from an earlier, more confident era; savor the interior for a taste of the old British *raj*.

South of Albert Park are the fine **Thurston Botanical Gardens**, opened in 1913, where tropical flowers such as cannas and plumbagos blossom. The original Fijian village of Suva once stood on this site. On the grounds of the gardens is the **Fiji Museum**. Small but full, this museum is renowned for its maritime displays: canoes, outriggers, the rudder from HMS *Bounty,* and *ndrua* steering oars that were manned by four Fijians. The collection of Fijian war clubs is outstanding. The history section is being greatly expanded as artifacts in overseas collections are returned to Fiji. The museum is open weekdays 0830-1630, admission 50 cents.

South of the gardens is **Government House**, residence of the president. The original building erected after 1882 burned after being hit by lightning in 1921, and the present edifice dates from 1928. The grounds cannot be visited. The sentry on ceremonial guard duty wears a belted red tunic and an immaculate white *sulu* (kilt). Military officers on duty here do not care to be photographed.

The seawall just opposite the sentry box is the perfect place to sit and enjoy the view across Suva Harbor to Mbengga Island (to the left) and the dark, green mountains of eastern Viti Levu punctuated by Joske's Thumb, a high volcanic plug (to the right). Take the Nasese bus around its loop through South Suva and back for a glimpse of the beautiful garden suburbs of the city.

University Of The South Pacific

Catch any bus eastbound along MacArthur or Gordon streets to reach this 78-hectare campus on a hilltop at Lauthala Bay. Founded in 1968 the USP is jointly owned by 11 Pacific countries for the purpose of building the skills needed back home. Although over 70% of the 2,500 full-time students are from Fiji, the rest are on scholarships from every corner of the Pacific. Since 1969 50% of all Fiji government scholarships have been reserved for indigenous Fijians. The USP's **Institute of Pacific Studies** (Box 1168, Suva) is the leading publisher of books written by Pacific islanders. There's a good library on campus.

Students from outside the Pacific islands pay F$4635 a year tuition to study at USP. There are minimum-entry qualifications and applications must be in by 31 Dec. for the following term. Many courses in the social sciences have a high level of content pertaining to Pacific culture. Postgraduate studies in a limited number of areas is available. To obtain a calendar, application for admission, and other materials send US$10 to: The Registrar, University of the South Pacific, Box 1168, Suva, Fiji Islands.

The USP is always in need of staff so if you're from a university milieu and looking for a chance to live in the South Seas, this could be it. The maximum contract is six years (and you need seven years residency to apply for Fijian citizenship). If your credentials are impeccable you should write to the registrar from home. On the spot it's better to talk to a department head about his/her needs before going to see the registrar.

Look for the pleasant canteen in the Student Union Building, or join the students for F$1.90 lunch and dinner in the dining hall just

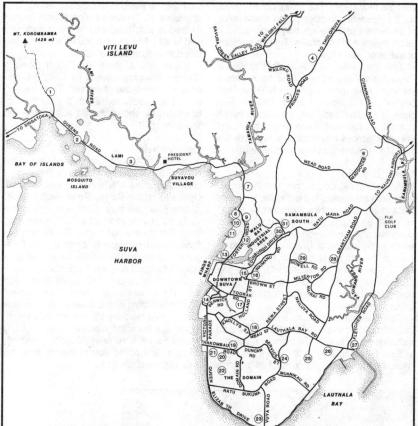

AROUND SUVA

1. cement factory
2. Tradewinds Marina/ Scubahire
3. Castle Restaurant
4. Fiji School of Medicine
5. Tamavua Reservoir
6. Queen Elizabeth Barracks
7. Suva Cemetery
8. Royal Suva Yacht Club
9. Suva Prison
10. Marine Department
11. Narain wharf
12. Carlton Brewery
13. Marine Pacific Ltd.
14. General Post Office
15. New Haven Motel
16. hospital
17. mosque
18. Suva Apts. Hotel
19. South Seas Private Hotel
20. Fiji Museum
21. Thurston Botanical Gardens
22. Government House
23. Pacific Theological College
24. South Pacific Bureau of Economic Cooperation (SPEC)
25. University of the South Pacific
26. National Stadium
27. Beach Road Park
28. Raiwangga market
29. Sangam Temple
30. Tanoa Guest House
31. Fiji Institute of Technology

past the new library. The food's not too good, but it's interesting to observe the mixed batch of students and the ways they cope with the inconvenience of tiny chairs. There's a choice of Indian or island food.

The area east of the university was a Royal New Zealand seaplane base before the land was turned over to USP. A little beyond the university, past the National Stadium, is Beach Road Park, the closest beach to town. It's too muddy and dirty to swim, but the view across Lauthala Bay is worth the stop. The Vatuwangga bus passes nearby.

North Suva

Suva's wonderful, colorful **market**, the largest retail produce market in the Pacific, is a good place to linger. If you're a yachtie or backpacker, you'll be happy to know that the market overflows with fresh produce of every kind. It's worth some time looking around. Have some kava at the *yanggona* kiosk in the market for F$1 a bowl (share the excess with those present). Unfortunately fumes, noise, and pollution from the adjacent bus station buffet through the market.

Continue north and turn right just before the bridge to reach the factory of **Island Industries Ltd.** Most of Fiji's copra is shipped to Suva for processing. At this plant the copra is crushed to extract the coconut oil which is then sent to the U.K. for further refining into vegetable oil. Crushed coconut meal for cattle feed is also produced at the factory and sold locally. Apply to the plant office for a free tour during business hours.

A little farther north on Foster Road is **Carlton Brewery**, owned by Carlton Breweries of Melbourne, Australia. They haven't started up regular tours yet, but the production manager shows visitors around Mon. to Thurs. at 1500.

Farther Afield

About 600 meters beyond the brewery is the vintage **Suva Prison** (1913), a fascinating colonial structure with high walls and barbwire. Opposite is the **Royal Suva Yacht Club**, where you can buy a drink, meet some yachties, and maybe find a boat to crew on. Their T-shirts are hot items. The picturesque **Suva Cemetery** is just to the north. The Fijian graves wrapped in colorful *sulus* and tapa cloth make good subjects for photographers.

Continuing west on Queen's Road, you pass **Suvavou** village, home of the original Fijian inhabitants of the Suva area, and Lami Town before reaching the **Tradewinds Hotel**, seven km from the market. Many cruising yachts tie up here (see "Services" below), and the view of the Bay of Islands from the hotel is particularly good.

Suva bowling club

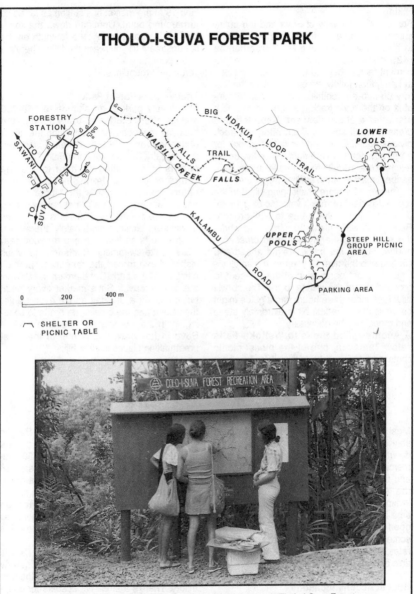

THOLO-I-SUVA FOREST PARK

FORESTRY STATION

TO SAWANI

TO SUVA

BIG NDAKUA LOOP TRAIL

WAISILA CREEK

FALLS TRAIL

FALLS

LOWER POOLS

UPPER POOLS

KALAMBU ROAD

STEEP HILL GROUP PICNIC AREA

PARKING AREA

0   200   400 m

⌢ SHELTER OR PICNIC TABLE

A good cross section of Fiji's tropical flora can be seen in Tholo-i-Suva Forest National Park near Suva.

Hiking

For a bird's-eye view of Suva and the entire surrounding area, spend a morning climbing to the volcanic plug atop **Mt. Korombamba** (429 meters). Take a Shore bus to the cement factory beyond the Tradewinds Hotel at Lami, then follow the dirt road past the factory up into the foothills. After about 45 minutes on the main track, you'll come to a fork just after a sharp descent. Keep left and cross a small stream. Soon after, the track divides again. Go up on the right and look for a trail straight up to the right where the tracks rejoin. It's a 10-minute scramble to the navigational marker at the summit from here.

There's a far more challenging climb to the top of **Joski's Thumb**, a volcanic plug 15 km west of Suva. Take a bus to Naikorokoro Road, then walk inland 30 minutes to where the road turns sharply right and crosses a bridge. Follow the track straight ahead and continue up the river till you reach a small village. Request permission of the villagers to proceed. From the village to the Thumb will take just under three hours and a guide might be advisable. The last bit is extremely steep and ropes may be necessary.

Another good trip is to **Wailoku Falls** below Tamavua, one of the nicest picnic spots near Suva. Take the Wailoku bus from lane 15 at the market bus station as far as its turnaround point. Continue down the road, cross a bridge, then follow a footpath on the left upstream till you reach the falls. There's a deep pool here where you can swim among verdant surroundings.

Tholo-i-Suva Forest Park

This lovely park at an altitude of 150-200 meters offers 3.6 km of trails through the beautiful mahogany forest flanking the upper drainage area of Waisila Creek. Enter from the Forestry Station along the Falls Trail. The park is so unspoiled it's hard to imagine you're only 11 km from Suva. A half-km nature trail begins near the Upper Pools. Aside from waterfalls and natural swimming pools there are thatched pavilions with tables at which to picnic. Unfortunately, there have been rip-offs so keep an eye on your gear while you're swimming. Thefts from previous visitors have forced the rangers to prohibit camping in the park. Get there on the Sawani bus which leaves Suva market every hour, but come on a dry day as it's even rainier than Suva and the creeks are prone to flooding. With the lovely green forests in back of Suva in full view, this is one of the most breathtaking places in all of Fiji.

ACCOMMODATIONS

Most of the decent places for travelers to stay are clustered on the south side of the downtown area near Albert Park. The commercially oriented hotels are near Marks St. and the market, while swingers gravitate to the establishments in the foothills up Waimanu Road. If you want to spend some time in Suva to take advantage of the city's good facilities and varied activities look for something with cooking facilities and weekly rates. Many functional apartments are available on a short term basis.

Budget Accommodations
Around Albert Park

The **South Seas Private Hotel** (GPO Box 157, Suva; tel. 22-195), 6 Williamson Road one block east of Albert Park, is owned by the same company as the Grand Pacific Hotel (see below), so South Seas guests may use their pool. The South Seas' 30 double rooms with fans and shared bath are F$6 pp. The hotel has a pleasant veranda and a large communal kitchen you may use to prepare your food. The no-nonsense Tongan lady who runs the hotel means business, so single men must behave themselves. It's often full.

A backpacker's oasis near Albert Park is the **Coconut Inn** (tel. 23-902), 8 Kimberly St., which charges F$5 for a bunk in the dormitory. There's a small flat upstairs for couples, F$14 d. The Inn offers cooking facilities and luggage storage. Though it does get crowded, this is just the place to meet other young budget travelers and exchange experiences. Buy some kava powder and have an evening grog session in the lounge. Ask Tambua to do the honors as master of ceremonies.

You can rent one of 12 self-contained apartments at **Pacific Grand Apartments** (Box 875, Suva; tel. 25-583), an older two-story building at 19 Gorrie St., for F$21 daily, F$100 weekly, or F$6 pp in the dorm. Cooking facilities are available.

For a longer stay rent an apartment by the month at **Pender Court** (31 Pender St., Suva; tel. 386-655). The 13 studios with kitchenette are F$200 a month plus service and utilities, while the six one-bedroom apartments with kitchen are F$350. The convenient location just a few blocks east of Albert Park makes this a very convenient place to settle in.

Twelve more self-contained units with cooking facilities are available at **Suva Apartments** (Box 12488, Suva; tel. 24-281), 17 Mbau St. a block or two farther east of Pender Court. They're $19 s, F$22 d daily, with weekly rates available.

Budget Accommodations Downtown

Women are accommodated at the big, modern **Y.W.C.A.** (Box 534, Suva; tel. 25-441) on Sukuna Park at F$8 pp—a good place to meet Fijian women. The main drawback is the loud late-night music from the disco across the street.

The **Metropole Hotel** (Box 404, Suva; tel. 24-010) on Usher St. opposite the market has 10 rooms with shared bath at F$10 s, F$16 d. Some hard drinking goes on in the public bar downstairs but the hotel is well run.

The 26-room **Suva Hotel** (Box 578, Suva; tel. 25-411; F$12.50 s, F$17 d, F$21 t) is similar, but the four noisy bars make it hardly a place for travelers. **Bhindi's Apts.** nearby at 55 Toorak Rd. has a row of self-contained units at F$85 a week.

Budget Accommodations Up Waimanu Road

The 20-room **Suva Oceanview Hotel** (tel. 312-129), 270 Waimanu Rd., charges F$12 s, F$15 d. It has a snack bar and a pleasant hillside location. Avoid the noisy rooms over the reception area.

Farther up the hill is the **New Haven Motel** (GPO Box 992, Suva; tel. 311-755), F$12 s, including breakfast. It's rather dirty and seems

to get a lot of couples for *very* short stays. The **Motel Crossroad Inn** (tel. 313-820), 124 Robertson Rd., and the **Motel Capital**, 91 Robertson Rd., also cater largely to people on the make. These three are not recommended for single women.

In contrast to these, **Tanoa House** (Box 704, Suva; tel. 381-575) in Samambula South, is a totally respectable guesthouse run by an ex-colonial from the Gilberts. The place has a garden with a view and you meet genuine island characters. The 10 rooms with shared bath are F$12 s, F$19 d for bed and breakfast. Other meals are available. It's situated across from the Fiji Institute of Technology near the end of Waimanu Road, too far to walk from downtown, but get there easily on the Samambula bus.

Medium-priced Hotels

If yesteryear decadence at fading colonial prices has an appeal don't miss the chance to stay at Suva's own 70-room **Grand Pacific Hotel** (Box 157, Suva; tel. 23-011), for decades the social center of the city. In 1914 the Union Steamship company built this charming white ediface to accommodate their trans-Pacific passengers. The rooms were designed to appear as shipboard staterooms, with upstairs passageways surveying the harbor like the promenade deck of a ship. All this elegance begins at only F$35 s, F$45 d for an a/c room in the old wing. Ask about the seven non-a/c economy rooms in the main building (F$20 s, F$28 d) and the "thrift" accommodations with shared bath in a four-room annex behind the hotel (F$15 dorm). Videos are shown free in the lounge nightly at 2000. Though the hotel bar is just the place for a gin and tonic you're best to take your meals elsewhere.

The **Southern Cross Hotel** (GPO Box 1076, Suva; tel. 314-233) is a high-rise concrete building at 63 Gordon Street. The 30 a/c rooms are F$48 s, F$54 d. The hotel restaurant serves delicious Fijian dishes and the lounge is a "safe," sedate nightspot.

The **Suva Peninsula Hotel** (Box 888, Suva; tel. 313-711) at the corner of Macgregor Rd. and Pender St. is a stylish four-floor building. The 39 a/c rooms run F$34 s, F$38 d. The Peninsula's Japanese restaurant is expensive but good.

Two apartment-hotels behind the Central Police Station are worth a try if you want cooking facilities. The **Sunset Apartment Motel** (Box 485, Suva; tel. 23-021) corner of Gordon and Murray streets is a normal four-story suburban apartment block with 12 self-contained two-bedroom apartments at F$28 s, F$38 d.

Nearby the **Townhouse Apartment Hotel** (Box 485, Suva; tel. 22-661), 3 Forster St., has 28 a/c units with cooking facilities beginning at F$47 s, F$56 d. It's a rather cramped five-story building with cars parked on the ground floor below, but there's a nice little bar on the roof.

Up in the Waimanu Road area the **Capricorn Apartment Hotel** (Box 1261, Suva; tel. 314-799), 7-11 St. Fort St. has 25 a/c units with cooking facilities and private balconies at F$40 s, F$50 d. It's very clean and comfortable, good value if you can find someone with whom to share. The three- and four-story apartment blocks are edged around the swimming pool.

Tropic Towers Apt. Motel (Box 1347, Suva; tel. 25-819), 86 Robertson Rd., has 34 a/c apartments with cooking facilities in a four-story building at F$35 s, F$45 d. Ask about cheaper units without air conditioning.

The President Hotel (Box 1351, Suva; tel. 361-033) is on a hill above Queen's Road between Suva and Lami. They have 44 rooms and will give a discount if you present your Y.H.A. card.

Upmarket Hotels

Suva's largest and most expensive hotel is the **Suva TraveLodge** (Box 1357, Suva; tel. 314-600) on the waterfront opposite the Government Buildings. The 132 a/c rooms begin at F$103 s, F$110 d. The swimming pool behind the two-story buildings compensates for the lack of a beach. The Sat. afternoon barbecues by the pool are enjoyable. Late at night and on Sun. their expensive restaurant will keep you from going hungry. This is the only Suva hotel where reservations are recommended.

The **Suva Courtesy Inn** (Box 112, Suva; tel. 312-300) at the corner of Malcolm and Gordon streets is a nine-story high-rise with 50 a/c rooms at F$87 s or d. All rooms face the harbor.

Camping

There's camping on **Nukulau**, a tiny reef island southeast of Suva. For many years Nukulau was the government quarantine station where most of the indentured laborers spent their first two weeks in Fiji. Now it's a public park. Get free three-day camping permits from the Dept. of Lands, Room 39, Government Buildings, during office hours. The island has toilets and drinking water, and the swimming is good. Problem is, the only access is the F$32 tourist boat (includes lunch) departing downtown Suva at 0930 when there are enough passengers. Contact **Coral See Cruises** (Box 852, Suva; tel. 386-319 or 381-570) for information. You're allowed to return to Suva a couple of days later at no extra charge. Mostly, Nukulau and nearby Makaluva Island attract **surfers**.

FOOD AND ENTERTAINMENT

Suva has many excellent, inexpensive restaurants. Three of the best are on Cumming St. in the heart of the duty-free shopping area. All post their menus on boards outside. One of the best is the **Shanghai Restaurant** upstairs, which serves Chinese and European dishes. The staff and surroundings are pleasant, and the food good and ample. You get free tea or coffee with the meal, but beer isn't sold until after 1800. Next door to the Shanghai is **Le Normandie** (French), and across the street the **Wan-Q** (Chinese), both a little more expensive than the Shanghai.

Despite its name **The Krauts**, 15 Cumming St. next to the Wan-Q, specializes in Fijian dishes. Try the reef fish cooked in coconut milk (F$3). It's three floors up, comfortable and attractive with a small terrace and a view over the city. Mitch, the owner, is a Fijian who bought the restaurant from a German couple. He also serves a few good German dishes. It's very good value though not well known.

The **Sichuan Pavilion Restaurant**, 6 Thompson St. is perhaps Suva's finest restaurant. Employees of the Chinese consulate frequent it for the spicy hot Chinese dishes. **Singh's Curry House**, in the arcade of the new block next to Dominion House, and **Geraldynes**, upstairs opposite the bridge near Cummings St., are both good.

If you just want a snack check out **Donald's Kitchen** in the arcade at 45 Cumming Street. This is an excellent place to take a break. One block over on Marks St. are cheaper Chinese restaurants, but did you come all the way to Fiji to put up with mediocre meals just to save 50 cents?

Several places offer good weekday lunchtime Chinese smorgasbords, especially the **Bamboo Terrace** on Thompson St. opposite the Fiji Visitors Bureau and the **Peking Restaurant** in the Pacific Arcade. The **Ming Palace Restaurant** is more expensive but very pleasant.

Two of the best Indian restaurants in the entire South Pacific are side-by-side at the corner of Pratt and Joske streets downtown: the **Hare Krishna Restaurant** specializes in luncheon vegetarian *thalis* and sweets, while the **Curry Place** next door offers non-vegetarian food. Study the menu carefully the first time you go into Hare Krishna, as two distinct all-you-care-to-eat offers are available and the prices vary considerably. Ask about the special lunch on Sat. which allows you to sample six different dishes. Both of these restaurants are highly recommended.

The **Lantern Restaurant**, also on Pratt St., is very comfortable and good value, but it's freezing cold in there. They have Chinese and European food.

The **Y.W.C.A. cafeteria** is the place to try native Fijian food, such as fish fried in coconut milk. You have to come early to get the best dishes. Another place where you may find Fijian food is the **Old Mill Cottage Cafe** on the street behind the Golden Dragon nightclub. At lunchtime they have curried freshwater mussels, curried chicken livers, fresh seaweed in coconut milk, taro leaves creamed in coconut milk, and fish cooked in coconut milk. Also stop by for afternoon tea.

Snack bars around town often sell large bottles of cold milk—cheap and refreshing. The **Castle Restaurant** (Chinese) in the Lami Shopping Center is the best place to eat near the Tradewinds Marina.

The very cheapest and most colorful places to eat in Suva are down near the market. At lunchtime Fijian women run a food market beside Princes Wharf, about F$1 a plate for real Fijian food. At night a dozen Indian food trucks park beside the market just opposite Burns Philp. Great curries.

ENTERTAINMENT

Movie houses are plentiful downtown, charging F$1 for a hard seat, F$1.50 for a soft seat. The selection of films is fairly good and they change every three days. The best time to be in Suva is around the end of Aug. or early Sept. when the **Hibiscus Festival** fills Albert

Park with stalls, games, and carnival revelers.

There are many nightclubs, all of which have cover charges of around F$3 and require neat dress, but nothing much happens until after 2200. The most interracial and relaxed of the clubs is **Chequers**, which has live music Tues. to Sat. after 2100. Gays will feel comfortable at **Lucky Eddie's** (daily except Sun.), 215 Victoria Parade, but it's not really a gay bar, as the Fijian girls present try to prove. The Lucky Eddie's cover charge is also valid for the more sedate **Rockefeller's Night Club** in the same building. The **Golden Dragon** (open Fri. and Sat. 0730-0100) is similar. The teenage set frequents the disco

at **Screwz** upstairs from the arcade opposite Sukuna Park (ask about happy hour here). **Traps**, 305 Victoria Parade, offers free admission (reasonable dress), jazz twice a week, and pitchers of beer anytime; they're open till 0200 weekends.

For real earthy atmosphere try the **Bali Hai**, the roughest club in Suva. Friday and Sat. nights the place is packed with Fijians (no Indians) and tourists are rare, so beware. If you're looking for action, you'll be able to pick a partner within minutes, but take care with aggressive males. The dancehall on the top floor is the swingingest, with body-to-body jive—the Bali Hai will rock you.

PRACTICALITIES

Sports And Recreation

Scubahire (GPO Box 777, Suva; tel. 361-088) at the Tradewinds Hotel Marina arranges full-day diving trips to the Mbengga Lagoon for US$70, including two tanks, weight belt, and backpack. Other equipment can be rented. Scubahire takes snorkelers out on all their dive trips for US$30 pp, gear included. The 65 km of barrier reef around the Mbengga Lagoon features multi-colored soft corals and fabulous sea fans at Side Streets and an exciting wall and big fish at Cutter Passage. Scubahire's five-day P.A.D.I. certification course (F$350) involves six boat dives, an excellent way to learn while getting in some great diving. A two-day resort course is US$125. You'll need to show a medical certificate proving you're fit for diving. Several readers have written in praising this company.

Scubahire will ferry you over to **Mosquito Island**, where the city maintains a beach and showers, for F$8 RT per group. A small admission fee is charged to the island.

The Suva **Olympic Swimming Pool** charges 50 cents admission; open Mon. to Fri. 1000-1800, Sat. 0800-1800 (April to Sept.), or Mon. to Fri. 0900-1900, Sat. 0600-1900 (Oct. to March). Lockers are available. Work off your excess energy at the roller skating rink on Greig St., only F$2 weekdays, skate rental included. The course record at

the 18-hole, par-72 **Fiji Golf Club** is 65.

A four-bed dormitory (F$10 pp) for **surfers** has opened in Suva; the boat to the surf break near the lighthouse at the pass into Suva harbor is only F$5 pp and takes five minutes to get there. For information write Marcus Oliver, Box 3338, Lami, Fiji Islands, or ask Tambua at the Coconut Inn (tel. 23-902).

Yacht races to Suva from Auckland and Sydney occur in April or May on alternate years, timed from the cruisers' return just after the hurricane season. There's a powerboat race from Suva to Levuka on the long weekend around 10 October.

The Fijians are a very muscular, keenly athletic people, who send champion teams far and wide in the Pacific. You can see rugby (April to Sept.) and soccer (March to Oct.) on Sat. afternoons at 1500 at the **National Stadium** near the University of the South Pacific. Rugby and soccer are also played at Albert Park Sat., and you could also see a cricket game here (mid-Oct. to Easter).

Shopping

Items of the best workmanship are sold in the **Government Handicraft Center** behind Ratu Sukuna House, MacArthur and Carnarvon streets. Familiarize yourself here with what is authentic in a relaxed fixed-price atmosphere before plunging into the hard-sell

Suva's business district adjoins Suva Harbor.

establishments. Another good place to start is the **Fiji Museum** shop, or try **Handicrafts of Fiji** (upstairs from the arcade), an outlet for a group of co-ops. The large **Curio and Handicraft Market** on the waterfront behind the post office is intended mostly for cruise-ship passengers; bargain hard here.

The **Hart Craft Shop** is a boutique selling the rather artsy productions of the local charity associations. (Notice the WW II air raid shelters across the street.) Some of the most off-beat places in Suva to buy things are the **pawn shops**, most of which are in the vicinity of the Suva Hotel. Ask for the behind-the-counter selection.

Cumming St. (site of the main Suva produce market until the 1940s) is Suva's **duty-free** shopping area. The wide selection of goods in the large number of shops makes this about the best place in Fiji to shop for

electrical and other imported goods. Expect to receive a 10-40% discount with bargaining. **Premier Electronic Co.**, 54 Cumming St., may offer the best prices, but *shop around* before you buy. Dealers with a sticker from the Fiji Duty Free Merchants Association in the window tend to be more reliable.

Be wary when purchasing gold jewelry as it might be fake. Never buy anything on the day when a cruise ship is in port—prices shoot up. And watch out for hustlers who will take you around to the shops and get you a "good price" after tempting you with the possibility of profits to be made by selling the items in New Zealand. The only profits will be your loss and their gain.

For clothing see the very fashionable hand-printed shirts and dresses at **Tiki Togs** across from the post office or their second location next to the Pizza Hut: you could

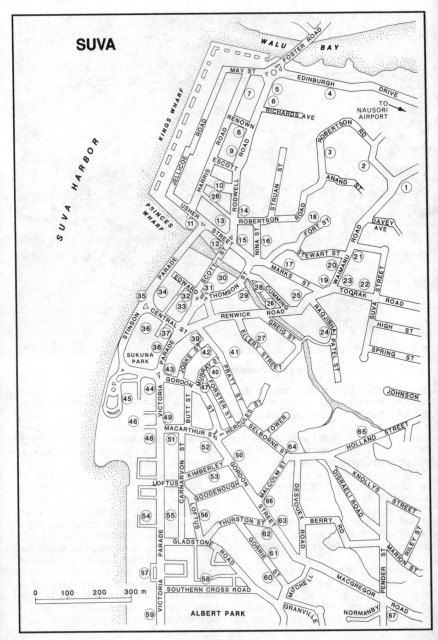

SUVA

WALU BAY

FOSTER ROAD

SUVA HARBOR

KINGS WHARF

PRINCES WHARF

JELLICOE ROAD

MAY ST

EDINBURGH DRIVE

TO NAUSORI AIRPORT

RICHARDS AVE

RENOWN ROAD

ESCOTT ROAD

HARRIS ROAD

RODWELL ROAD

USHER STREET

ROBERTSON RD

ROBERTSON ROAD

ANAND ST

DAVEY AVE

STRUAN ST

NINA ST

FORT ST

STEWART ST

WAIMANU ROAD

SUVA STREET

MARKS ST

TOQRAK ROAD

HIGH ST

SPRING ST

RAQIBBAI PATEL ST

GREIG ST

RENWICK ROAD

CUMMING ST

THOMSON ST

SCOTT ST

EDWARD STREET

CENTRAL ST

STINSON PARADE

VICTORIA PARADE

SUKUNA PARK

ELLERY STREET

JOHNSON

GORDON ST

JOSKE ST

MURRAY ST

PRATT ST

FORSTER ST

BUTT ST

MACARTHUR ST

HERCULES ST

SELBORNE ST

TOWER

HOLLAND STREET

DISRAELI ROAD

KNOLLYS STREET

CARNARVON ST

KIMBERLEY ST

GORDON STREET

MALCOLM ST

DESVOUEX ROAD

BERRY RD

MARION STREET

RILEY ST

LOFTUS ST

GOODENOUGH ST

THURSTON ST

GORRIE ST

PENDER ST

MACGREGOR ROAD

GLADSTONE ROAD

SOUTHERN CROSS ROAD

MITCHELL

GRANVILLE

NORMANBY

ALBERT PARK

0   100   200   300 m

SUVA

1. Oceanview Hotel
2. Crossroad Inn
3. Tropic Towers Apt. Motel
4. Island Industries Ltd.
5. Bali Hai Cabaret
6. Phoenix Theater
7. Union Maritime Ltd.
8. Health Office
9. buses for Lautoka
10. bus station
11. Kaunitoni Shipping (Maritime Checkers)
12. Metropole Hotel
13. market
14. Morris Hedstrom store
15. Burns Philp Supermarket
16. Wong's Shipping
17. Century Theater
18. Capricorn Hotel
19. Suva Hotel
20. Handicrafts of Suva
21. Alankar Theater
22. Bhindi's Apartments
23. Lilac Theater
24. D. Chung Shipping
25. Chequer's Nightclub
26. public toilets
27. Hart Craft Shop
28. Shanghai Restaurant
29. Morris Hedstrom Supermarket
30. Harbor Center
31. Fiji Visitors Bureau
32. General Post Office
33. Thomas Cook Travel
34. Curio and Handicraft Center
35. Coral See Cruise Landing
36. Y.W.C.A.
37. Air Pacific Office
38. Regal Theater
39. Hare Krishna Restaurant
40. Townhouse Apt. Hotel
41. Catholic Cathedral
42. police station
43. Tuvalu High Commission
44. Fiji International Telecommunications office
45. Suva Civic Auditorium
46. Suva Olympic Pool
47. Sunset Apt. Motel
48. Suva City Library
49. Fiji Air/Lucky Eddies
50. Southern Cross Hotel
51. Government Handicraft Center
52. Anglican Cathedral
53. Coconut Inn
54. Immigration Office
55. Golden Dragon
56. U.S. Embassy
57. TraveLodge Hotel
58. Government Buildings
59. Grand Pacific Hotel
60. Fiji Arts Council
61. Pacific Grand Apartments
62. Gordon St. Medical Center
63. Forestry Dept.
64. The Playhouse
65. Hindu Temple
66. Courtesy Inn
67. Suva Peninsula Hotel

come out looking like a real South Seas character at a very reasonable price.

The **Philatelic Bureau** at the main post office sells the stamps of Tuvalu, Pitcairn, and the Solomons, as well as those of Fiji. **Lotu Pasifika Productions** (Box 208, Suva) on Thurston St. near the Government Buildings sells books on island social issues and Nuclear-free Pacific posters.

In Suva beware of the seemingly friendly sword and mask sellers (usually toting a canvas bag) who will approach you on the street, ask your name, then quickly carve it on a sword and demand F$15 for a set that you could buy at a Nandi curio shop for F$5. The masks and swords themselves have nothing to do with Fiji.

Services

Thomas Cook Travel next to the post office will change foreign currency Sat. 0830-1200 at the usual rate. The **Fiji International Telecommunications** office on Victoria Parade is open 24 hours a day for trunk calls and telegrams. There's a row of public telephones outside the post office, most out of service.

The **Immigration office** (for extensions of stay, etc.) is behind the Labor Dept. Building (open Mon. to Fri. 0800-1300/1400-1600; tel. 211-325). Cruising yachties wishing to tour the Lau Group must first obtain permission from the prime minister. Fijian Affairs gives approval to cruise the other Fijian islands. Right after the 1987 military coups they weren't giving permission to anyone (out of fear of gunrunning), but things may have quieted down by now.

Australia, Britain, Canada, China, France, India, Israel, Japan, Korea, Malaysia, New Zealand, Papua New Guinea, Tuvalu, and the U.S. have diplomatic missions in Suva. The U.S. Embassy (Box 218, Suva; tel. 314-466) is at 31 Loftus Street. Almost everyone needs a visa to visit Australia and these are available at the Australian Embassy, eighth floor, Dominion House (tel. 313-844), near the Fiji Visitors Bureau.

Mooring charges for **yachts** at the Tradewinds Hotel (tel. 361-166) are F$15 a week per boat to tie up alongside (includes water, electricity, dinghy pontoon, telephone message service, use of hotel pool, etc.). There's a notice board by the pool for people seeking passage or crew for yachts. At the Royal Suva Yacht Club (tel. 23-666) it costs F$15 a week for such amenities as mooring privileges, warm showers, laundry facilities, cheap drinks, Sun. barbecues, and the full use of facilities by the whole crew. There have been reports of thefts off boats anchored here, so watch out.

Hunts Travel (Box 686, Suva; tel. 24-671) in the Dominion Building arcade behind the Fiji Visitors Bureau is the place to pick up air tickets. They often know more about Air Pacific flights than the Air Pacific employees themselves!

The **Fiji Society** (Box 1205, Suva) can help researchers on Fiji and the other Pacific islands. Contact them locally through the Fiji Museum. The **Fiji Arts Council**, 34 Gorrie St., can be of assistance to visiting musicians and artists.

The **Indian Cultural Center** above the Bank of Baroda on Marks St. shows free films Thurs. at 1830 and arranges cultural events such as music and dance. The program is posted on the board downstairs. There are courses on Indian music, dance, etc., and cultural events can be arranged for visiting groups (write GPO Box 1134, Suva). The center also has a library (open Mon. to Fri. 0830-1300/1400-1700).

Suva's only **laundromat** (open Mon. to Fri. 0900-1700, Sat. 0900-1200) is in the Raiwangga Market Shopping Arcade (catch the Raiwangga bus). The machines are in Jeff's Pawn Shop.

Health

You can see a doctor at the Outpatients Dept. of the **Colonial War Memorial Hospital** (tel. 313-444) for F$5 (tourists) or 50 cents (locals). It can be extremely crowded so take along a book to read while you're waiting for them to call your number. You'll receive better attention at the **Gordon St. Medical Center**, Gordon and Thurston streets (consultations F$8). There's a female doctor here. Nearby is **Dr. Mitchell's Medical Clinic**, 96 Gordon Street. The **J.P. Bayly Clinic** opposite the Phoenix Theater is a church-operated low-income clinic.

The **Health Office** (open Tues. and Fri. 0830-0930) past the market gives tetanus, polio, cholera, typhoid, and yellow fever vaccinations.

Information

The **Fiji Visitors Bureau** (tel. 22-867) is in the old customs house in front of the post office on Thompson St., open Mon. to Fri. 0830-1630, Sat. 0830-1200. The **Ministry of Information**, Ground Floor, New Wing, Government Buildings, hands out a few official booklets on the country. Across the parking lot in the same complex is the Maps and Plans Room of the **Lands and Surveys Division**, which sells excellent maps of Fiji (open Mon. to Thurs. 0900-1300/1400-1530, Fri. 0900-1300/1400-1500). Carpenters Shipping in the Harbor Center sells navigational charts (F$12 each).

The **Suva Public Library** is worth a look (open Mon., Tues., Thurs., Fri., 1000-1900, Wed. 1200-1900, Sat. 0900-1300). Visitors can use the library upon payment of a refundable deposit. This library opened in 1909 thanks to a grant from American philanthropist Andrew Carnegie. The **Desai Bookshop** on Pier St. opposite the post office has the best selection of books on Fiji. There's a good second-hand book exchange upstairs in the building at 45 Marks Street. The **Seamen's Mission** (open weekdays 1200-1400) near the main wharf trades paperback books, one for one.

TRANSPORT

Although nearly all international flights to Fiji arrive at Nandi, Suva is still the most important transportation center in the country. Inter-island shipping crowds the waterfront, and if you can't find a ship going your way at precisely the time you want to travel, Fiji Air flies to all the major Fiji islands, while Air Pacific services Tonga, Samoa, and New Zealand, both from Nausori Airport. Make the rounds of the shipping offices listed below then head down to the wharf to check the information. Compare the price of a cabin and deck passage and ask if meals are included.

A solid block of buses await your patronage at the market bus station near the harbor, with continuous local service to Lami and Raiwangga, among others, and frequent long-distance departures to Nandi and Lautoka.See "Getting Around By Bus" in the Introduction. Most of the points of interest around Suva are accessible on foot. If you wander too far, jump on any bus headed in the right direction and you'll end up back in the market. Taxis are also easy to find and relatively cheap.

Ships To Other Countries
Burns Philp Shipping (above Burns Philp Supermarket) are agents for the monthly Banks Line service to Lautoka, Noumea, Honiara, Kieta, Port Moresby, and on to Europe. They cannot sell you a passenger ticket; they can only tell you when the ship is due in and where it's headed. It's up to you to make arrangements personally with the captain. You may get on if there are any empty cabins.

The **Fijian Shipping Agency** in the Honson Building opposite the Fiji Visitors Bureau handles passenger bookings for the MV *Fijian* trip from Suva to Auckland every three weeks, about F$350 OW.

Union Maritime, 80 Harris Rd., are agents for the monthly Kiribati ship to Funafuti (F$70 deck) and Tarawa (F$94 deck). Meals are included in the fares. The **Tuvalu Embassy** has a ship to Funafuti two or three times a year, which then cruises the Tuvalu Group (F$29 deck, F$58 cabin to Funafuti).

Marine Pacific Ltd., upstairs near the dry dock at Walu Bay, handles Warner Pacific Line ships to Tonga and Samoa. Passengers are sometimes accepted but you must bring your own food.

Carpenters Shipping in the Harbor Center near the Fiji Visitors Bureau are agents for the MV *Moana II,* which about every two months sails from Suva to Futuna and Wallis (F$85 OW), then on to Noumea. Again, they can't sell the ticket but will tell you when the ship is expected in and you book with the captain. This is a beautiful trip, not at all crowded between Fiji and Wallis. Book a cabin, however, if you're going right through to Noumea.

Sofrana Line ships sometimes accept work-a-passage crew for New Zealand, Australia, or any other port when they need hands. You must arrange this with the captain.

The Wed. issue of the *Fiji Times* carries a special section on international shipping though most of the services listed don't accept passengers. You can also try to sign on as crew on a yacht. Try both yacht anchorages in Suva: put up a notice, ask around, etc.

Ships To Other Islands
Wong's Shipping Co. (Box 1269, Suva; tel. 311-888), Suite 6, first floor, Epworth Arcade off Nina St. (open Mon. to Fri. 0800-1700, Sat. 0800-1000) has six ships to different parts of Fiji with departures every other day. There are two ships a week to Savusavu, Taveuni, and Rambi (F$25 deck, F$35 cabin, each); weekly departures for Koro (F$20 deck, F$30 cabin); a monthly service to the Lau Group (F$38 deck, F$48 cabin to Vanua Mbalavu). Wong's is the biggest domestic

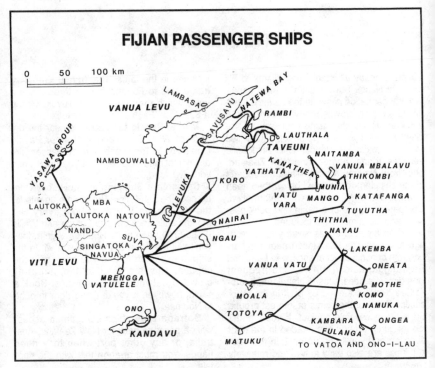

FIJIAN PASSENGER SHIPS

shipping company in Fiji, so check with them first. All fares include meals, but cabin passengers get better food and facilities.

Patterson Brothers (Private Mail Bag, Suva; tel. 315-644) opposite Wong's takes reservations for the Suva-Natovi-Nambouwalu-Lambasa bus-ferry-bus combination which departs Suva Post Office Mon. to Sat. at 0500 and Lambasa at 0700. The fare is F$20 Suva to Nambouwalu, F$24 right through to Lambasa, an excellent 10-hour trip. Another Patterson Bros. ship links Natovi to Ngau, Koro, Savusavu, and Taveuni weekly.

North West Shipping (Box 5312, Raiwangga; tel. 385-388) operates a ferry service from Suva to Savusavu twice a week (F$20 OW). Some trips call at Levuka, Koro, and Taveuni. Their boat also goes to Kandavu (F$20) weekly. North West has the advantage over Patterson in that their ships leave right from Suva rather than Natovi, a 1½-hour bus ride north. On the down side their services aren't as reli-

able as those of Patterson. Be there early.

Another good place to try is **D. Chung Shipping Co.** (tel. 315-666), 24 Raojibhai Patel St. (upstairs). Chung has weekly service to Kandavu (F$20 deck) and Ngau (F$20 deck), fortnightly to Moala (F$25 deck), and every six weeks to Kambara, Namuka, and Komo in Lau (F$76 RT deck). All fares include basic meals.

Also check at the Narain Wharf in Walu Bay for private ships to different islands. Also at Walu Bay, the **Marine Dept.** handles government barges to all the Fiji islands, and passenger fares are generally lower than on the private ships but no meals are included. Departures are listed on a blackboard at their office. The government barge to Rotuma leaves approximately once a month (F$32 OW deck). Ask about boats to Western Samoa and Tokelau here.

Kaunitoni Shipping (Box 326, Suva; tel. 312-668) at Princes Wharf handles the *Kaunitoni*, which services the Lau Group to the east.

There are different trips to the northern, central, and southern Lau islands, F$234 for tourists and F$156 for locals roundtrip in a cabin, meals included. Tourists are not allowed to travel deck class on this ship due mostly to the complaining attitude of previous European deck passengers, who expected red-carpet treatment while paying the least possible. Though not cheap, it's a good way to see a cross section of Lau in seven to nine days. A compromise would be to take the *Kaunitoni* as far as Lakemba (F$54) or Vanua Mbalavu (F$53) and fly back on Fiji Air.

Ask on the smaller vessels tied up at **Princes Wharf** for passage to Nairai (F$20), Ngau (F$20), Kandavu (F$20), etc. Don't believe the first person who tells you there's no boat going where you want—*ask around*. If you're planning a long voyage by inter-island ship, a big bundle of kava roots to captain and crew as a token of appreciation for their hospitality works wonders.

To Ovalau Island
The most popular trip is the bus/launch combination to Levuka on Ovalau via Natovi (F$9 straight through). The bus leaves from behind the post office in Suva Mon. through Sat. at 0830; you leave Levuka on the return trip Mon. through Sat. at 0800. Reserve your seat on the bus at Budget Rent-A-Car (open daily 0730-1700) on Foster Road near Carlton Brewery. Otherwise try Thomas Cook Travel in downtown Suva. Reservations are recommended on weekends and public holidays. Fiji Air flies from Nausori to Levuka (F$20) two or three times a day.

Tours And Trips
Orchid Island Cultural Center (Box 1018, Suva; tel. 311-800), seven km northwest of Suva, offers a good synopsis of Fijian customs through demonstrations, dancing, and informative exhibits. Although the visit is invariably superficial and rushed, Orchid Island does afford a glimpse into traditions such as the kava ceremony, tapa and pottery-making, etc., and the historical displays and miniature zoo are good. See and photograph Fiji's rare banded and crested iguanas up close. Replicas of a Fijian war canoe and

Fiji's emerald-green banded iguana is the most striking reptile of the Pacific.

thatched temple are on the grounds. Two-hour tours of the center are available every morning except Sun. and the F$11.50 pp cost includes transportation, admission, and entertainment (Orchid Island can only be visited on the tour). Bookings can be made through any travel agency in Suva. Though not as slick as Pacific Harbor's Cultural Center, Orchid Island has personal touches its counterpart lacks.

The **Fiji Rucksack Club** (Box 2394, Govt. Bldgs., Suva) offers noncommercial outings from Suva every weekend, and visitors are welcome to participate upon payment of a F$2 temporary membership fee. These trips offer an excellent opportunity to meet some local expats and see the untouristed side of Fiji. The Fiji Visitors Bureau will be able to put you in touch with the club.

AROUND NAUSORI

NAUSORI

In 1881 the Rewa River town of Nausori, 19 km northeast of Suva, was chosen as the site of Fiji's first large sugar mill, which operated until 1959. In those early days it was believed incorrectly that sugar cane grew better on the wetter eastern side of the island. Today cane is grown only on the drier, sunnier western sides of Viti Levu and Vanua Levu. The old sugar mill is now a rice mill and storage depot as the Rewa Valley has become a major rice-producing area. Today Nausori is Fiji's fifth largest city (population 14,018 in 1986) and the headquarters of Central Division. The nine-span bridge across the river here was built in 1937.

Nausori is better known for its large international airport three km southeast, built as a fighter strip to defend Fiji's capital during WW II. It's a good place to stay if your flight leaves very early the next morning. The business area is compact so it's easy to attend to odds and ends like getting a haircut, last-minute shopping at the small stores and the few duty-free shops, and taking in a movie at one of the three cinemas. **Rewa Pawn Shop** opposite the Mobil station sells off-beat souvenirs such as large mats and old tapa cloth. You could have trouble getting these through Customs back home.

Accommodations And Food

The **Hotel Nausori** (Box 67, Nausori; tel. 48-833) beside the rice mill has seven rooms with private bath and hot water at F$15 s, F$18 d. **Joe's Restaurant** on the back street opposite the bus station is very reasonable. Have a beer in unaccustomed comfort at the **Whistling Duck** pub nearby. Better yet, have a bowl of grog at the **Nausori Kava Saloon** farther back from the bus station.

From Nausori

Buses to the airport and Suva are fairly frequent, but the last bus to Suva is at 2130. You can also catch buses here to Lautoka and Natovi (for Levuka).

Take a bus to **Nakelo Landing** to explore the **Rewa River Delta**. Many outboards leave from here to take villagers to their riverside homes. Passenger fares are under a dollar for short trips. Larger boats leave sporadically from Nakelo for Levuka, Ngau, and Koro, but finding one would be pure chance. Some also depart from nearby **Wainimbokasi Landing**.

Livai Fiji Ethnic Tours (tel. 313-908) runs a boat tour (F$22 pp) of the Rewa Delta, with stops at Nailili Catholic Mission to visit St. Joseph's Church, Nambua village where Fijian pottery is still made, and a Hindu temple. This is a refreshing change of pace.

OFFSHORE ISLANDS

Mbau Island

Mbau, a tiny, eight-hectare island just east of Viti Levu, has a special place in Fiji's history: this was the seat of High Chief Cakobau who used European cannons and muskets to subdue most of western Fiji in the 1850s. At its pinnacle Mbau had a population of 3,000, hundreds of war canoes to guard its waters, and over 20 temples on the island's central

Tanoa, the cannibal king of Mbau: Tanoa was about 65 years of age in 1840 when the United States Exploring Expedition under Lt. Charles Wilkes toured Fiji. His rise to power threw the island into several years of strife, as Tanoa had to do away with virtually every minor chief who challenged his right to rule. With long colorful pennants playing from the mast and thousands of Cypraea ovula shells decorating the hull, his 30-meter outrigger canoe was the fastest in the region. One of Tanoa's favorite sports was overtaking and ramming smaller canoes at sea. The survivors were then fair game for whoever could catch and keep them. At feasts where most nobles were expected to provide a pig, Tanoa always furnished a human body. Wilkes included this sketch of Tanoa in volume three of the Expedition's monumental Narrative, published in 1845.

plain. After the Battle of Verata on Viti Levu in 1839, Cakobau and his father, Tanoa, presented 260 bodies of men, women, and children to their closest friends and allied chiefs for gastronomical purposes. Fifteen years after this slaughter, Cakobau converted to Christianity and prohibited cannibalism on Mbau. In 1867 he became a sovereign, crowned by European traders and planters desiring a stable government in Fiji to protect their interests.

Sights Of Mbau

The great stone slabs which form docks and seawalls around much of the island once accommodated Mbau's fleet of war canoes. The graves of the Cakobau family and many of the old chiefs lie on the hilltop behind the school. The large, sturdy, stone church located near the provincial offices was the first Christian church in Fiji. Inside its nearly one-meter-thick walls, just in front of the altar, is the old sacrificial stone once used for human sacrifices, today the baptismal font. Now painted white, this font was once known as King Cakobau's "skull crusher." It's said a thousand brains were splattered against it. Across from the church are huge ancient trees and the thatched Council House on the site of the onetime temple of the war god Cagawalu. Ratu Sir George Cakobau, governor general of Fiji from 1973-82, has a large traditional-style home on the island. You can see everything on the island in an hour or so.

Getting There

Take the Mbau bus from Nausori to Mbau Landing. There are punts to cross over to the island: F$1 at high tide from the old landing, F$2 at any time from the new landing.

Note that Mbau is not considered a tourist attraction and from time to time visitors are prevented from going to the island. It's important to get someone to invite you across, which they'll do willingly if you show a genuine interest in Fijian history. Like all Fijians, the people of Mbau are very friendly people. Bring a big bundle of *waka* for the *turanga-ni-koro* and ask permission very politely to be shown around. There could even be some confusion about who's to receive the *sevu sevu* as everyone on Mbau's a chief! If, however, you're told to contact the Office for Fijian Affairs in Suva just depart gracefully as that's only their way of saying no. After all, it's up to them.

Viwa Island

Before Cakobau adopted Christianity in 1854 Methodist missionaries working for this effect resided in Viwa Island just across the water from Mbau. Here the first Fijian New Testament was printed in 1847; the Rev. John Hunt, who did the translation, lies buried in the graveyard beside the church which bears his name.

Viwa is a good alternative if you aren't invited to visit Mbau itself. To reach the island, hire a punt at Mbau Landing for about F$5. If you're lucky, some locals will be going and you'll be able to get a ride for less. A single Fijian village stands on the island.

Tomberua Island

Tomberua Island Resort (Michael Dennis, Box 567, Suva; tel. 49-177) on a tiny island off the east tip of Viti Levu caters to elderly, well-heeled guests. The 14 thatched *mbures* (F$233 s, F$263 d, meals extra) are designed in the purest Fijian style, yet it's all very luxurious. Don't expect tennis courts or a golf course here though: the small size means peace and quiet. Deep-sea fishing is additional. Tomberua is out of eastern Viti Levu's wet belt so it doesn't get a lot of rain like nearby Suva. The transfer from Nakelo landing to Tomberua is F$36 pp.

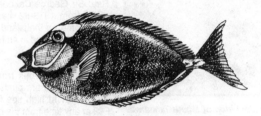

The surgeonfish gets its name from the knife-like spines just in front of its tail. Extreme care must be taken in handling the fish to avoid severe cuts.

CENTRAL VITI LEVU

THE CROSS-ISLAND HIGHWAY

Vunindawa

If you have a few days to spare, consider exploring the river country northwest of Nausori. The main center of Naitasiri Province is Vunindawa on the Wainimala River. There are five buses a day from Suva to Naluwai, where you cross the river on a free government punt then walk the last bit into Vunindawa. It's a big village with four stores, a hospital, post office, police station, two schools, and a provincial office.

Go for a swim in the river or borrow a horse to ride around the countryside. Stroll two km down the road to Waindawara, where there's another free punt near the point where the Wainimbuka and Wainimala rivers unite to form the mighty Rewa River. Take a whole day to hike up to Nairukuruku and Navuniyasi and back.

Regular bus service operates along the Cross-Island Highway, with routes from both Suva and Tavua at either end connecting at Monasavu in the middle. Buses depart Suva for Monasavu at 0800 and 1300 daily. If you want to make a connection at Monasavu for Nandarivatu or Tavua, you'll have to catch the 0800 bus. The 0800 bus to Monasavu passes Naluwai, across the river from Vunindawa, at about 1000. This bus passes Mbalea, trailhead of the Trans-Viti Levu Trek, about noon. A bus leaves Tavua for Monasavu at about 1500 daily, passing through Nandarivatu. We've heard that bus service via Monasavu is now greatly reduced, so check.

River-running

There's an exciting bamboo raft (mbilimbili) trip through the Waingga Gorge between Naitauvoli to Naivuthini, two villages on the Cross-Island Highway west of Vunindawa. Two men with long poles guide each raft through the frothing rapids as the seated visitor views towering boulders enveloped in jungle. The charge for the two-hour ride is F$25 pp, but reservations must be made in advance as an individual mbilimbili will have to be constructed for you. (There's no way to get a used mbilimbili back up to Naitauvoli.)

Write Mr. Joeli Bose, Naitauvoli village, Wainimala, Naitasiri, P.A. Naikasanga, Fiji Islands, at least two weeks ahead, giving the exact date of your arrival in the village and the number in your party. Mere Nawaqatabu at the Fiji Visitors Bureau in Suva can also arrange this trip for you in advance for a small consideration. No trips are made on Sunday. If you plan to spend the night at Naitauvoli, specify whether you require imported European-style food, or will be satisfied with local village produce. If you stay overnight a *sevu sevu* and monetary contribution are expected in addition to the F$25 pp for the raft trip.

Monasavu Hydroelectric Project

The largest development project ever undertaken in Fiji, this massive F$234 million scheme at Monasavu on the Nandrau Plateau near the center of Viti Levu took 1,500 men and six years to complete by 1985. This earthen dam, 82 meters high, was built on the Nanuka River to supply water to the four 20-megawatt generating turbines at the Wailoa Power Station on the Wailoa River, 625 meters below. The dam forms a lake 17 km long, and the water drops through a 5.4-km tunnel at a 45 degree angle, one of the steepest engineered dips in the world. Overhead transmission lines carry power from Wailoa to Suva and Lautoka, and Monasavu is capable of filling Viti Levu's needs well into the 1990s representing huge savings on imported diesel oil.

Mount Victoria

The two great rivers of Fiji, the Rewa and the Singatoka, originate on the slopes of Mt. Victoria (Tomanivi), highest mountain in the country (1,323 meters). The climb begins near the bridge at Navai, 10 km from Nandarivatu. Turn right up the hillside a few hundred meters down the jeep track then climb up through native bush on the main path all the way to the top. Beware of misleading signboards. There are three small streams to cross; no water after the third. Bright red epiphytic orchids *(Dendrobium mohlianum)* are sometimes in full bloom. There's a flat area up there where you could camp—if you're willing to take your chances with Mbuli, the devil king of the mountain. On your way down, stop for a swim at the largest stream. Allow about six hours for the roundtrip. Local guides are available. Mount Victoria is on the divide between the wet and dry sides of Viti Levu and from the summit you should be able to distinguish the contrasting vegetation in these zones.

For experienced hikers there's a rugged two-

THE TRANS–VITI LEVU TREK

day trek from the Cross-Island Highway to Wainimakutu, up and down jungle river valleys through the rainforest. It will take a strong, fast hiker about three hours from Mbalea on the highway to Nasava, then another four over the ridge to Wainimakutu. The Trans-Viti Levu Trek passes through several large, Fijian villages and gives you a good cross section of village life.

On this traditional route, you'll meet people going down the track on horseback or on foot. Since you must cross the rivers innumerable times, the trek is probably impossible for visitors during the rainy season (Dec. to April) although the locals still manage to do it. If it's been raining, sections of the trail become a quagmire stirred up by horses' hoofs. Hiking boots aren't much use here; you'd be better off with shorts and an old pair of running shoes in which to wade across the rivers. There are many refreshing places to swim along the way. Some of the villages have small trade stores, but you're better off carrying your own food. Pack some *yanggona* as well. You can always give it away if someone invites you in.

But remember, you are not the first to undertake this walk; the villagers have played host to track-walkers many, many times. Some previous hikers have not shown much consideration to local residents along the track. Unless you have been specifically invited, do not presume automatic hospitality. If a villager provides food or a service, be prepared to offer adequate payment. This applies equally to the Singatoka River Trek. Camping

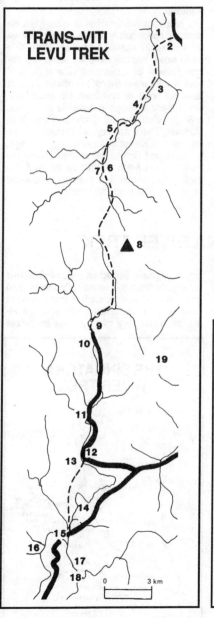

is a good alternative, so take your tent if you have one. Hopefully, the locals will soon recognize the popularity of these treks and set up simple resthouses along the way for trekkers to use.

The Route

Take the Monasavu bus to **Mbalea**, which is just before Lutu. From Mbalea walk down to the Wainimala River, which must be crossed three times before you reach the bank opposite Sawanikula. These crossings can be dangerous and well-nigh impossible in the rainy season, in which case it's better to stop and wait for some local people who might help you across. From Sawanikula it's not far to **Korovou**, a fairly large village with a primary school, clinic, and two stores. Between Korovou and **Nasava** you cross the Wainimala River 14 times, but it's easier because you're farther upstream. Try to reach Nasava on the first day. If you sleep at Korovou you'll need an early start and a brisk pace to get to the first village south of the divide before nightfall on the second day.

TRANS–VITI LEVU TREK

1. Lutu
2. Mbalea
3. Sawanikula
4. Korovou
5. Matawailevu
6. Nasava
7. Nasauvere
8. Mt. Naitarandamu
9. Wainimakutu (Nasua)
10. Nanggarawai
11. Saliandrua
12. Navunikambi
13. Waintava
14. Wainuta Falls
15. Namuamua
16. Nuku
17. Nukusere
18. Sambata
19. Korombasambasnga Range

From Nasava, follow the course of the Waisomo Creek up through a small gorge and past a waterfall. You zigzag back and forth across the creek all the way up almost to the divide. After a steep incline you cross to the south coast watershed. There's a clearing among the bamboo groves on top where you could camp but no water. Before **Wainimakutu** (Nasau) the scenery gets better as you enter a wide valley with Mt. Naitarandamu (1,152 meters) behind you, and the jagged outline of the unscaled Korombasambasanga Range to your left. Wainimakutu is a large village with two stores and bus service to Suva twice a day at 0600 and 1300.

Namosi

The bus from Wainimakutu to Suva goes via **Namosi**, spectacularly situated below massive Mt. Voma (927 meters) with sheer stone cliffs on all sides. You can climb Mt. Voma in a day from Namosi for a sweeping view of much of Viti Levu. It's steep but not too difficult. Allow at least four hours up and down. Mr. Anani Lorosio at Namosi village is available as a guide (F$10). Visit the old Catholic Church at Namosi. There are copper deposits at the foot of the Korombasambasanga Range, which Rupert Brooke called the "Gateway to Hell," 14 km north of Namosi by road. No mining has begun due to depressed world prices and high production costs.

THE SINGATOKA RIVER TREK

Nandarivatu

One of the most rewarding trips you can make on Viti Levu is the three-day hike south across the center of the island from Nandarivatu to Korolevu on the Singatoka River. There are many superb campsites along the trail. Nandarivatu, on the Cross-Island Highway, is an important forestry station; its 900-meter altitude means a cool climate and a fantastic panorama of the north coast from the ridge. An excellent viewpoint is just above the District Officer's residence. This is the source of the Singatoka River.

While you're at Nandarivatu make a side-trip to Mt. Lomalangi (Mt. Heaven), which has a fire tower on top which provides a good platform for viewing Mt. Victoria. Actually the tower seems about to collapse but you might still risk climbing up onto its shaky roof. It's an hour's hike to the tower past the Forestry Training Center; the governor general's swimming hole is also on the way. Pine forests cover the land.

Practicalities

Nandarivatu is a good place to catch your breath before setting out on the trek. The **Forestry Rest House** at Nandarivatu charges F$4, but you must reserve in advance at the Forestry Dept. in Suva or Lautoka. The rest-

house originally served as a summer retreat for expats from the nearby Vatukoula gold mine. When booking, explain that you don't mind sharing the facilities with other travelers, otherwise they might reserve the whole

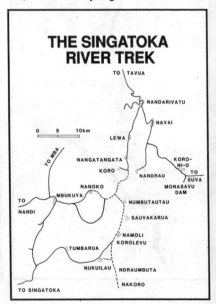

THE SINGATOKA RIVER TREK

building (nine beds) just for you, or turn you away for the same reason. Also ask about camping permits for this area. Some canned foods are available at the canteen opposite the resthouse. Bring most of the food you'll need for the hike from Suva or Lautoka. Cabin crackers are handy.

The Route

Follow the dirt road south from Nandarivatu to **Nangatangata**. Fill your canteen at Nangatangata; the trail ahead of you is rigorous and no water is to be found. From Nangatangata walk about one hour. When you reach the electric high-power line, where the road turns right and begins to descend toward Koro, look for the well-worn footpath ahead. The trail winds along the ridge, and you can see as far as Mba. The primeval forests which once covered this part of Fiji were destroyed long ago by the slash-and-burn agricultural techniques of the Fijians.

When you reach the pine trees, the path divides, with Nanoko to the right and **Numbutautau** down to the left. If you decide to make for Nanoko beware of a very roundabout loop road on the left. The Rev. Thomas Baker, the last missionary to be clubbed and devoured in Fiji (in 1867), met his fate at Numbutautau. Jack London wrote a story, "The Whale Tooth," about the death of the missionary.

Numbutautau gets more than its share of hikers looking for a place to stay. A simple guesthouse would make things easier for all concerned and would provide a little income for the villagers. Suggest it to them. Nangatangata, Namoli, and Korolevu have also been visited far too often for it to be pure Fijian hospitality anymore: a monetary *sevu sevu* spiced with a bundle of *waka* are in order. Camping is an excellent alternative, but please don't spoil things by littering or causing fires.

The Numbutautau-Korolevu section involves 22 crossings of the Singatoka River, which is easy enough in the dry season (cut a bamboo staff for balance) but almost impossible in the wet (Dec. to April). During the rainy season it's best to turn right and head to Nanoko, where you may be able to find a carrier to Mbukuya or all the way to Nandi. There's a bus service between Mbukuya and Mba. Still, it's a fantastic trip down the river to **Korolevu** if you can make it. Hiking boots will be useless in the river so wear a pair of old running shoes. From Korolevu you can take a carrier to Tumbarua, where there are four buses a day to Singatoka.

The Korolevu villagers can call large eels up from a nearby pool with a certain chant. A few hours' walk from Korolevu are the **pottery villages**, Ndraumbuta and Nakoro, where traditional, long Fijian pots are still made. The pots are not sold, but you can trade mats or salt for one.

NORTHERN VITI LEVU

Korovou To Natovi And Beyond

Korovou is an engaging small town 31 km north of Nausori on the east side of Viti Levu at the junction of King's Road and the road to **Natovi**, terminus of the Ovalau and Vanua Levu ferries. Its crossroads position in the heart of Tailevu Province makes it an important stop for buses plying the northern route around the island. (**Note:** since "korovou" means "new village" there are many places called that in Fiji—don't mix them up.) The large dairy farms in this area were set up just after WW I. The very enjoyable **Tailevu Hotel** (tel. 43-28) in Korovou has 10 rooms beginning at F$14 s, F$18 d. The hotel's public bar can get wild.

At **Nanggatawa**, eight km north of Natovi, there's a camping area near a good beach (but no surf). Ask about this place at the Coconut Inn in Suva, which owns the property. For a sweeping view of the entire Tailevu area climb **Mt. Tova** (647 meters) in a day from Silana village, eight km northwest of Nanggatawa.

At Wailotua #1, 20 km west of Korovou, is a large **cave** (admission F$2) right beside the village, easily accessible from the road. One stalactite in the cave is shaped like a six-headed snake. From Wailotua King's Road follows the Wainimbuka River north almost all the way to Viti Levu Bay.

Ra Province

The old Catholic Church of St. Francis Xavier at **Naiserelangi** on a hilltop above Navunimbitu Catholic School on King's Road about 25 km southeast of Rakiraki was beautifully decorated with frescoes by Jean Charlot in 1962-63. Typically Fijian motifs such as the *tambua, tanoa,* and *yanggona* blend in the powerful composition behind the altar. Father Pierre Chanel, who was martyred on Futuna Island in 1841, appears on the left holding the weapon which killed him, a war club. Christ and the Madonna are portrayed in black. The church is worth stopping to see, and you'll find an onward bus, provided it's not too late in the day. Ask the driver.

The two-story **Rakiraki Hotel** (Box 31, Rakiraki; tel. 94-101) has 36 a/c rooms with fridge and private bath at F$47 s, F$53 d. The Penang Sugar Mill, erected at Rakiraki in 1880, is connected by an 11-km cane railway to Ellington Wharf where the sugar is loaded aboard ships. Navatu Rock a few kilometers west of Rakiraki was the jumping-off point for the disembodied spirits of the ancient Fijians. A fortified village once stood on its summit.

The **Nakauvandra Range** towering south of Rakiraki is the traditional home of the Fijian serpent god Degei, who is said to dwell in a cave on the summit of Mt. Uluda (866 meters). This "cave" is little more than a cleft in the rock. To climb the mountain hire a guide at Tongowere village between Rakiraki and Tavua.

Nananu-i-ra Island

Off the northernmost tip of Viti Levu, this is a good place to spend some time amid perfect tranquility and beauty without the commercialization of the resorts off Nandi. Here too the climate is dry and sunny.

Kontiki Island Lodge (Box 87, Rakiraki) offers shared accommodations in three six-bed bungalows at F$7.50 pp. All have fridge and full cooking facilities, but it's necessary to take all your own supplies as there's no store or village on the island. If you run out groceries can be ordered, but it's best to bring everything with you when you come. The boat to Nananu-i-ra costs F$8 RT pp (20 minutes). Contact Empire Taxi (tel. 94-320) in Rakiraki for transport to Volivoli tidal flat (F$6 for the car). Kontiki is in touch with Empire several times a day and will send their boat over to pick you up, but you have to wade out. Enjoy the beach, snorkel, and rest—four nights is the average stay. Recommended.

The 219-hectare property adjacent to Kontiki is owned by Sanford Kent of Carlsbad, California. Mr. Kent has written us several times requesting that we ask Kontiki guests not to trespass on his property. Please do comply with his wishes. Actually Kontiki is

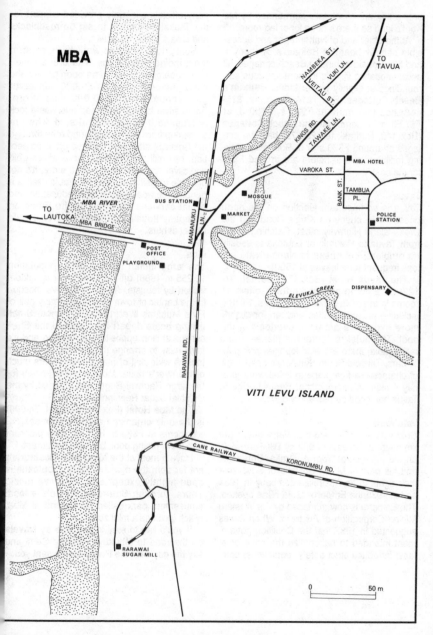

MBA

TO TAVUA

NAMBEKA ST.
VUKI LN.
VEITAU ST.
KINGS RD.
TAWAKE LN.
MBA HOTEL
VAROKA ST.
BANK ST.
TAMBUA PL.
POLICE STATION

MBA RIVER
BUS STATION
MOSQUE
MARKET
MAMANUKU LN.

TO LAUTOKA
MBA BRIDGE

POST OFFICE
PLAYGROUND

ELEVUKA CREEK
DISPENSARY

RARAWAI RD.

VITI LEVU ISLAND

CANE RAILWAY
KORONUMBU RD.

RARAWAI SUGAR MILL

0   50 m

only a tiny enclave totally surrounded by Mr. Kent's land so there's not a lot of leg room.

At the other end of Nananu-i-ra and accessible only by boat are Betham's, Anthony's, and MacDonald's Nananu Beach cottages, all accommodating visitors in more spacious surroundings at slightly higher tariffs. **Betham's Beach Cottages** (Box 1244, Suva; tel. 315-448) has four units at F$25 s, F$30 d, or F$7.50 in the dorm. **Nananu Beach Cottages** (Box 140, Rariraki; tel. 22-672) has five cottages at around F$30 s or d. Both offer cooking facilities, and transfers are around F$25 for the boat.

Tavua

Tavua is an important junction on the north coast where buses on King's Road and the Cross-Island Highway meet. Catching a bus from Tavua to Rakiraki or Lautoka is usually no problem, but buses to Nandarivatu are less frequent (one leaves at 1500).

The **Tavua Hotel** (Box 47, Mba; tel. 91-122) on a hilltop behind the town, offers 11 rooms in the main building at F$14 s, F$18 d including private facilities and fan, or slightly more expensive a/c units overlooking the pool. The hotel restaurant is pleasant and reasonable; there are also lounges and public bars. This old South Seas-style hotel is full of character, a fine place to break your journey if night is approaching. **Eagle Lodge** in Tavua has good curries and videos.

Vatukoula

Gold was first discovered at Vatukoula, eight km south of Tavua, in 1932 by Bill Borthwick, an old prospector from Australia. Borthwick and his partner Mr. P. Costello of Suva sold their rights to an Australian company in 1934 and in 1935 the **Emperor Gold Mine** opened. The Emperor is now managed by the Western Mining Corporation of Australia. When it was suggested in 1987 that the Coalition government intended to nationalize the mine or at least introduce strict safety regulations, com-

pany officials allegedly provided support for the Taukei extremists to set up roadblocks and create public disorders.

Some 1,000 miners work here, most of them indigenous Fijians. The ore is mined both underground and in an open pit, and the mine presently extracts 50,000 ounces of gold annually from 500,000 tons of ore. Some silver is also produced and waste rock is crushed into gravel and sold. The ore comes up from the underground area through the Smith Shaft. There's also a crushing section, ball mill, and flotation area where gold and silver are separated from the ore. It's not possible to visit the mine. Vatukoula itself is a genuine company town with education and social services provided by the Emperor. Company housing consists of WW II-style Quonset huts.

Mba

The large Indian town of Mba (population 10,255 in 1986) on the Mba River is seldom visited by tourists. As the attractive mosque in the center of town indicates, nearly half of Fiji's Muslims live in Mba Province. Small fishing boats depart from behind the Shell service station opposite the mosque and it's fairly easy to arrange to go along on all-night trips. A wide belt of mangroves covers much of the river's delta. Mba is better known for the large Rarawai Sugar Mill, opened by the Colonial Sugar Refining Co. in 1886.

The **Mba Hotel** (Box 29, Mba; tel. 74-000) is the only organized accommodations, 13 a/c rooms at F$25 s, F$30 d, very pleasant with a swimming pool, bar, and restaurant.

Have a meal at the **Ming Wah Restaurant** not far from the mosque. **Club Tropicana** is open nightly except Sun. with live music Thurs. through Saturday. There's a local amusement park called **Merryland** at Mba, which includes a mini zoo.

If you'd like to stay in a village try **Navala** on the road to Mbukuya; ask for Semi and say the guy from the Peace Corps sent you.

AROUND LAUTOKA

LAUTOKA

Fiji's second largest city (population 39,061 in 1986), Lautoka is the main center of the sugar industry, a major port, and Western Division headquarters. It's an amiable place with a row of towering royal palms along its main street. Though Lautoka grew up around the Fijian village of Namoli it's a predominantly Indian town today. Ferries to the couple of offshore resorts in the Malolo Group depart from Lautoka, and this is the gateway to the Yasawa Islands. Lautoka offers a rambunctious night life (though not as good as Suva's), but it's also a religious city with all the main religions of India (except the Jains and Buddhists) well represented. The mosque is also very prominent, located in the center of town. Unless you're into tourist-oriented activities Lautoka is a good alternative to staying in Nandi.

SIGHTS OF LAUTOKA AND VICINITY

Sugar Mill
Before the 1987 military coups the Lautoka Sugar Mill (founded in 1903) offered free tours during the crushing season (June to Nov.). Then the mill was reclassified as a potential target for sabotage and the tours were stopped. You can see quite a bit of this mill, one of the largest in the Southern Hemisphere, from outside even if you're not allowed in. Ask before taking photos.

Sikh Temple
Both males and females must cover their heads (handkerchiefs are all right) when they visit the Sikh Temple. Sikhism began in the Punjab of northwest India in the 16th C. as a

prominent Krishna temple in the South Pacific. The images inside on the right are Radha and Krishna, while the central figure is Krishna dancing on the snake Kaliya to show his mastery over the reptile. The story goes that Krishna chastised Kaliya and exiled him to the island of Ramanik Deep, which Fiji Indians believe to be Fiji. (Curiously, the native Fijian people have also long believed in a serpent-god named Degei who lived in a cave in the Nakauvandra Range.) The two figures on the left are incarnations of Krishna and Balarama. At the front of the temple is a representation of His Divine Grace A.C. Bhaktivedanta Swami Prabhupada, founder of the International Society for Krishna Consciousness (ISKCON).

The big event of the week at the temple is the Sun. evening *puja* (prayer) from 1630-2030, followed by a vegetarian feast. Visitors are encouraged to join in the singing and dancing. Take off your shoes and sit on the white marble floor, men on one side, women on the other. The female devotees are espe-

His Divine Grace A.C. Bhaktivedanta Swami Prabhupada, founder of the International Society for Krishna Consciousness

reformed branch of Hinduism much influenced by Islam: for example, Sikhs reject the caste system and idolatry. The teachings of the 10 gurus are contained in the *Granth,* a holy book prominently displayed in the temple. The Sikhs are easily recognized by their beards and turbans. There is a *dharamshala* (hostel) in the temple where sensitive visitors may spend the night, but cigarettes, liquor, and meat are forbidden. There's a communal kitchen. Weekdays lunch is served after the noon service. Make a contribution to the temple when you leave.

Hare Krishna Temple

The Sri Krishna Kaliya Temple on Tavewa Ave. (open daily until 2030) is the most

The Sunday afternoon festival and feast at Lautoka's Hare Krishna Temple, fifth largest in the South Pacific, is worth attending.

cially stunning in their beautiful *saris*. Bells ring, drums are beaten, conch shells blown, and stories from the *Vedas, Srimad Bhagavatam,* and *Ramayana* are acted out as everyone chants, "*Hare Krsna, Hare Krsna, Krsna Krsna, Hare Hare, Hare Rama, Hare Rama, Rama, Rama, Hare, Hare*". It's a real celebration of joy and a most moving experience. At one point children will circulate with small trays covered with burning candles on which it is customary to place a modest donation; you may also drop a dollar or two in the yellow box in the center of the temple. You'll be readily invited to join the feast later and no more money will be asked of you.

If you are interested in learning more about Vedic philosophy, there are several spiritual teachers resident in the temple ashram who would be delighted to talk to you about the *Bhagavad-gita,* and who can supply literature for a nominal fee. It's also possible to stay at the temple.

North Of Lautoka

Timber is becoming important as Fiji attempts to diversify its economy away from sugar. One of the largest reforestation projects yet undertaken in the South Pacific is the **Lololo Pine Scheme**, eight km off King's Road between Lautoka and Mba. There's a shady picnic area along a dammed creek at the forestry station where you could swim, but even if you don't stop, it's worthwhile to take the roundtrip bus ride from Lautoka to see this beautiful area and learn how it's being used.

East Of Lautoka

Ambatha village east of Lautoka is the perfect base for hiking into the **Mount Evans Mountains** behind Lautoka. Guides are available. Take a *sevu sevu* of *yanggona* roots and pay F$2 pp a day hiking tax to the *turanga-ni-koro*. Four waterfalls are near the village and **Table Mountain**, with sweeping views of the coast and Yasawas, is only an hour away. More ambitious hikes to higher peaks are possible. The landscape of wide green valleys set against steep slopes is superb.

You can get there by taking the Tavakumba bus as far as Ambatha junction, then hik-

ing another 10 km to the village. A better idea is to hire a carrier direct to Ambatha from Lautoka market for about F$10. Fiji-style accommodations are provided in the village for F$10 pp including basic meals. It's all part of a local income-generating project so you'll be well received. Avoid arriving in Ambatha on Sun., the traditional day of worship and rest.

South Of Lautoka

A popular legend invented in 1893 holds that **Viseisei** village between Lautoka and Nandi (frequent buses) is the oldest settlement in Fiji. It's told how the first Fijians, led by chiefs Lutunasobasoba and Degei, came from the west, landing their great canoe, the *Kaunitoni,* at Vunda Point where the oil tanks are now. A Centennial Memorial (1835-1935) in front of the church commemorates the arrival of the first Methodist missionaries in Fiji. Opposite the memorial is a traditional Fijian *mbure*—the residence of the present king of Vunda. Near the back of the church is another monument topped by a giant war club.

All this is only a few minutes' walk from the bus stop, but you're expected to have someone accompany you (Fijian villages are private property). Ask permission of anyone you meet at the bus stop and they will send a child with you. You could give him/her a pack of chewing gum as you part. Nearby is a **Memorial Cultural Center** where souvenirs are sold to cruise ship passengers. There's a fine view of Nandi Bay from the Center. Dr. Timoci Bavadra, former prime minister of Fiji deposed by the Rabuka coup in 1987, hails from Viseisei.

A couple of kilometers from the village on the airport side of Viseisei, just above Lomolomo Public School, are two **British six-inch guns** set up here during WW II to defend the north side of Nandi Bay. It's a fairly easy climb to them from the main highway and you get an excellent view from the top.

Scuba Diving

The closest scuba locale to Lautoka is **Tivoa Island** (20 km RT), which has clean clear water (except when it rains), abundant fish, and beautiful coral. Farther out is **Vomolailai Island** (50 km RT), a sheer wall covered with

the guns of Lomolomo on
a hilltop between Lautoka
and Nandi

Gorgonian soft coral, visibility 30 meters plus. The **Mana Main Reef** off Mana Island (65 km RT) is famous for its drop-offs. It has turtles, fish of all descriptions, plus the occasional crayfish. Visibility on this reef is never less than 25 meters. At **Yalombi** on Waya Island (100 km RT) in the Yasawas see cabbage coral, whip coral, and giant fan corals in the warm, clear waters teeming with fish.

Diver Services Fiji (Box 502, Lautoka; tel. 60-496) has a dive shop on Vitongo Parade beside Union Travel where you can arrange scuba trips and rent snorkeling gear. Tank air fills at offshore islands can also be arranged. Six-day trips to Waya Island in the Yasawas are F$380 pp for scuba divers, F$280 pp for snorkelers, including basic accommodations and meals. Divers should call for free pickup at Nandi/Lautoka hotels.

PRACTICALITIES

Accommodations

The **Sugar City Hotel** (Box 736, Lautoka; tel. 60-172) on Nathula St. charges F$6 pp in the dorm (four beds) or F$12.50 s, F$16.50 d for a private room with bath. It's rather noisy at night.

More appealing is the clean, quiet **Sea Breeze Hotel** (Box 152, Lautoka; tel. 60-717) on the waterfront near the bus station, from F$17 s, F$27 d for one of the 26 rooms with private bath.

Also recommended are the 42 rooms at the **Cathay Hotel** (Box 239, Lautoka; tel. 60-566), which features a swimming pool. The charge is F$18 s, F$22 d with a/c and private bath, F$10 s, F$16 d with fan, or F$6 pp in the dorm. All food and drink here is very expensive.

To be close to the action, stay at the 36-room **Lautoka Hotel** (Box 51, Lautoka; tel. 60-388) which has several good bars and night clubs on the premises. There's also a pool. There are six cheaper rooms (shared bath) at F$15 s, F$20 d, and more expensive rooms with waterbeds (F$66 s, F$73 d).

The **Waterfront Hotel** (Box 4653, Lautoka; tel. 64-777), a two-story building on Marine Dr., has 20 a/c rooms at F$53 s, F$60 d.

Lautoka's most colorful lodging without doubt is the **Lautoka Budget Hotel**, formerly the Fiji Guest House and once the Lautoka Police Station (cells downstairs). Hookers on the beat outside are still brought in and the management is understanding. Peep holes between rooms! A reasonable snack bar is attached. It's hot and noisy, and at F$12 s, F$15 d (shared bath) not cheap. Be prepared after a night of revelry for the *muezzin* of the mosque across the street who calls the faithful to prayer at the crack of dawn. Don't leave your luggage here while you go to the Yasawas.

At The Beach

There are two beach hotels between Lautoka and Nandi airport, both two km off the main road. They are also alike in offering dormitory accommodations with good cooking facilities, fridge, swimming pool, and nearby stores. The **Saweni Beach Hotel** (Box 239, Lautoka;

LAUTOKA

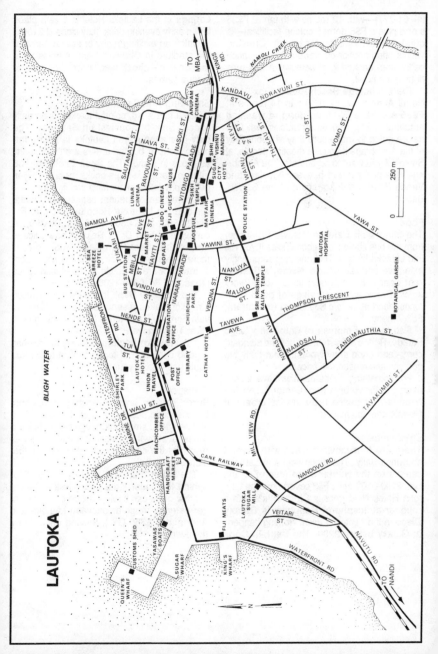

tel. 61-777)—with 12 rooms with fan at F$35 s or d plus a F$6 dorm (cooking facilities)—is quieter and has a better beach. Cruising yachts often anchor off Saweni Beach—much better than anchoring at Lautoka. A bus runs right to the hotel.

The **Anchorage Beach Resort** (Box 9472, Nandi Airport; tel. 62-009) has 14 rooms at F$65 s or d, a F$15 pp dorm, a washing machine (F$1), and panoramic views. Call before going to make sure they're open. Stay at the Anchorage if you like meeting people, at Saweni if you want to regenerate. The Anchorage Beach Resort is between Viseisei and Vunda Point a few km south of the Saweni Beach.

Food

The **Ming Wah Cafe** on Yasawa St. across from the bus station is a good choice if you roll into Lautoka hungry. Their menu is surprisingly extensive and reasonable. **Narsey's Restaurant** nearby has the best Indian food—very spicy. Enjoy ample servings of good Cantonese food at the a/c **Sea Coast Restaurant**; F$3-7 menu.

Also try the **Empress of China** on Vitongo Parade. **Renee's Restaurant** has the standard curry- and chop suey-type stuff but tasty big portions and reasonable prices.

For something a little earthier, have a bowl of grog at the **Rabnia Pool Center**, 32 Namoli Avenue. For dessert, try the ice cream at **Gopals** near the market.

Entertainment

There are four movie houses with several showings daily. The disco scene in Lautoka centers on the **Hunter's Inn** (open Fri. and Sat. 2100-0100 only; F$3 cover) near the Lautoka Hotel. Next door is **Cinderella's** with a rougher atmosphere. Roughest is **Galaxy Disco** in the center of town. Nothing happens at Galaxy before 2200. The **Captain Cook Lounge** at the Lautoka Hotel is a safe place for an early evening drink (they close at 2100).

Catch an exciting rugby or soccer game at the stadium in Churchill Park. Admission is reasonable—check locally for the times of league games.

Shopping And Services

Lautoka has a big, colorful market, open daily except Sun. but busiest on Saturday. The duty-free shopping in Lautoka is poor compared to Suva but the sellers aren't as pushy as those in Nandi. The **Book Exchange**, 36 Vitongo Parade, swaps books, or buy a Fijian geography textbook for facts and figures.

There's an outpatient service and dental clinic at the **Lautoka Hospital** (Mon. to Fri. 0800-1600, Sat. 0800-1100; tel. 60-399). A consultation with Dr. Y. Raju, whose office is across the street from Desai Bookstore, is more convenient. Vaccinations for international travelers are available at the Health Office (Tues. and Fri. 0800-1200).

The **Forestry Dept.** in the Dept. of Agriculture Bldg. takes reservations for the Nandarivatu Forestry Rest House (see "The Singatoka River Trek" above).

The **Western Regional Library** nearby has a good collection of topographical maps you could use to plan your trip.

Transport

Buses, carriers, taxis—everything leaves from the bus stand beside the market (see p. 77). If you can get a small group together try hiring a fishing boat over to Treasure Island or another resort for the day. This will be much cheaper than a tour.

The **Fijian Shipping Agency** (tel. 63-940) behind the liquor store opposite the Beachcomber office can book passage on a passenger-carrying freighter between Lautoka and Auckland (F$350 OW), leaving once every three weeks.

CRABS OF THE PACIFIC

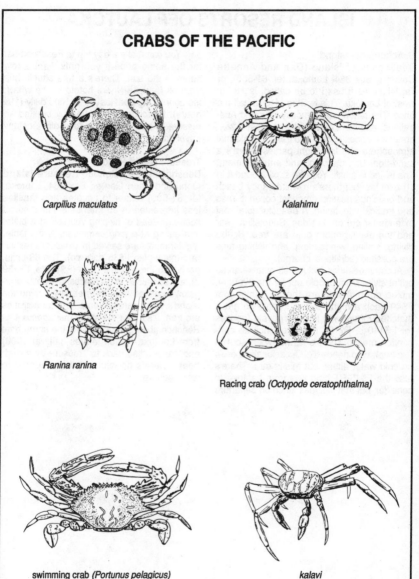

Carpilius maculatus

Kalahimu

Ranina ranina

Racing crab (Octypode ceratophthalma)

swimming crab (Portunus pelagicus)

kalavi

ISLAND RESORTS OFF LAUTOKA

Beachcomber Island

Beachcomber Island (Dan and Annette Costello, Box 364, Lautoka; tel. 61-500), or Tai Island as it used to be called, is 18 km west of Lautoka. This is Club Med at half the price. The resort caters mostly to young Australians, and it's a good place to meet travelers of the opposite sex. You'll like the informal atmosphere and late-night parties: there's a sand-floor bar, dancing, and entertainment. The island is small. You can stroll around it in 10 minutes, but there's a white sandy beach and buildings nestled amongst coconut trees and tropical vegetation. A beautiful coral reef extends far out on all sides. Snorkeling gear and the glass-bottom boat are free. Scuba diving, sailing, windsurfing, and fishing trips are possible (additional charge).

Accommodations include all meals served buffet style. Most people opt for the big open mixed dormitory where the 32 bunks cost F$49 each a night, but you can also get a thatched *mbure* with fan and private facilities for F$140 s, F$191 d. Prices include self-service meals. There's no hot water, but in this heat, who needs it? Occasionally there's no cold water either, but this is rare. There's also the F$45-RT boat ride from Lautoka to consider, but that includes lunch on departure day. You can make a day trip to Beachcomber for the same price if you only want a few hours in the sun. There's a free shuttle bus from all Lautoka/Nandi hotels to the wharf; the connecting boat leaves at 1000 daily (1 1/2 hours). Beachcomber is heavily booked so reserve ahead at their Lautoka office or any travel agency.

Treasure Island Resort

Beachcomber's neighbor **Treasure Island** (John and Pearl Gerber, Box 364, Lautoka; tel. 61-500) caters to couples and families less interested in an intense singles' social scene. Instead of helping yourself at a buffet and eating at a long communal picnic table, regular meals are served in Treasure's restaurant (meal plan F$35 daily pp). The 68 units, each with three single beds (F$132 s, F$159 d), are contained in 34 functional duplex bungalows packed into the greenery behind the island's white sands. Some nautical activities are free. It's under the same management as Beachcomber, so guests take the same boat from Lautoka (which leaves daily at 1000) and are shuttled back to Treasure by speedboat. There's no wharf so be prepared to wade ashore.

THE YASAWA ISLANDS

The Yasawas are a chain of 16 main volcanic islands and dozens of smaller ones stretching 80 km in a north-northeast direction roughly 35 km off the west coast of Viti Levu; they offer beautiful, isolated beaches, cliffs, bays, and reefs. In the lee of Viti Levu, the Yasawas are dry and sunny. The waters are crystal clear and almost totally shark-free. The group was romanticized in two movies titled "The Blue Lagoon": a 1949 original starring Jean Simmons and the 1980 remake with Brooke Shields. It was from the north end of the Yasawas that two canoe-loads of cannibals appeared in 1789 and gave Capt. William Bligh and his 18 companions a chase less than a week after the famous mutiny.

Two centuries later, increasing numbers of cruise ships ply the chain. Though an abundance of luxury resorts dot the islands off Nandi there aren't many regular inexpensive places to stay. The usual thing for backpackers is to visit Tavewa (see below) by village boat from Lautoka. Visiting any of the other islands usually involves some local contact, a sevu sevu of yanggona (which doesn't grow in the Yasawas) for the chief, and observing the etiquette outlined under "Staying In Villages" in the Introduction. You'll also have to take most of your own food.

Waya Island

The 579-meter peak on Waya is the highest in the Yasawas. A sheer mass of rock rises above **Yalombi** village, which also has a beautiful beach. At low tide you can wade from here across to neighboring Wayasewa Island: there's good snorkeling here. A remarkable 354-meter-high volcanic thumb overlooks the south coast of Wayasewa. Also from Yalombi it's a 30-minute hike across the ridge to Natawa village on the east side of Waya. There's a deserted beach another 20 minutes north of Natawa.

For a place to stay at Yalombi ask for Miss Andi or her brother Monasa who rent *mbures* at F$10 pp. The huts are usually used by scuba divers sent over by **Dive Expeditions Ltd.** (Box 502, Lautoka; tel. 60-496).

Captain William Bligh: In 1789, after being cast adrift by the mutineers on his HMS Bounty, Capt. Bligh and 18 others in a seven-meter longboat were chased by two Fijian war canoes through what is now called Bligh Water. His men pulled the oars desperately, heading for open sea, and managed to escape the cannibals. They later arrived in Timor, finishing the most celebrated open-boat journey of all time. Captain Bligh did some incredible charting of Fijian waters along the way.

Tavewa Island

Tavewa is a small island about two km long with a population of around 50 souls. There's no store, telephones, or electricity. Tall grass covers the hilly interior, there's a beach on the southeast side where the bathing is excellent, and there's a good fringing reef. This is free-hold land so there's no chief on Tavewa.

In the past we've recommended that travelers visiting Tavewa stay with Auntie Lucy Doughty and Auntie Amelia, who put up guests for around F$10 pp. Unfortunately numerous contradictory complaints about these two places have come in from readers who felt they'd been "used." Evidently the food they contributed didn't come back to them in their meals and there was tampering with the agreed-upon prices. Auntie Lucy even set up a small store to resell the supplies and kava contributed by guests!

Still, Tavewa's a good island to visit if you don't mind a non-Fijian atmosphere and a lack of privacy. The snorkeling in the sur-

rounding waters is great! If you stay at Auntie Lucy's it's probably best to camp (F$5 pp), but consider hanging on to all of your own food and only paying at the end of your visit. Check out the accommodations Lucy offers in the house and ask if you can cook. Ask other travelers who've visited Tavewa recently.

So far all the reports about **David and Kara Doughty's Place** have been good. They've put up several *mbures* for travelers (F$10 pp) between Auntie Lucy's and the small church. Camping is F$5 pp. Bring your own food with you, especially green vegetables. Unlike the others, David and Kara will invite you to join in family activities. The results of David's fishing trips often appear at dinner and he'll take you to a scenic cave for much less than some of the other people on the island want. In the evening you can sit around drinking kava with David, playing backgammon, or (if you're a woman) helping Kara weave a mat. Recommended.

To get to Tavewa ask for the weekly Nathula boats, such as the *Calm Sea, Babale, Tai Vo, Ratu Levu, Andi Sulva, Vatuvula,* or *Nukunindreke.* Take all your own food, one kilo of kava, and a *sulu* to cover up. Don't promise to stay with anyone in particular. Once on Tavewa you can size up the situation. It's a six- to 10-hour trip from Lautoka to Tavewa.

Beware of an old guy from this island named Moses who has misled numerous travelers in the past. He claims to be the "ratu" of Tavewa (untrue) and says he can arrange your trip there. This means you give him money for the food, boat, kava, etc. He'll simply pocket half the money and give you very basic supplies (if you see him again at all). You'll later be charged extra for the boat. We've also heard of a tipsy scammer named Joe from another island who hustles travelers around Lautoka market and bus station. Never pay anyone like this cash in advance.

Impressions

Lucy Barefoot of Queensland, Australia, sent us this comment:

We took a trip out to the Yasawas but got ripped off (as did others we met). First the agreement was to be that we would buy

village house, Nathula, Yasawa Island

kava, food, and pay a small amount of money to stay with the locals. Later the chief told us we shouldn't have paid any money, only brought food and kava. I had money stolen by the family we stayed with (others too), then the last straw was to be asked to pay extra (i.e,. much more than agreed) to get back by boat. No way out of that one! It left a terrible taste in the mouth, especially trusting them and having the money stolen. Incidentally, the family we stayed with had done quite well out of these extra monies—proper beds, radio, etc. We would have preferred the money to go to those who needed it most!

Peter Goodman of New York sent this:

I met up with a guy who invited me to his village, Wayalevu on Waya. It became clear the next morning that he had been sent into Lautoka by the family to get groceries, i.e., find a tourist, invite him home—the Santa Claus Syndrome. He was a nice guy and I expected to stay for a week or so, so I didn't mind forking over F$50-60 for groceries. Still, the whole thing left me with a bad taste in my mouth. I could see that he too was uncomfortable with the situation, but there we were. As the week progressed I felt very nickel and dimed.

"Hey, Peter, let's go fishing!"
"Yeah, great!" I said.
"Okay...oh, hey, we need $10 for benzine."
Then I'd either have to fork it out or look like an ogre.
"You don't want to go fishing?" he'd ask, smile disappearing.

After five days of this I moved over to Yalombi and fell in love with the place. What a beach! And the mountains! I got a kick out of knowing that one of them's named Eisenhower. I mean, here's this glorious place, sun shining, tide rolling in, the kids going off to school...and there's good ol' Mt. Eisenhower looking over us! I stayed at Andi's Rest House. She has a refrigerator, for those thinking about bringing beer.

Others

Naviti (33 square km) is the largest of the Yasawas. It's king, one of the group's highest chiefs, resides at Soso. The church there houses fine woodcarvings. Every Wed. at noon the people of Soso gather to sell shells to the button factory. On the hillside above Soso are two caves containing the bones of

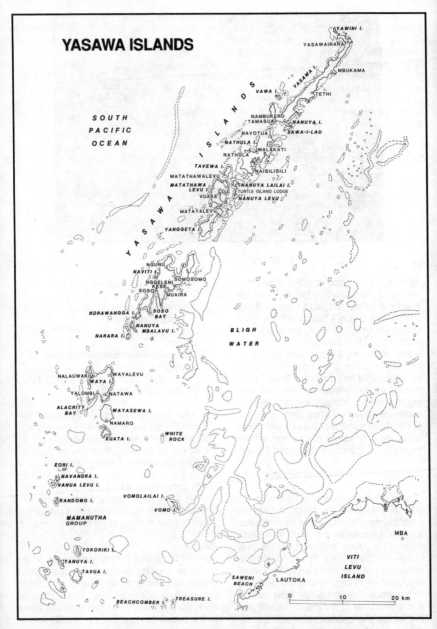

YASAWA ISLANDS

YAWINI I.

YASAWAIRARA

MBUKAMA

VAWA I.   *YASAWA I.*

TETHI

I S L A N D S

NAMBUKERU
TAMASUA   *NANUYA I.*

NAVOTUA   *SAWA-I-LAU*

NATHULA I.

NATHULA   MALAKATI

NAISILISILI

TAVEWA

MATATHAWALEVU

*MATATHAWA
LEVU*   *NANUYA LAILAI I.*
TURTLE ISLAND LODGE

VUAKE   *NANUYA LEVU*

MATAYALEVU

YANGGETA I.

S O U T H

P A C I F I C

O C E A N

Y A S A W A

NGUNU

NAVITI I.   SOMOSOMO

NGGELENI
KESE

SOSO   MUAIRA

NDRAWANGGA I.   *SOSO
BAY*

*NANUYA
MBALAVU I.*

NARARA I.   B L I G H

W A T E R

NALAUWAKI   WAYALEVU

WAYA I.

YALOMBI   NATAWA

*ALACRITY
BAY*   *WAYASEWA I.*

NAMARO

KUATA I.   *WHITE
ROCK*

EORI I.

NAVANDRA I.

VANUA LEVU I.

KANDOMO I.   *VOMOLAILAI I.*

VOMO I.

*MAMANUTHA
GROUP*

MBA

TOKORIKI I.

YANUYA I.   V I T I

TAVUA I.   L E V U

I S L A N D

*SAWENI
BEACH*   LAUTOKA

BEACHCOMBER I.   *TREASURE I.*   0   10   20 km

ancestors. Yawesa, the secondary boarding school on Naviti, is a village in itself. There's no wharf on Naviti so you must wade ashore from the boat.

On the island of **Sawa-I-Lau** is a large limestone cave illuminated by a crevice at the top. There's a clear, deep pool in the cave where you can swim, and an underwater opening leads back into a smaller, darker cave (bring a light). A Fijian legend tells how a young chief once hid his love in this cave when her family wished to marry her to another. Each day he brought her food until both could escape to safety on another island. All the cruise ships stop at this cave. If you get there on your own, pay F$1 pp to the chief of Nambukeru village just west of the cave to visit.

The Tui Yasawa, highest chief of the group, resides at Yasawairara village at the north end of **Yasawa Island**. The most remote of the Yasawas is **Viwa**, squatting alone 25 km northwest of Waya. Traditional Fijian pottery is made in the village on **Yanuya Island** in the Mamanutha Group. Of the 13 Mamanutha islands only it and nearby Tavua have Fijian villages.

Permissions

Before going to the Yasawas you're expected to get a free permit from the district officer in the Dept. of Agriculture and Fisheries building beside the public library (open Mon. to Fri. 0800-1300/1400-1600). He will only issue the permit if you have an invitation from the village you intend to visit. You don't need a permit or letter to go to Tavewa, which is freehold land.

Getting There

Village boats from the Yasawas arrive at Lautoka's Queen's Wharf and the old jetty near Fiji Meats on Wed. or Thurs., and depart on Fri. or Sat. morning. This means you must spend either five or 12 days in the Yasawas. The fare is F$10-15 pp OW. There are always Yasawans around Lautoka market on Fridays.

Turtle Island

If you've been looking for the South Pacific's ultimate resort, it may be **Turtle Island Lodge** (Richard Evanson, Box 9317, Nandi Airport; tel. 72-780) on 200-hectare Nanuya Levu in the middle of the Yasawa Group. Only 12 fan-cooled, two-room *mbures* grace Turtle, and American owner-resident Richard Evanson, who bought the island in 1972 for half a million dollars, swears there'll never be more. The 24 guests (mixed couples only, please) pay US$480 d a night, but that includes all meals *and* drinks. You'll find the fridge in your cottage well stocked with beer, wine, soft drinks, and champagne, re-filled daily, and no extra bill to pay when you leave. Sports such as sailing, snorkeling, canoeing, windsurfing, glass-bottom boating, deep-sea fishing, cata-maraning, horseback riding, guided hiking, and moonlight cruising are all included in the tariff. They'll even do your laundry at no charge.

If you want to spend the day on an uninhabited island, just ask and they'll drop you off. Later someone will be back with lunch and a cooler of wine or champagne. Otherwise use any of the dozen secluded beaches on the main island, including one a few steps from your door. Meals are served at your cottage or taken at the community table; every evening Richard hosts a small dinner party. He's turned down many offers to develop the island with hundreds more units or to sell out for a multi-million-dollar price. That's not Richard's style and he's quite specific about who he *doesn't* want to come: "Trendies, jet-setters, obnoxious imbibers and plastic people won't get much out of my place. Also, opinionated, loud, critical grouches and anti-socials should give us a miss." Of course, all this luxury has a price. Aside from the per diem it's another US$480 per couple for roundtrip seaplane transportation to the island from Nandi. There's also a six-night minimum stay, but as nearly half the guests are repeaters, that doesn't seem to be a problem. It's just the place for a quiet, relaxing holiday. (Turtle Island is off limits to anyone other than hotel guests.)

THE LOMAIVITI GROUP

The Lomaiviti or "Central Fiji" Group lies in the Koro Sea near the heart of the archipelago, east of Viti Levu and south of Vanua Levu. Of its nine main volcanic islands Ngau, Koro, and Ovalau are among the largest in Fiji. Lomaiviti's climate is moderate, neither as wet and humid as Suva nor as dry and hot as Nandi. The population is mostly Fijian, engaged in subsistence agriculture and copra making.

The old capital island Ovalau is by far the best known and most visited of the group. Naingani has a tourist resort all its own, but Koro and Ngau are seldom visited due to a lack of facilities for visitors. Ferries ply the Koro Sea to Ovalau, while onward ferries run to Savusavu a couple of times a week. Fiji Air also flies frequently to Ovalau, but only a couple of times a week to Koro and Ngau.

OVALAU ISLAND

Ovalau, a large volcanic island just east of Viti Levu, is the main island of Lomaitviti Group. Almost encircled by high peaks, the Lovoni Valley in the center of Ovalau is actually the island's volcanic crater and about the only flat land. The crater's rim is pierced by the Mbureta River which escapes through a gap to the southeast. The highest peak is Nandelaiovalau (626 meters) behind Levuka, meaning "the top of Ovalau."

LEVUKA

The town of Levuka on Ovalau's east side was Fiji's capital until the shift to Suva in 1881. Founded as a whaling settlement in 1830, Levuka became the center for European traders in Fiji. The cotton boom of the 1860s brought new settlers and Levuka quickly grew into a boisterous town with over 50 hotels and taverns along Beach Street.

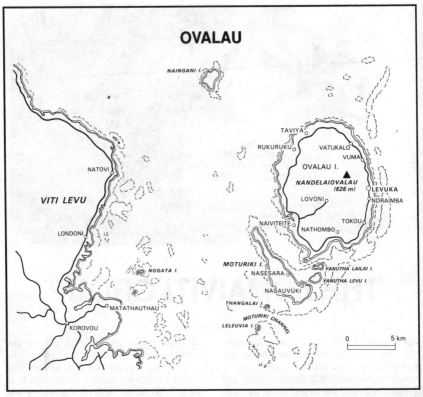

OVALAU

Escaped convicts and debtors fleeing creditors in Australia swelled the throng until it was said that a ship could find the reef passage into Levuka by following the empty gin bottles floating out on the tide. The honest traders felt the need for a stable government so in 1871 Levuka became capital of Cakobau's Kingdom of Fiji. The disorders continued with certain elements forming a "Ku Klux Klan" defiant of any form of Fijian authority.

On 10 Oct. 1874, a semblance of decorum came as Fiji was annexed by Great Britain. A municipal council was formed in 1877. Ovalau's central location seemed ideal for trade and sailing boats could easily reach the port from Lau or Vanua Levu. Yet the lush green hills which rise behind the town saw that its downfall as colonial planners saw that

there was no room for the expansion of their capital. In Aug. 1882 Governor Sir Arthur Gorden moved his staff to Suva. After a hurricane in 1886 Levuka's devastated buildings were not replaced.

Levuka remained the collection center for the copra trade right up until 1957. When that industry also moved to Suva, the town seemed doomed. With the establishment of a fishing industry in 1964 things picked up and today it's a minor educational center, the headquarters of Eastern Division, and a low-profile tourist center. The false-fronted buildings and covered sidewalks along Beach St. give this somnolent town of 2,871 inhabitants (1986) a 19th-century, Wild West flavor. It's a perfect base for excursions into the mountains, along the winding coast, or out to the barrier reef one km offshore. Levuka is one of the most peaceful, pleasant, and picturesque places in Fiji.

SIGHTS

Near Queen's Wharf is the old Morris Hedstrom Ltd. store, erected in 1878 by Percy Morris and Maynard Hedstrom, great-granddaddy of today's Pacific-wide Morris Hedstrom chain. In 1980 the building was restored and converted into a **museum and library** (closed Sun.) where cannibal forks vie with war clubs and clay pots for your attention. Ask at the museum about guided walking tours of historic Levuka.

Stroll along Levuka's sleepy waterfront. The **Church of the Sacred Heart** with its square stone clock tower was erected by French Marist Fathers who arrived in 1858. When you reach the former movie house, turn left onto Hennings St. and head inland on the left side of Tongonga Creek to the

Levuka Public School (1879), the birthplace of Fiji's present public educational system. Other Levuka firsts include the first newspaper (1869), the first Masonic Lodge (1875), and the first bank (1876) in Fiji. Farther up Bath Road the creek has been dammed to create a pond. Continue straight up and you'll eventually reach the source of the town's water supply.

As you come back down the hill, on your left across the small bridge is the **Ovalau Club**. Despite the Members Only sign you're welcome to go in. On the wall by the bar is a framed letter from Count Felix von Luckner, the WW I German sea wolf. Von Luckner left the letter and some money at the unoccupied residence of a trader on Katafanga Island in the Lau Group from which he took some provisions. In the letter Count von Luckner identifies himself as Max Pemberton, an English writer on a sporting cruise through the Pacific. The old Town Hall (1898) and Masonic Lodge adjoin the Club. A few blocks north of

view of Levuka, as seen from Gun Rock

The Provincial Council meeting place at Levuka is built like a traditional Fijian chief's mbure.

the club past the Royal Hotel are the 199 steps up **Mission Hill** to an old Methodist school and a fine view.

On a low hill farther north along the waterfront is a **war memorial** to British residents of Levuka who died in WW I. Before Fiji was ceded to Britain the Cakobau government headquarters was installed on this hill. The Anglican Church (1904) beyond has period stained-glass windows.

North Of Levuka

Follow the coastal road north from Levuka to the second yellow bridge, where you'll see the old **Methodist church** (1869) on the left. In the small cemetery behind the church is the grave of the first U.S. consul to Fiji, John Brown Williams. For the story of Williams' activities see the introduction to this chapter. Across the bridge and beneath a large *ndilo* tree is the tomb of an old king of Levuka. The large house in front of the tree is the residence of the present Tui Levuka.

Directly above is **Gun Rock**, which was used as a target in 1849 to show Cakobau the efficacy of a ship's cannon so he might be more considerate to resident Europeans. The early Fijians had a fort atop the Rock to defend themselves against the Lovoni hill tribes. Ask permission of the Tui Levuka (the "Roko") or a member of his household to climb Gun Rock for a splendid view of Levuka. If a small boy leads you up and down, it wouldn't be out of place to give him something for his trouble. From the summit, let your eyes follow the horizon from right to left with the islands of Ngau, Mbatiki, Nairai, Wakaya, Koro, Makongai, and Vanua Levu respectively in view.

Continue north on the road, round a bend, pass the ruin of a large concrete building, and you'll reach a cluster of government housing on the site of a cricket field where the Duke of York (later King George V) played in 1878. There's a beautiful deep pool and waterfall behind **Waitovu** village, about two km north of Levuka. You may swim here but please don't skinny-dip; this is offensive to the local people and has led to serious incidents in the past. Since they're good enough to let you use this idyllic spot which they own, it's common courtesy to respect their wishes.

South Of Levuka

The **Pacific Fishing Company** tuna cannery is south of the main wharf. A Japanese cold-storage facility opened here in 1964, the cannery in 1976. In 1986 the Japanese company involved in the joint venture pulled out, turning the facility over to the government. The cannery is supplied by Asian purse seine and longline fishing boats and pole-and-line ships of the government-owned Ika Corporation.

The **Cession Monument** is a little farther along; the Deed of Cession which made Fiji a British colony was signed here by Chief Cakobau in 1874. A traditional *mbure* used for Provincial Council meetings is on the other side of the road.

When you reach Ndraimba village (two km), take the road to the right before the four condominiums and follow a path for 4½ hours through enchanting forests and across clear streams to **Lovoni** village. The trail is no longer used by the locals and requires attentiveness to follow. Swim and picnic, then catch the 1500 bus from Lovoni back to Levuka. In 1855 the fierce Lovoni tribesmen Ovalau burned Levuka. They continued to threaten Levuka right up until 1871 when they were finally captured during a truce and sold to European planters as laborers. In 1875 the British government allowed the survivors to return to their valley where their descendants live today.

If you forego this hike and continue on the main road, you'll come to an old cemetery a little south of Ndraimba. A few km farther is the **Devil's Thumb**, a dramatic volcanic plug towering above **Tokou** village, one of the scenic highlights of Fiji. Catholic missionaries set up a printing press at Tokou in 1889 to produce gospel lessons in Fijian. In the center of the village is a sculpture of a lion made by one of the early priests. It's five km back to Levuka.

Just off the south end of Ovalau is tiny Yanutha Lailai Island where on 14 May 1879 the first 463 indentured Indian laborers to arrive in Fiji landed from the ship *Leonidas*. They spent two months in quarantine on Yanutha Lailai to avoid the introduction of cholera or smallpox into Fiji. Later Nukulau Island off Suva became Fiji's main quarantine station.

PRACTICALITIES

Accommodations

Levuka hasn't yet been blemished by an up-market hotel; instead there's a choice of five inexpensive places to stay. The first hotel you come to after disembarking is the **Old Capital Inn** (Box 50, Levuka; tel. 44-057), a favorite of budget travelers who want to be with their counterparts where the action is. The Inn has six double rooms at F$9 pp and a 16-bed dormitory at F$5, breakfast included. There's no hot water.

Also recommended is the **Mavida Guest House** (Box 91, Levuka; tel. 44-051; F$9 pp bed and breakfast) on the waterfront near the Levuka Club. Mavida is in a spacious colonial house with five guest rooms and cooking facilities.

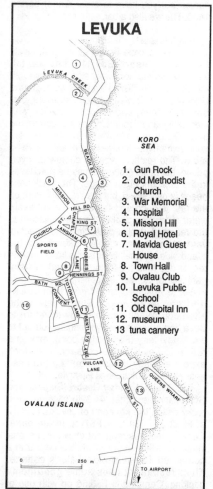

LEVUKA

KORO SEA

1. Gun Rock
2. old Methodist Church
3. War Memorial
4. hospital
5. Mission Hill
6. Royal Hotel
7. Mavida Guest House
8. Town Hall
9. Ovalau Club
10. Levuka Public School
11. Old Capital Inn
12. museum
13 tuna cannery

OVALAU ISLAND

0   250 m

TO AIRPORT

For the Somerset Maugham flavor, stay at the 14-room **Royal Hotel** (Box 7, Levuka; tel. 44-024). Built in 1852 and renovated in the 1890s, this is Fiji's oldest operating hotel. Ceiling fans revolve above the potted plants and rattan sofas in the lounge. The colonial atmosphere and impeccable service make it about the best value in Fiji (F$12 s, F$17 d, F$22 t). The 15 rooms are pleasant, and much-needed mosquito nets are provided. There's also a F$6 dorm. Good meals are served but you have to order dinner before 1400. There's also a bar.

A Beach Resort

The perfect escape from it all is quiet, lovely **Rukuruku Resort** (Box 112, Levuka; tel. 312-507) on the northwest side of Ovalau 20 km from Levuka. There's a large campground (F$5 pp) complete with toilets, showers, barbecue, kitchen, and an open pavilion with electric lighting. Dormitory-style accommodations (F$10 pp) are also available, or rent your own private four-person *mbure* for F$35 a day. The restaurant/bar is somewhat overpriced, but basic groceries may be purchased in the adjacent Fijian village. The black-sand beach is only so-so, but the snorkeling out on the reef is good and there's a natural freshwater swimming pool in the river adjacent to the resort. A vanilla plantation and beautiful verdant mountains cradle Rukuruku on the island side. A small boat is available to charter for day trips (F$40 for the boat) to Naingani Island, the reef, or for fishing.

Get to Rukuruku on a carrier from Levuka (F$1 pp), no service on Sun. or late in the afternoon. When you're ready to return to Suva, the resort launch will shuttle you out to the Natovi ferry (F$5 for the boat), making a return to Levuka unnecessary. Just don't expect a flashy tourist hotel like the ones near Nandi—Rukuruku is Fiji-style.

The **Ovalau Holiday Resort** (Stephen and Rosemary Diston; tel. 44-329) at Vuma on a rocky beach five km north of Levuka, is F$12 s, F$22 d, F$30 t, or F$7 pp in the dorm. Cooking facilities, and hot showers are provided, and there's the Mbula Beach Bar in a converted 150-year-old whaler's cottage. Their restaurant does some good home cooking. Camping is F$3.50 pp with use of the dorm facilities.

Food And Entertainment

There's a restaurant at the **Old Capital Inn** where everyone gathers for dinner. Otherwise try the curry house on the waterfront or **Matts Korna**. The Chinese restaurant on Beach St. is reasonable and you can eat with chopsticks if you want.

Andy Zender, a young Swiss from Zurich, runs the **Koro Sea Noodle Shop** (tel. 44-365) on the main drag in Levuka. The tasty French and Italian dishes have a Fijian touch: instead of spinach leaves, Andy uses *ndalo*. Specialties include spaghetti, lasagna, and ravioli, but try the *kokonda* and ask about lobster. Beer and wine are available, as is chocolate cake or fresh fruit and ice cream for dessert. Have a look through the visitors' book while you're there.

Although the sign says Members Only, visitors are welcome at the **Ovalau Club** (cheap beer). Stop in for a drink at the **Royal Hotel** (1882) to absorb some of the atmosphere of old Levuka. To have dinner here you must put in your order before 1700.

Transport

Fiji Air has flights several times a day from Nausori to Mbureta airport on Ovalau (F$20). Once a week the flight continues on to Koro (F$18). Book the Koro flight well ahead. Standby fares are available on the flights back to Nausori but they don't like giving them to tourists. Fiji Air has a minibus from their Levuka office to the airstrip for F$2.50 pp.

There's sometimes a ship direct from Levuka to Nambouwalu, Vanua Levu, very early Mon. mornings. Ask at the **Patterson Bros.** office on the waterfront beside the market in front of the Royal Hotel. Also inquire about the Suva-Savusavu ferry which calls at Levuka on Fri. northbound and Tues. southbound. Village boats leave sporadically for Mbatiki, Nairai, and Koro.

For details of the bus/launch service between Suva and Levuka see "Suva—Transport" above. Book your seat on the express bus back to Suva at **Mantels Store** next to the Ovalau Visitors Bureau (recommended on holidays).

Small outboards to **Moturiki Island** depart Nangguelendamu Landing most afternoons (50 cents). You can charter one to take you over anytime for about F$10. The best beaches are on the east side of Moturiki. Camping is officially discouraged but possible.

Due to steep hills on the northwest side of Ovalau there isn't a bus around the island. Northbound they go as far as historic St. John's College, while those headed south don't reach farther than Viro. Carriers run as far as Rukuruku village (F$1) along a beautiful, hilly road. Go in the morning.

Tours

Emosi Show, manager of the Old Capital Inn, offers many good trips. He does a land tour around Ovalau with lunch at Rukuruku for F$10. His reef tour (F$5 pp) is great for swimming and snorkeling, and he'll show you sharks if you ask. Five people are required for either of these tours. Ask Emosi about a visit to **Leleuvia Island**, a lovely isolated reef island with nothing but coconut trees and sandy beaches. He charges F$25 pp for the trip over and the first night with meals; additional days are F$13 each. A day trip to Leleuvia with lunch is about F$15 pp. Water is in short supply on Leleuvia, so you bathe with a bucket. Emosi drops off as many people as he can, so it does get crowded. Emosi will also do charters to Naingani or Makongai if enough people are interested. If you'd like to climb the peak which towers behind Levuka just ask; Emosi will arrange a guide for a nominal amount. Problem is, when Emosi's out of town on business, activities are suspended.

Tuni Tours (tel. 44-329) also does the minibus tour around Ovalau and provides transfers to Rukuruku Resort. Ask at the **Ovalau Visitors Bureau** on the main street. The Royal Hotel books day trips to **Yanutha Lailai Island** at F$18 pp, plus F$6 pp a night if you want to sleep there. Meals are served.

OTHER ISLANDS OF THE LOMAIVITI GROUP

Naingani

Naingani, 11 km off Viti Levu, is a lush tropical island near Ovalau on the west end of the Lomaiviti Group with beautiful beaches and one Fijian village in the southwest corner. **Mystery Island Resort** (Box 12539, Suva; tel. 44-364), formerly known as Islanders Village or Naingani Island Resort, offers 22 fan-cooled units. Rates vary according to size of the accommodations: F$60 s or d, F$90 for up to four, F$150 for up to six, F$200 for up to eight. Lower off-season rates apply from mid-Sept. to May (excepting Christmas)—ask. Also ask about their F$10-pp dormitory. The F$60 studios don't have cooking facilities but all of the larger villas do, so bring food. The resort meal plan is F$25 pp daily. Sporting activities such as windsurfing are also charged extra. This is a good place for families. To get there ask at their Suva office at 46 Gordon St. opposite the public library. There's a minibus/launch connection from Suva daily at 1000 for F$30 RT; the daily launch to Levuka is also F$30 pp RT.

Makongai

Makongai shares a figure eight-shaped barrier reef with neighboring Wakaya. From 1911 to 1969 this was a leper colony staffed by Catholic nuns which also received patients from various other Pacific island groups. Many of the old hospital buildings still stand. Today Makongai is owned by the Dept. of Agriculture, which runs an experimental sheep farm there. The anchorage is in Dalithe Bay on the northwest side of the island.

Wakaya

Chief Cakobau sold Wakaya to Europeans in 1840 and it has since passed through many hands. In 1862 David Whippy set up Fiji's first sugar mill on Wakaya. At one time the Pacific Harbor Corporation had grandiose plans to develop Wakaya for condo-tourists, but these have proved impractical. In 1985 American interests bought the island for US$6 million. Red deer imported from New Caledonia run wild across Wakaya. A high cliff on the west coast is known as Chieftain's Leap for a young chief who threw himself over the edge to avoid capture by his foes.

The German raider, Count Felix von Luckner, was captured on Wakaya during WW I. His ship the *Seeadler* had foundered on a

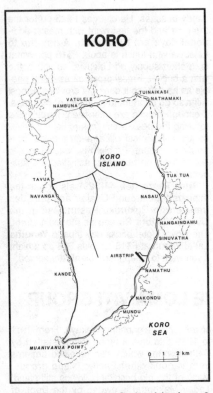

KORO

villages are on Mbatiki but due to hazardous reefs there's no safe anchorage for ships. Fine baskets are made here.

Nairai

Seven Fijian villages are found on this 336-meter-high island between Koro and Ngau. The inhabitants are known for their woven handicrafts. Hazardous reefs stretch out in three directions and in 1808 the brigantine *Eliza* was wrecked here. Among the survivors was Charles Savage who served as a mercenary for the chiefs of Mbau for five years until falling into the clutches of Vanua Levu cannibals.

Koro

Koro is an eight- by 16-km island shaped like a shark's tooth. A ridge traverses the island from northeast to southwest, reaching 561 meters near the center. High jungle-clad hillsides drop sharply to the coast. The best beach is along the south coast between Mundu and the lighthouse at Muanivanua Point. Among the 14 large Fijian villages, the government center with post office, hospital, and schools is at **Nasau**.

NGAU

reef at Maupihaa in the Society Islands on 2 Aug. 1917. The 105 survivors (prisoners included) camped on Maupihaa while von Luckner and five men set out in an open boat on Aug. 23 to capture a schooner and continue the war. On 21 Sept. 1917 they found a suitable ship at Wakaya. Their plan was to go aboard as passengers and capture it, but a British officer and four Indian soldiers happened upon the scene. Not wishing to go against the rules of chivalry and fight in civilian clothes, the count gave himself up and was interned at Auckland as a prisoner of war. He later wrote a book, *The Sea Devil*, about his experiences.

Mbatiki

Mbatiki has a large interior lagoon of brackish water surrounded by mud flats. Four Fijian

The road to **Vatulele** village on the north coast climbs from Nasau to the high plateau at the center of the island. The coconut trees and mangos of the coast are replaced by great tree ferns and thick rainforest. Mr. Amena Tave, chief of Vatulele village, can arrange accommodations for visitors or give you a place to camp.

At **Nathamaki** village, in the northwest corner of Koro, turtle-calling is still practiced. The caller stands on Tuinaikasi, a high cliff about a kilometer west of the village and repeats the prescribed words to bring the animals to the surface. The ritual does work although the turtles are becoming scarce and only one or two may appear. If anyone present points a finger or camera at a turtle, they quickly submerge. Actually, it's not possible to photograph the turtles as magic is involved (the photos wouldn't show any turtles). You're so high above the water you'd need the most powerful telephoto lens just to pick them out, anyway.

The track south between Nathamaki and Tua Tua runs along a golden palm-fringed beach. There's a cooperative store at **Nangaindamu** where you can buy *yanggona* and

supplies. Koro kava is Fiji's best. A 30-minute hike up a steep trail from the co-op brings you to a waterfall and idyllic swimming hole. Keep left if you're on your own (a guide would be preferable).

The ship from Suva anchors off Nangaindamu (no wharf). Koro has an unusual inclined **airstrip** on the east side of the island near Namathu village. You land uphill, take off downhill. Several carriers meet the flights (F$1 to nearby villages, F$2 to the farthest).

Ngau

Ngau is the fifth-largest island in Fiji, with 16 villages and 13 settlements. There's a barrier reef on the west coast, only a fringing reef on the east. There's a hot-spring swimming pool close to the P.W.D. depot at **Waikama**. From Waikama hike along the beach and over the hills to **Somosomo** village. If you lose the way, look for the creek at the head of the bay and work your way up it until you encounter the trail. There's a bathing pool in Somosomo with emerald-green water.

A road runs from Somosomo to **Sawaieke** village, where the Takalaingau, high chief of Ngau, resides. The remnants of one of the

Mangroves (Rhizophora) *flourish along Fijian shorelines. The many spidery stilt roots, which anchor and support the tree, allow it to breathe more easily in the oxygen-poor environment. As* saltwater floods the mud flats, the mangroves serve to reclaim new land and create a specialized habitat. Where mangroves have been cleared coastal fisheries decline.

only surviving pagan temples *(mbure kalou)* in Fiji is beside the road at the junction in Sawaieke. The high stone mound is still impressive.

It's possible to climb **Mt. Ndelaitho** (760 meters), highest on the island, from Sawaieke in three or four hours. The first hour is the hardest. From the summit there is a sweeping view. MacGillivray's Fiji petrel, a rare seabird of the albatross family, lays its eggs underground on Ngau's jungle-clad peaks. Only two specimens have ever been taken: one by the survey ship *Herald* in 1855, and a second by Dick Watling of Nandi in 1984.

The co-op and government station (hospital, post office, etc.) are at **Nggarani** at the north end of Ngau. Two ships a week arrive here from Suva on an irregular schedule, but there is no wharf so they anchor offshore. The wharf at **Waikama** is used only for government boats.

There are a number of waterfalls on the east coast, the best known behind **Lekanai** and up Waimboteingau Creek, both an hour's walk off the main road. The "weather stone" is on the beach, a five-minute walk south of **Yandua** village. Bad weather is certain if you step on it or throw a stone at it.

To arrange accommodations ask at the Fiji Air office in Suva. Tom Koroi, driver of the carrier (F$2) serving the airstrip, can provide accommodations in Waikama village at F$10 pp including all meals. Tom connects with another carrier down the east coast to Lamiti. The airstrip is on Katundrau Beach at the south end of Ngau.

The leatherback (Dermodhelys coriacea), *one of four species of sea turtles found in Fiji, is the only turtle which cannot retract its head or limbs. Its shell is a leathery skin rather than a horny plate. The seven lengthwise ridges on its back and five on its underside make it easily recognizable. Leatherbacks can grow up to 2.5 meters long and weigh up to a ton. In the Fiji Islands all leatherbacks and their eggs are fully protected year-round under the Fisheries Act.*

VANUA LEVU

Though only half as big as Viti Levu, Vanua Levu ("Great Land") has much to offer. The transport is good, scenery varied, people warm and hospitable, and often you'll have the whole island to yourself—few tourists visit as it's not as heavily promoted as Nandi/Singatoka/Suva. Fijian villages are numerous all the way around the island—here you'll be able to experience real Fijian life. Make an effort to get off the beaten track and visit Fiji's second largest island (5,556 square km).

The drier northwest side of Vanua Levu features sugar cane fields, while on the damper southeast side copra plantations predominate with a little cocoa around Natewa Bay. Toward the southeast it's more a bucolic beauty of coconut groves dipping down toward the sea. Majestic bays cut into the island's south side, and one of the world's longest barrier reefs flanks the north coast. There are some superb locations here just waiting to be discovered both above and below the waterline.

Fiji Indians live in the large market town of Lambasa and the surrounding cane-growing area; most of the rest of Vanua Levu is Fijian. Together Vanua Levu, Taveuni, and adjacent islands form Fiji's Northern Division, which is subdivided into three provinces: the west end of Vanua Levu is Mbua Province; most of the north side of Vanua Leva is Mathuata Province; and the southeast side of Vanua Levu and Taveuni are Thakaundrove Province.

Nambouwalu
The ferry from Viti Levu ties up to the wharf at this friendly little government station near the south tip of Vanua Levu. From here it's 137 km by bus to Lambasa, 141 km to Savusavu. There are no restaurants or hotels at Nambouwalu but **Mr. Sukha Prasad**, a jolly ol' boy, runs a very basic *dharamshala* (guesthouse) with cooking facilities near the wharf. He doesn't charge, but make a contribution upon departure.

Another possibility is the lovely **Government Rest House** on the hillside. They have two rooms where you can cook at F$5 pp. Make reservations with the district officer in Mbua (tel. 6, Nambouwalu). If the Rest House

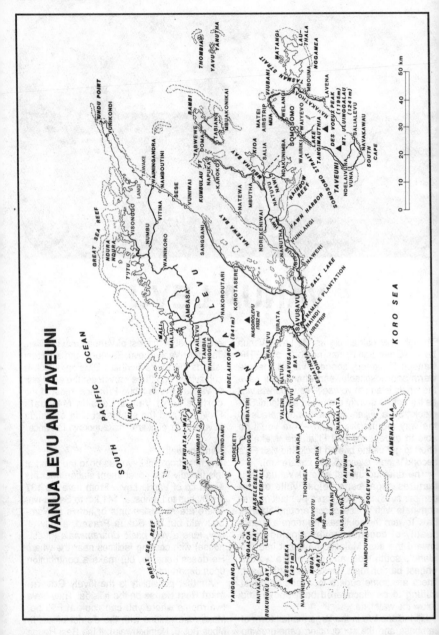

VANUA LEVU AND TAVEUNI

the death of Charles Savage

is booked, ask the D.O.'s clerk if you may camp on the grounds.

The large Patterson Bros. car ferry sails from Natovi on Viti Levu to Nambouwalu daily except Sun. around 0730, F$16 for the four-hour trip. From Nambouwalu the same boat departs for Natovi daily except Sun. at noon. Patterson Bros. runs an express bus from Nambouwalu to Lambasa (four hours—F$4) for ferry passengers. This bus is quicker and cheaper than the four regular buses to Lambasa (five hours—F$5), which make numerous detours and stops.

The Road To Lambasa

This twisting, tiring bus ride takes you past Fijian villages, rice paddies, and cane fields. The early sandalwood traders put in at **Mbua Bay**, and the dry open countryside west of Mbua stretches out to Seseleka (421 meters). About 13 km west of Lekutu, near the bay on the north side of the narrow neck of land which joins the Naivaka Peninsula to the main island, is Dillon's Rock. In Sept. 1813 a party of Europeans took refuge here after being ambushed during a raid on a nearby village.

After witnessing Swedish mercenary Charles Savage being killed and eaten by enraged Fijian warriors when he descended to negotiate a truce, Capt. Peter Dillon of the *Hunter* and two others managed to escape to their boat by holding a musket to the head of an important chief and walking between the assembled cannibals. Nukungasi Beach on Ngaloa Bay is three km off the main highway just south of Lekutu postal agency (keep right).

About five km north of Lekutu Secondary School, one km off the main road (bus drivers know the place), are Fiji's most-accessible yet least-known waterfalls, the **Naselesele Falls**. This is a perfect place to picnic between buses, with a nice grassy area where you could camp. The falls are most impressive during the rainy season, but the greater flow means muddy water so swimming is best in the dry season. There's a large basalt pool below the falls and nobody lives in the immediate vicinity. You'll probably have the place to yourself. Much of this part of the island has been reforested with pine.

Farther east the road passes a major rice-growing area and runs along the Ndreketi

River, Vanua Levu's largest. A rice mill at Ndreketi and citrus project at Mbatiri are features of this area. In the Seanggangga settlement area between Mbatiri and Lambasa about 60 square km of native land was cleared and planted with sugar cane during the 1980s.

LAMBASA

Lambasa is a busy Indian market town which services Vanua Levu's major cane-growing area. It's Fiji's third-largest city with 16,736 (1986) inhabitants and the Northern Division headquarters. Built on a delta where three rivers enter the sea, maritime transport is limited to small boats able to navigate the shallow Lambasa River. Large ships must anchor off Malau, 11 km away. Lambasa's lack of an adequate port has hindered development.

Other than providing a good base from which to explore the surrounding countryside and a place to spend the night, Lambasa has little to interest the average tourist. That's its main attraction: since few visitors come there's adventure in the air, good food, and fun places to drink (for males). It's not beautiful but it is real and the bus ride that brings you here is great.

SIGHTS

There's a library in the **Civic Center** near Lambasa bus station. The **Lambasa Sugar Mill**, opened in 1894 a kilometer east of town, is in operation from May to December. Walk a little farther along the road for a view of **Three Sisters Hill** to the right.

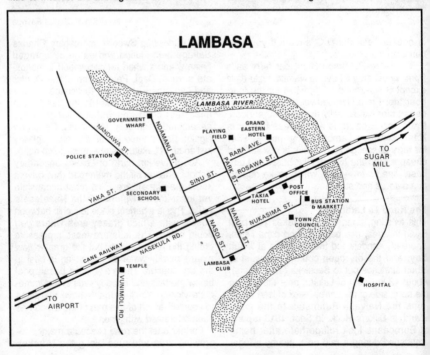

Anyone with an interest in archaeology should take the short ride on the Nakoroutari bus to **Wasavula** on the southern outskirts of Lambasa. Parallel stone platforms bearing large monoliths are found among the coconut trees to the east of the road. This site is not well known, so just take the bus to Wasavula, get off, and ask.

Other easy side trips with frequent bus service include the Fiji Forests plant at **Malau**, where Lambasa's sugar production is loaded, and the **Wainggele hot springs** (no bathing) beyond the airport. If you're a surfer ask about hiring a boat out to the **Great Sea Reef** north of Kia Island 40 km northwest of Lambasa.

Near Lambasa

You can get a view of much of Vanua Levu from atop **Ndelaikoro** (941 meters), 25 km south of Lambasa. There's no public transport, but you might swing a ride by asking the telecommunications engineer in the building behind the Lambasa Post Office if any of his staff is going to the summit to service the equipment. Only a four-wheel drive vehicle can make it to the top.

PRACTICALITIES

Accommodations

The single-story **Grand Eastern Hotel** (Box 641, Lambasa; tel. 81-022) has 25 non-a/c rooms with fans and shared bath at F$11 s, F$16 d.

The **Lambasa Club** has two rooms available at F$6 pp, men only. Also try the **Farmers Club** on the main street, where an a/c room with private bath (but no windows) is F$10 s, F$14 d.

The **Lambasa Guesthouse** (Shiv Narayan Sharma) on Nanuku St. near the center of town is F$6 s, F$12 d.

Riverview Accommodation on Namara St. beyond the police station charges F$10 s, F$15 d for a room with shared bath in a new concrete building.

The **Takia Hotel** (Box 7, Lambasa; tel. 81-655) above the shopping area right in the middle of town has 34 rooms from F$28 s, F$38 d.

Food And Entertainment

Best for the money is the **Wun Wah Cafe** across from the bus station. The **Midtown Cafe** opposite Diamond Theater is also passable. **Singh's Restaurant** is a poor third but the only one likely to be open for dinner.

Naidu's Nite Club and Restaurant near the Grand Eastern Hotel serves a reasonable curry lunch made more appealing by the cold beer; it has music and dancing Fri. and Sat. around 2200. There are three movie houses in Lambasa.

Transport

Air Pacific has service two or three times a day from Lambasa to Suva (F$43). **Sunflower Airlines** flies direct to Nandi (F$62) daily, and to Taveuni (F$31) three times a week. A local bus shuttles between the airport and town.

Patterson Bros. has an office in the arcade beside the Takia Hotel, where you can book your bus/ferry/bus ticket through to Suva (F$22) via Nambouwalu and Natovi.

Rental cars are available from **Paul's Rent-A-Car** (Box 7, Lambasa; tel. 81-655) at the Takia Hotel and **Northern Rentals** (Box 364, Lambasa; tel. 81-973). Few roads on Vanua Levu are paved and obtaining gasoline outside the two main towns is difficult.

There are four regular buses a day to Nambouwalu (F$5) and another four to Savusavu (three hours—F$3). The ride from Nambouwalu to Lambasa is dusty and tiring so if time is short catch a morning flight from Suva to Lambasa and an afternoon bus on to Savusavu, the best part of the trip. Otherwise stay in Savusavu and make Lambasa a day trip. The 0700 Lambasa-Savusavu bus connects with the bus/ferry service to Taveuni, making it possible to go straight through from Lambasa to Taveuni in a day. It's a very beautiful ride over the Waisali saddle between the Korotini and Valili mountains and along the palm-studded coast.

Savusavu is a picturesque small town opposite Nawi Island on Savusavu Bay. This is one of the most scenic spots in Fiji—the view across to the mountains of southwestern Vanua Levu and down the coast towards Nambouwalu is superlatively lovely.

SAVUSAVU

Savusavu is Vanua Levu's main port and cruising yachts often rock at anchor offshore. The surrounding mountains and reefs make Savusavu a well-protected hurricane refuge. In the 1860s Europeans arrived to establish coconut plantations. They mixed with the Fijians and although business went bust in the 1930s, their descendants and Fijian villagers still supply Savusavu's small mill with copra, giving this side of Vanua Levu a pleasant agricultural air. Savusavu is also the administrative center of Thakaundrove Province.

The one main street by the bay consists of a motley collection of Indian and Chinese shops, parked taxis, loitering locals, and the odd tourist. Visit the small **hot springs** boiling out among fractured coral behind Burns Philp. Residents use the springs to cook native vegetables (bathing is not possible). Follow the road six km southwest from Savusavu to Lesiatheva Point. **Nukumbalavu Beach** stretches along the south coast from the point as far east as the airstrip. Just off the point is tiny Naviavia Island, which you can wade to at low tide—a good place to picnic or even camp.

PRACTICALITIES

Accommodations In Savusavu
Savusavu Bay Accommodation (Lal Chand and Suresh Chand, Box 290, Lambasa; tel. 86-100) near the hot springs in Savusavu has four a/c rooms at F$20 s or 'd and seven standard rooms at F$10 s, F$15 d. Cooking facilities are provided and there's a restaurant downstairs. On the roof is a terrace where travelers can wash and dry their clothes or just sit and relax. It's in walking distance from the ferry landing.

David M. Lal's Holiday House (Box 65, Savusavu; tel. 86-150), just up from the hot springs behind Burns Philp, has bed and breakfast for F$10 s, F$15 d (shared bath), and there's a well-equipped kitchen. The place is clean; no alcoholic beverages are allowed on the premises. Ask David if you

may borrow his bicycle.

The **Hot Springs Hotel** (Box 208, Savusavu; tel. 86-111) on the hillside just above downtown Savusavu, is named for the nearby thermal springs and steam vents. The 48 a/c rooms begin at F$66 s, F$78 d. There's no beach nearby. This two-story hotel has had numerous changes of ownership and name during the past few years, which needn't detract from its utility as a convenient, medium-priced choice. Friday and Sat. nights there's live music in the hotel bar.

Accommodations Around Savusavu
The **Na Koro Resort** (Box 12, Savusavu; tel. 86-188) on the peninsula of Savusavu Bay five km from Savusavu town, opened in mid-1987. The 20 thatched cottages with fan are F$168 s, F$188 d and the price includes sailing, windsurfing, snorkeling gear, and other activities. It's affiliated with the Quality Inns chain of Australia. **Pacific Island Divers** at Na Koro offers scuba diving, scuba instruction, and yacht charters with diving.

Lesiatheva Point Beach Apartments (Rhonda and Glenn Mulligan, Box 57, Savusavu; tel. 85-250) on the point five km from Savusavu, has several plain, functional apartments each with one double room and two bunk beds. Cooking facilities are provided, as is free transportation to the shops in town weekdays. Rates are F$32 s, F$40 d, F$50 t. The weekly rate for an entire apartment is F$200 s, F$250 d, F$300 t. There's a discount if you pay in cash within 24 hours of arrival. Ask about camping on a small nearby island. Lesiatheva would make a good base from which to explore the surrounding area while settling in for a restful, inexpensive week.

The most up-market place around Savusavu is **Namale Plantation** (Liz and Curly Carswell, Box 244, Savusavu; tel. 86-117), a working copra plantation 10 km east of Savusavu. The superb food and homey atmosphere amid exotic landscapes and refreshing white beaches make this one of

*Lesiatheva Point
Beach Apartments*

Fiji's most exclusive resorts. The seven thatched *mbures* run F$158 s, F$190 d—meals F$34 pp extra. The mosquito nets over the beds, ceiling fans, and louvered windows give the units a rustic charm. Rental cars are available at Namale. Namale caters only to in-house guests—there's no provision for sightseers who'd like to stop in for lunch.

Kontiki Resorts (Postal Agency, Savusavu; tel. 86-262) on the Hibiscus Highway 15 km east of Savusavu, has 16 thatched bungalows with cooking facilities from F$60 s or d, F$70 t including Continental breakfast. Groceries are available at normal prices in the resort shop. Set in a coconut grove near a sandy beach, Kontiki has many interesting caves, pools, trails, falls, ponds, lakes, and jungles to explore in its vicinity. Scuba diving is available: F$55 for one tank, F$75 for two tanks. The four-day certification course is F$360. A dive site known as "Dream House" is right at their front door. The snorkeling is fine, as well. There's also a swimming pool, 18-hole golf course, a pontoon anchored out on the reef, and many activities. Your host, Robin Mercer, is the author of *A Field Guide to Fiji's Birds.*

Food

Have a meal at the **Pingho Cafe** opposite the market or try the more modern **Wing Yuen Restaurant** farther along. At **Tommy** **Tucker's** behind the market Vuki prepares good local food; her husband Abram is an excellent diver. Drinkers can repair to the **Planters Club** toward the wharf. The weekend dances at the club are local events.

Transport

Fiji Air flies into Savusavu daily from Nausori (F$41), while **Sunflower Airlines** has daily flights to Savusavu from Nandi (F$68) and Taveuni (F$31). The airstrip is beside the main highway, three km east of town. The airport bus is about F$1 or take a taxi for F$2.50.

Northwest Shipping runs the ferries *Princess Ashika* and *Spirit of Free Enterprise* from Suva to Savusavu twice a week, a 12-hour trip. The ferries sometimes call at Levuka and Koro en route. The car ferry *Ovalau* also arrives from Suva weekly.

Numerous taxis congregate at Savusavu market. Four buses a day run from Savusavu to Lambasa (F$3). The 1030 bus from Savusavu to Napuka connects at Mbutha Bay with the daily ferry to Taveuni (F$3), which departs Natuvu around 1300. It's a beautiful trip but can be rough if the wind is up. The five-hour bus/boat connection goes straight through from Savusavu to Taveuni so use a toilet before leaving and bring along a snack.

Emerald Yacht Charters (Private Box, Savusavu) based at Savusavu has four skippered yachts for hire. Due to hazardous reefs in this area bareboat charters are not available. Ask about all-day or sunset cruises on these boats.

ALONG THE HIBISCUS HIGHWAY

This lovely coastal highway runs 77 km east from Savusavu to Natuvu, then up the east side of Vanua Levu to the old Catholic mission station of **Napuka** at the end of the peninsula. Old frame mansions remaining from the heyday of the 19th-century planters can be spotted among the palms. **Mbutha Bay** is a recognized "hurricane hole" where ships can find shelter during storms.

Large red prawns inhabit a saltwater crevice in the center of a tiny limestone island off **Naweni** village between Savusavu and Natuvu. The villagers believe the prawns are the spirit

Urumbuta and call them up by singing,

> *Keitou onggo na marama ni vuna*
> *keitou mai sara Urumbuta*
> *I tumba i tumba e*
> *I tumba i tumba e*

The island is accessible on foot at low tide, but a *sevu sevu* must first be presented to the chief of Naweni for permission to visit (no photos). Local guides must also be compensated. Ask to be shown the weather stone on the beach and, perhaps, a second pool of prawns on the other side of the village.

There are petroglyphs *(vatuvola)* on large stones in a creek near **Ndakunimba** village, 10 km south of Natuvu (no bus service). Look for a second group of rock carvings a couple of hundred meters farther up the slope. The figures resemble some undeciphered ancient script.

OFFSHORE ISLANDS

Kioa

The Taveuni ferry passes between Vanua Levu and Kioa, home of some 300 Polynesians from Vaitupu Island, Tuvalu (the former Ellice Islands). In 1853 Captain Owen of the ship *Packet* obtained Kioa from the Tui Cakau and it has since operated as a coconut plantation. In 1946 it was purchased by the Ellice Islanders who were facing overpopulation on their home island.

The people live at **Salia** on the southeast side of Kioa. The women make baskets for sale to tourists, while the men go out fishing alone in small outrigger canoes. If you visit, try the coconut toddy *(kalevi)* or more potent fermented toddy *(kamangi)*. Kioa and nearby Rambi are the only islands in Fiji where the government allows toddy to be cut.

Rambi

In 1855 a Tongan army conquered Fijian rebels on Rambi at the request of the Tui Cakau on Taveuni. On their departure a few years later this chief sold the island to Europeans to cover outstanding debts. In 1941 the British government purchased Rambi Island from the Australian firm Lever Brothers for 25,000 pounds to serve as a new home for the Micronesian Banabans of Ocean Island (Banaba) in Kiribati, whose home island was being ravaged by phosphate mining. The war began before they could be resettled and it was not until Dec. 1945 that the move was made. Today the Banabans are citizens of Fiji and live among Lever's former coconut plantations at the northwest corner of the island. The Rambi Island Council administers the island.

The island reaches a height of 472 meters and is well wooded. The former Lever headquarters is at Tabwewa, while the airstrip is near Tabiang. Rambi's other two villages are Uma and Mbuakonikai. At Nuku between Uma and Tabwewa is a post office and small guest house. For permission to visit wire the chairman of the Rambi Island Council explaining your interest in the island.

Fiji Air flies direct to Rambi from Nausori (F$66) twice a week. Ask about flights from Savusavu to Rambi. A chartered speedboat from Karoko on Vanua Levu to Tabiang on Rambi costs F$15-20 each way.

The Banabans

The Banaban people on Rambi are from Banaba, a tiny, six-square-km raised atoll 450 km southwest of Tarawa in the Gilbert Islands, since 1979 part of the independent Republic of Kiribati. Like Nauru, Banaba was once rich in phosphates, but from 1900-1980 the deposits were exploited by British interests. Britain declared Banaba part of the Gilbert and Ellice Islands Protectorate in 1900, just after the phosphates were discovered. It's said British protection was more for the phosphates than for the inhabitants.

The phosphate company made an agreement with the guileless Micronesian islanders to exploit the mineral for 999 years, in exchange for 50 pounds sterling a year—it's unlikely the locals back then had any idea what it was all about. They learned fast, however, and in 1909 refused to lease the company any additional land because of the poor terms. The British government arranged a somewhat better deal, but in 1916 changed the protectorate to a colony so the Banabans could not withhold their land again. In 1928 the resident commissioner, Sir Arthur Grimble, signed an order expropriating the rest of the land against the Banabans' wishes.

The islanders continued to receive their tiny royalty right up until WW II. The British evacuated Banaba in early 1942, abandoning the islanders to the tender mercy of the advancing Japanese who occupied the island in Aug. 1942. They deported the starving inhabitants to Nauru, Tarawa, and the Caroline Islands and committed the usual atrocities including mutilations, beheadings, and crucifixions. When peace came, the British decided to resettle all 2,000 surviving Banabans on Rambi Island, which seemed a better place for them than their mined-out homeland.

During the 1960s the Banabans saw the much better deal Nauru was getting from the Australians, and demanded reparations from the British for laying waste to their island. In 1966 Mr. Tebuke Rotan, a Methodist minister and son of the Banaban chief, journeyed to London to press the case. After some 50 visits to the Foreign and Commonwealth offices, he was offered (and rejected) 80,000 pounds sterling compensation. In 1971 the Banabans sued for damages in the British High Court. After lengthy litigation, the British government in 1977 offered the Banabans an *ex gratia* payment of A$10 million, in exchange for a pledge that there would be no further legal action.

At this point the Banabans asked that their island be separated from the rest of Kiribati and joined to Fiji, their present country of citizenship. Gilbertese politicians, anxious to protect their fisheries zone and wary of the dismemberment of the country, lobbied against this, and the British rejected the proposal. Finally, in 1981 the Banabans accepted the A$10 million, plus interest, from the British. The present Kiribati government rejects all further claims from the Banabans, asserting that it's something between them and the British. The Banabans still resent what happened while British are simply trying to forget the whole thing. (For more information on Rambi and the Banabans see *On Fiji Islands* by Ronald Wright.)

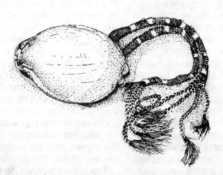

golden cowry pendant: *The golden cowry (Cypraea aurantium), which the Fijians call* mbuli kula, *is one of the rarest of all seashells. On important ceremonial occasions, high chiefs would wear the shell around the neck as a symbol of the highest authority. This example in the Fijian Museum was collected in the mid-19th century by one of the first Methodist missionaries.*

TAVEUNI

This long, green island covered with coconut trees is Fiji's third largest (470 square km). Only eight km across the Somosomo Strait from Vanua Levu's southeast tip, Taveuni is known as the Garden Island of Fiji for the abundance of its flora. Taveuni's surrounding reefs and those off nearby Vanua Levu are one of the world's top dive sites. The strong currents in the strait nurture the corals but can make diving a tricky business for the unprepared. These waters are also famous for deep-sea fishing. Because the Taveuni is free of the mongoose, there are many wild chickens, *kula* parrots, and orange doves making this a special place for birders.

The island's 16-km-long, 1,000-meter-high volcanic spine causes the prevailing tradewinds to dump colossal amounts of rainfall on the island's southeast side and considerable quantities on the northwest side. At 1,241 meters Uluinggalau in southern Taveuni is the second highest peak in Fiji. Des Voeux Peak (1,195 meters) in central Taveuni is the highest point in the country accessible by road. The Euro-

pean discoverer of Fiji, Abel Tasman, sighted this ridge on the night of 5 Feb. 1643. The almost inaccessible southeast coast features plummeting waterfalls, soaring cliffs, and crashing surf. The people live on the island's gently sloping northwest side.

The deep, rich volcanic soil nurtures indigenous floral species such as *Medinilla spectabilis,* which hang in clusters like red sleigh bells, and the rare *tangimauthia (Medinilla waterousei),* a climbing plant with red-and-white flower clusters 30 cm long. *Tangimauthia* grows only around Taveuni's 900-meter-high crater lake and on Vanua Levu. It cannot be transplanted and flowers only in mid-December. The story goes that a young woman was fleeing from her father who wanted to force her to marry a crotchety old man. As she lay crying beside the lake, her tears turned to flowers. Her father took pity on her when he heard this and allowed her to marry her young lover.

Taveuni today is about the most beautiful, scenic, and friendly island in Fiji.

The ruins of the century-old Bilyard Sugar Mill at Salialevu, Taveuni, lie incongruously in the midst of today's coconut plantation. In the early days, planters believed sugar grew best in a wet tropical environment such as that at southeast Taveuni. Sugarfields in the Rewa Valley near Suva fed another mill at Nasusori, which now processes rice. Today all of Fiji's sugar is grown on the sunny, dry, northwest sides of Viti Levu and Vanua Levu, with bustling sugar mills at Lambasa, Rakiraka, Mba, and Lautoka.

Southern Taveuni

The post office, hospital, and government offices are on a hilltop at **Waiyevo** above the Castaway Hotel. Tiny Korolevu Island off Waiyevo is haunted. The 180th degree of longitude passes through a point just south of Waiyevo marked by a signboard. One early Taveuni trader overcame the objections of missionaries to his doing business on Sunday by claiming the international date line ran through his property and if it was Sunday at the front door it was already Monday around back. Similarly, European planters got their native laborers to work seven days a week by having Sunday at one end of the plantation, Monday at the other. An 1879 ordinance ended this by placing all of Fiji west of the date line, so you're no longer able to stand here with one foot in the past and the other in the present. Beyond the date line a couple of condo developments stand out like pimples on the side of Taveuni.

At **Vuna** the lava flows have formed pools beside the ocean which fill up with fresh water at low tide and are used for washing and bathing. Good snorkeling on the reef. Take a bus south to **Navakawau** village at the southeast end of the island. Hike northeast for an hour and a half along a dirt track through the coconut plantations from Navakawau to **Salialevu**, site of the Bilyard Sugar Mill (1874-96), one of Fiji's first. In the 1860s European planters tried growing cotton on Taveuni, turning to sugar when the cotton market collapsed. Later copra was found to be more profitable. Some of Fiji's only Australian magpies (large black-and-white birds) inhabit this plantation. A tall chimney, boilers, and other equipment remain below the school at Salialevu.

From Salialevu, another road climbs over the island to **Ndelaivuna**, a tiring two hours. The bus comes up this road from the northwest coast as far as Ndelaivuna, so you could also start from there and do the above in reverse.

Northern Taveuni

Somosomo is the chiefly village of Thakaundrove and seat of the Tui Cakau: Ratu Sir Penaia Ganilau, the president of Fiji, hails from here. The large hall in the village was erected for a 1986 meeting of the Great Council of Chiefs. Missionary William Cross, one of the creators of today's system of written Fijian, is buried in this village.

Take a bus around the north tip of the island to **Mbouma** to see the famous waterfall (admission F$2 pp). The track to the falls leads along the right bank of the second stream south of Mbouma. The falls plunge 20 meters into a deep pool, where you could swim. The villagers at Mbouma are very friendly. Some of the Mbouma buses go on to **Lavena**, a beautiful area with another waterfall and a sandy beach.

To The Interior

The trail up to lovely **Lake Tangimauthia** high in the mountainous interior, begins behind the Mormon church at Somosomo. The first half is the hardest. You'll need a full day to do a roundtrip and a guide (F$10-20) will be necessary as there are many trails to choose from. You must wade for a half hour through knee-deep mud in the crater to reach the lake's edge. Much of the lake's surface is vegetation covered and the water is only five meters deep.

The adventuresome might try hiking to Lake Tangimauthia from Lavena on the southeast coast, or southwest from Lavena to Salialevu, lesser-known but feasible routes. Intrepid kayakers sometimes paddle the 20 km down the backside of Taveuni past countless cliffs and waterfalls.

An easier climb is up the jeep track from the Marist school one km south of Waiyevo to the telecommunications station on **Des Voeux Peak**. This is an all-day trip with a view of Lake Tangimauthia as a reward (clouds permitting). The less ambitious will settle for the short hike up to the cross above the Marist mission.

PRACTICALITIES

Accommodations And Food

Kaba's Guest House (Box 4, Taveuni) at Somosomo charges F$12 s, F$15 d for a bed in one of three double rooms with shared facilities. You can cook but fruit and vegetables are hard to find. Check in at Kaba's Supermarket across the street. The supermarket also has a huge selection of videos you can rent to play on the guesthouse VCR. You may camp behind the guesthouse and use the facilities for half price.

Camp in **Tom Valentine's Compound** at Mua, two km southwest of Matei airstrip. It's F$3 per tent per night with use of kitchen, toilets, shower, water tank, a clear pool behind the house, spring water, a beach, volleyball court, and good snorkeling on the reef offshore. Fishing trips can be arranged. Tom likes to play cards with you in his house. If you require any information about the area just ask Horace.

Just a kilometer south of the airstrip between Dive Taveuni and Tom Valentine's place is **Beverly Camping Ground**, run by Bill Madden. It's F$4 pp (own tent) or F$5 pp (Bill's tent). Cooking facilities are available in a nearby *mbure* but bring food. Bill can supply fresh fruit and vegetables. It's a clean, quiet place on a great beach with excellent snorkeling.

Maravu Plantation Resort (Postal Agency, Matei, Taveuni; tel. 87-401A) is a village-style resort in a coconut grove a kilometer south of the airport opposite Dive Taveuni. It has eight *mbures* with ceiling fans at F$95 s, F$148 d. The meal plan at the resort restaurant is F$30 pp extra. There's also a bar and swimming pool. Non-guests must make reservations to eat here (the food is good).

Castaway Gardens Taveuni (Box 1, Taveuni; tel. 87-286) three km south of Somosomo has 31 a/c rooms in a main two-story building at F$54 s, F$60 d. This used to be Taveuni's premier hotel but has been neglected. The Castaway offers a restaurant, bar, evening entertainment, excursions, and watersports.

Mr. Seru Ledua puts up visitors in his home for F$10 pp including all meals. For basic accommodations (F$6 pp) at Mbouma village on the east side of the island ask for Mikaele Rusa.

Clusters of small shops sell groceries at Somosomo and Wairiki, a couple of km north and south of Waiyevo respectively.

Scuba Diving

Dive Taveuni (Ric and Do Cammick, Postal Agency, Matei, Taveuni; tel. 87-406M) arranges scuba diving off Taveuni (F$60 for two tanks

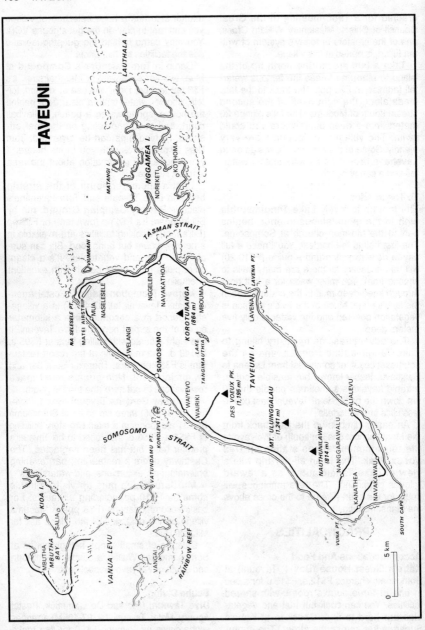

TAVEUNI

LAUTHALA I.

MATANGI I.

NGGAMEA I.

NDREKETI

KOTHOMA

TASMAN STRAIT

NA SELESELE PT.

VUIMBANI I.

MUA

NASELESELE

NGGELENI

NAVAKATHOA

MBOUMA

Matei Airstrip

WELANGI

SOMOSOMO

KOROTURANGA (864 m)

Lake TANGIMAUTHIA

WAIYEVO

WAIRIKI

DES VOEUX PK. (1,195 m)

LAVENA

LAVENA PT.

TAVEUNI I.

SALIALEVU

Korolevu I.

VATUNDAMU PT.

SOMOSOMO STRAIT

MT. ULUINGGALAU (1,241 m)

NAUTHUNILAWE (814 m)

NANGGARAWALU

KANATHEA

NAVAKAWALU

VUNA PT.

SOUTH CAPE

KIOA I.

SALIA

MBUTHA MBUTHA BAY

VANUA LEVU

VANGAI

RAINBOW REEF

0   5 km

including lunch). Ten divers are accommodated in five pleasant *mbures* at Dive Taveuni's premises just southwest of Matei airstrip across from Maravu Plantation Resort. They'll take you to the fabulous 31-km **Rainbow Reef** off the south coast of eastern Vanua Levu, where you'll see turtles, fish, overhangs, crevices, and soft corals all in five to 10 meters of water. Favorite dive sites here include White Sandy Gulley, Jack's Place, Pot Luck, Blue Ribbon Reef, Jerry's Jelly, Coral Garden, and especially the White Wall. The Cammicks pioneered scuba diving in this area.

Getting There

Matei airstrip at the north tip of Taveuni is serviced daily by **Fiji Air** from Nausori (F$56) and **Sunflower Airlines** from Nandi (F$79) and Savusavu (F$31). Sunflower also arrives from Lambasa (F$31) three times a week. Flights out of Taveuni can be heavily booked. You get superb views of Taveuni from the plane; sit on the right side going up, the left side coming back.

A good compromise is to fly direct to Taveuni from Viti Levu and return overland to Suva via Vanua Levu. The ferry to Natuvu on Vanua Levu leaves Waiyevo daily at 0800 (F$3), connecting with a bus to Savusavu on the other side. A ferry direct from Taveuni to Suva operates weekly.

Buses on Taveuni run north to Mbouma and south to Navakawau, leaving Waiyevo at 0900, 1230, and 1700. The service is reliable on Mon., Fri., and Sat., unreliable Tues., Wed., and Thurs., and nonexistent on Sunday. Taxis are available but are somewhat more expensive than elsewhere and may have to be called.

OFFSHORE ISLANDS

Nggamea Island, just three km east of Taveuni, is the 12th largest island in Fiji. It's 10 km long with lots of lovely bays and secluded white sand beaches. Land crabs *(lairo)* are gathered in abundance during their migration to the sea in late Nov. or early December. The birdlife is also rich due to the absence of the mongoose. Outboards from villages on Nggamea land near Navakathoa village on

the northeast side of Taveuni. Best time to try for a ride over (F$3 pp) is Thurs. or Fri. afternoons. Vatusongosongo village on Nggamea is inhabited by descendants of blackbirded Solomon islanders.

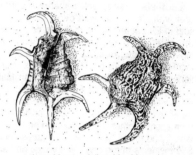

the spider conch (Lambis chiragra)

Turtle Island in the Yasawas, with its luxury resort, was mentioned above. Well, Fiji's other top upmarket hideaway is the **Qamea Beach Club** (Postal Agency, Matei, Taveuni; tel. 87-220) on the west side of Nggamea. Their 10 very pleasant thatched *mbures* with fans and fridges go for F$227 s, F$243 d (no children under 12) and the meal plan is another F$53 pp a day. The boat transfer from Taveuni airport is F$38 pp. Activities such as windsurfing, snorkeling, sailing, outrigger canoeing, hiking, and night fishing are included in the basic price, but scuba diving is F$45 per tank. Some of the best dive sites in the world are close at hand. To prevent Qamea from deteriorating into a scuba camp, half the resort's beds are reserved for nondivers who'll be satisfied with the superb snorkeling right off the beach or who came mainly to relax. Owners Frank and Jo Kloss of Silicon Valley, California, arrived by yacht in 1982 and built the place from scratch with the help of the locals. They call it "island living gone luxurious."

Matangi Island (Box 83, Waiyevo, Taveuni; tel. 87-260) just north of Nggamea is being developed as a scuba base camp. Divers are accommodated in neat thatched *mbures* well spaced among the coconut palms below Matangi's high jungly interior. Dive tours to Matangi are arranged by Aqua-

Trek (110 Sutter St., Suite 608, San Francisco, CA 94104 USA; tel. 415-339-2550) at US$1089 pp a week double occupancy. The price includes meals and five days of diving, but airfare is extra.

Lauthala Island, which shares a barrier reef with Nggamea, was depopulated and sold to Europeans in the mid-19th century by the chief of Taveuni after the inhabitants sided with Tongan chief Enele Ma'afu in a local war. Today it's owned by New York publisher and multimillionaire businessman Malcolm Forbes. In 1972 Forbes bought 12-square-km Lauthala from the Australian company Morris Hedstrom for US$1 million. He then spent another US$5 million on an airstrip, wharf, and roads. The thatched *mbures* of the 350 residents of the one Fijian village on Lauthala were replaced by red-roofed cement-block houses with running water. Forbes's private residence at the top of a hill overlooks the village, the inhabitants of which work for him making copra. Mr. Forbes and his overseer are the only chiefs and anyone who misbehaves is promptly booted off the island.

Now Mr. "Capitalist Tool" Forbes has kindly deigned to share his island with eight tourists who stay in four a/c cottages, each with living room, bar, and kitchen. A private cook prepares guests' meals in their cottages; dinner is served in the plantation house. The price is US$2365 pp plus tax for seven nights (the minimum stay), all meals, "a reasonable supply" of liquor, sports, scuba diving, deep-sea fishing, and the 300-km trip from Nandi in Forbes's private plane included.

THE LAU GROUP

Lau is by far the most remote part of Fiji, its 57 islands scattered over a vast area of ocean between Viti Levu and Tonga. Roughly half of them are inhabited. Though all are relatively small, they vary from volcanic islands, to uplifted atolls, to some combination of the two. Vanua Mbalavu (52 square km) and Lakemba (54 square km) are the largest and most important islands of the group. Tongan influence has always been strong in Lau, and due to Polynesian mixing the people have a somewhat lighter skin color than other Fijians. Historically the chiefs of Lau have always had a political influence on Fiji far out of proportion to their economic or geographical importance.

Once accessible only after a long sea voyage on infrequent copra-collecting ships, four islands in Lau (Lakemba, Vanua Mbalavu, Moala, and Thithia) now have regular air service from Nausori. There are organized accommodations on Lakemba and Vanua Mbalavu; the latter is the more rewarding of the two. Similarly, Moala is a large mountainous island with much to offer, while there is little for the average visitor on Thithia. Both government and private ships circulate through Lau, usually calling at five or six islands on a single trip. To experience what life in the group is really about, try to go at least one way by ship (see "Suva—Transport" for details).

NORTHERN LAU

VANUA MBALAVU

The name means the "long land." The southern portion of this unusual, seahorse-shaped island is mostly volcanic, while the north is uplifted coral. An unspoiled environment of palm-fringed beaches backed by long grassy hillsides and sheer limestone cliffs, this is a wonderful area to explore. There are varied vistas and scenic views on all sides. To the east is a barrier reef enclosing a lagoon 37 by 16 km. The Bay of Islands at the northwest end of Vanua Mbalavu is a recognized hurricane shelter. The villages of Vanua Mbalavu are impeccably clean, the grass cut and manicured. Large mats are made on the island and strips of pandanus can be seen drying before many of the houses.

In 1840 Commodore Wilkes of the U.S. Exploring Expedition named Vanua Mbalavu and its adjacent islands enclosed by the same barrier reef the Exploring Isles. In the days of sail, Lomaloma, the largest settlement, was an important Pacific port. The early trading company Hennings Brothers had its headquarters here. The great Tongan warlord Enele Ma'afu conquered northern Lau from the chiefs of Vanua Levu in 1855 and made Lomaloma the base for his bid to dominate Fiji. A small monument flanked by two cannon on the waterfront near the wharf recalls the event. Fiji's first public botanical garden was laid out here over a century ago

but nothing remains of it. History has passed Lomaloma by. Today it's only a sleepy big village with a hospital and a couple of general stores. Some 400 Tongans live in Sawana, the south portion of Lomaloma village, and many of the houses have the round ends characteristic of Lau.

Sights

Copra is the main export and there's a small coconut oil mill at **Lomaloma**. A road runs inland from Lomaloma up and across the island to **Ndakuilomaloma**. From the small communications station on a grassy hilltop midway, there's an excellent view.

Follow the road south from Lomaloma three km to **Narothivo** village, then continue two km beyond to the narrow passage separating Vanua Mbalavu and Malata islands. At low tide you can easily wade across to **Namalata** village. Alternatively, work your way around to the west side of Vanua Mbalavu where there are isolated tropical beaches. There's good snorkeling in this passage.

There are **hot springs** and **burial caves** among the high limestone outcrops between Narothivo and Namalata, but you'll need a guide to find them. This can be easily arranged at Nakama, the tiny collection of houses closest to the cliffs, upon payment of a F$2 pp fee. Small bats inhabit some of the caves.

Rent a boat (F$15) to take you over to the **Raviravi Lagoon** on Susui Island, the favorite picnic spot near Lomaloma for the locals. The beach and snorkeling are good and there's even a cave if you're interested. **Munia Island** is a privately owned coconut plantation where paying guests are accommodated in two *mbures*.

Events

A most unusual event occurs annually at Masomo Bay, west of **Mavana** village, usually around Christmastime. For a couple of days the Mavana villagers, clad only in skirts of *ndrauninggai* leaves, enter the waters and stir up the muddy bottom by swimming around clutching logs. No one understands exactly why and magic is thought to be involved, but this activity stuns the *yawi* fish which inhabit

VANUA MBALAVU

BAY OF ISLANDS
NAMBAVATU
VUTUNA
AVEA
ANDAVATHI I.
DAKUIRASIA
TOTA
MATAVURA
MASOMO BAY
MAVANA
NDALITHONI
YANUTHALOA
MALAKA
AIRPORT
NARUARUA
MUAMUA
MUALEVU
BOITATHE
VANUA LEVUKANA MBALAVU
URUONE
ISLAND
LOMALOMA
YANUYANU
LAGOON
NAROTHIVO
NAKAMA
NAMALATA
RAVIRAVI LAGOON
MALATA
SUSUI
SUSUI
URONA
MUNIA

0 2 4 km

the bay, rendering them easy prey for the waiting spearmen. Peni, the *mbete* (priest) of Mavana, controls the ritual. No photos are allowed.

Accommodations
Mr. Poasa Delailomaloma and his brother Laveti operate a charming traditional-style resthouse in the middle of Lomaloma village. A bed and all meals is F$12.50 pp. If you'd like to camp ask Alfred Miller, the Fiji Air agent, if he knows of a place. Bread is baked locally.

Getting There
Fiji Air flies in from Nausori (F$75 OW) weekly. The flights are heavily booked so reserve your return journey before leaving Suva. The bus from the airstrip to Lomaloma is 50 cents. After checking in at the airstrip for departure you'll probably have time to scramble up the nearby hill for a good view of the island. Boat service from Suva is only every couple of weeks.

Several carriers a day run from Lomaloma north to Mualevu (40 cents), and some carry on to Mavana (70 cents).

OTHER ISLANDS OF NORTHERN LAU

After setting himself up at Lomaloma on Vanua Mbalavu in 1855 Chief Ma'afu encouraged the establishment of European copra and cotton plantations and several islands are freehold land to this day. **Kanathea**, to the west of Vanua Mbalavu, is owned by the Australian firm, Morris Hedstrom. **Mango Island**, a copra estate formerly owned by English planter Jim Barron, was purchased by the Tokyu Corporation of Japan in 1985 for F$6 million.

In 1983 **Naitamba Island** was purchased from TV star Raymond Burr by the California spiritual group, Johannine Daist Communion (750 Adrian Way, San Rafael, CA 94903 USA), for US$2,100,000. Johannine Daist holds four- to eight-week meditation retreats on Naitamba for long-time members of the Communion. The communion's founder and teacher, Baba Da Free John, the former Franklin Albert Jones who attained enlightenment in Hollywood in 1970, resides on the island.

There's a single Fijian village and a gorgeous white beach on **Yathata Island**. **Kiambu Island** right next to Yathata is owned by Hollywood millionaire Jay Johnson, who runs a retreat there for fellow holders of megabucks. **Vatu Vara** to the south, with its soaring interior plateau, golden beaches, and azure lagoon, is privately owned and unoccupied much of the time. The circular, 314-meter-high central limestone terrace, when viewed from the sea, gave it its other name, Hat Island. There is reputed to be buried treasure on Vatu Vara.

Katafanga to the southeast of Vanua Mbalavu was at one time owned by Harold Gatty, the famous Australian aviator who founded Fiji Airways (later Air Pacific) in 1951.

Weekly Fiji Air flights from Nausori call at **Thithia**, between Northern and Southern Lau. Several Fijian villages are found on Thithia and land is leased to European companies for copra planting. Fiji's only black and white Australian magpies have been introduced to Thithia and Taveuni.

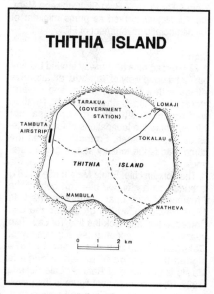

THITHIA ISLAND

TARAKUA (GOVERNMENT STATION)

LOMAJI

TAMBUTA AIRSTRIP

TOKALAU

THITHIA ISLAND

MAMBULA

NATHEVA

0   1   2 km

Wailangi Lala, northernmost of the Lau Group, is a coral atoll bearing a lighthouse which beckons to ships entering Nanuku Passage, the northwest gateway to Fiji.

CENTRAL AND SOUTHERN LAU

LAKEMBA

Lakemba is a rounded, volcanic island reaching 215 meters. The fertile red soils of the rolling interior hills have been planted with pine, but the low coastal plain, with eight villages and all the people, is covered with coconuts. To the east is a wide lagoon enclosed by a barrier reef. In the olden days the population lived on Delai Kendekende, an interior hilltop well suited for defense.

The original capital of Lakemba was Nasanggalau on the north coast. The present inhabitants of Nasanggalau retain strong Tongan influence. When the Nayau clan conquered the island their paramount chief, the *Tui Nayau*, became ruler of all of central and southern Lau from his seat at Tumbou. From 1970 to 1987 Ratu Sir Kamisese Mara, the *Tui Nayau*, served as prime minister of the democratic government of Fiji.

Sights
A 29-km road runs all the way around Lakemba. Get a good view of **Tumbou**, an attractive village with a hospital, wharf, and several stores, from the Catholic church. Tumbou was originally situated at Korovusa just inland, where the foundations of former houses can still be seen. Further inland on the same road is the forestry station and a nursery.

The Tongan chief Enele Ma'afu (died 1881) is buried on a stepped platform behind the Provincial Office near Tumbou's wharf. In 1869 Ma'afu united the group into the Lau Confederation and took the title Tui Lau. Two years later he accepted the supremacy of Cakobau's Kingdom of Fiji and in 1874 signed the cession to Britain. Alongside Ma'afu is the grave of Ratu Sir Lala Sukuna (1888-1958), an important figure in the development of indigenous Fijian self-government.

The first Methodist missionaries to arrive in Fiji landed on the beach just opposite the burial place on 12 Oct. 1835. Here they invented the present system of written Fijian.

Coconut Factory
Four km west of Tumbou is the coir (husk fiber) and coconut oil factory of the **Lakemba Cooperative Assn.** at Wainiyambia. Truckloads of coconuts are brought in and dehusked by hand. The meat is removed and sent to the copra driers. The coconut oil is pressed from the copra and exported in drums. The dry pulp remaining after the extraction is bagged and sold locally as feed for pigs. The husks are flattened and soaked, then fed through machinery which separates the fiber. This is then made into twine, rope, brushes, and door mats, or bundled to be used as mattress fiber. Nothing is wasted. Behind the factory is Wainiyambia Beach, one of the most scenic on Lakemba.

Nasanggalau And Vicinity
The best limestone caves on the island are near the coast on the northwest side of Lakemba, 2.5 km southwest of Nasanggalau. **Oso Nambukete** is the largest; the entrance is behind a raised limestone terrace. You walk through two chambers before reaching a small, circular opening about one meter in diameter which leads into a third. The story goes that women attempting to hide during pregnancy are unable to pass through this opening, thus giving the cave its name, the "Tight Fit to the Pregnant" Cave.

Nearby is a smaller cave, **Nggara Mbulo** (Hidden Cave), which one must crawl into. Warriors used it as a refuge and hiding place in former times. The old village of Nasanggalau was located on top of the high cliffs behind the caves at Ulu-ni-koro. The whole area is owned by the Nautonggumu clan of Nasanggalau, and they will arrange for a guide to show you around for about F$5. Take a flashlight and some newspapers to spread over the openings to protect your clothing.

Each Oct. or Nov. the Nasanggalau people perform a shark-calling ritual. A month before a priest *(mbete)* plants a post with a piece of tapa tied to it in the reef. He then keeps watch to ensure that no one comes near the area while performing a daily kava ceremony. When the appointed day arrives the caller wades out up to his neck and repeats a chant. Not long after a large school of sharks led by a white shark arrives and circles the caller. He led them to shallow water where all but the white shark were formally killed and eaten. This event still takes place today.

East Of Tumbou

Two less impressive caves can be found at Tarakua, southeast of Tumbou. **Nggara-ni-pusi** has a small entrance but opens up once you get inside. **Delaiono Cave** is just below a huge banyan tree; this one is easier to enter and smaller inside.

The best beach near Tumbou is **Nukuselal**, which you can reach by walking east along the coastal road as far as the P.W.D. workshops.

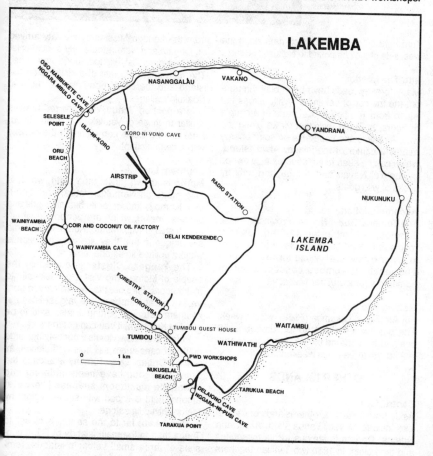

LAKEMBA

The Tumbou Guest House (Lakemba) is typical of the simple yet comfortable accommodations available on the outer islands.

Turn right onto the track which runs along the west side of the compound to Nukuselal Beach.

Into The Interior
Many forestry roads have been built throughout the interior of Lakemba. Walk across the island from Tumbou to Yandrana in a couple of hours, enjoying excellent views along the way. A radio station operates on solar energy near the center of the island. **Aiwa Island**, which can be seen to the southeast, is owned by the Tui Nayau and is inhabited only by flocks of wild goats.

Accommodations
The **Tumbou Guest House** (Provincial Office, Tumbou, Lakemba; tel. 42-090) has four rooms at F$8 pp bed/breakfast, F$4 extra for lunch or dinner. Call ahead for reservations. The locals at Tumbou concoct a potent homebrew (umburu) from cassava.

Getting There
Fiji Air flies to Lakemba (F$68) twice a week. The bus from the airstrip to Tumbou is 50 cents. Buses around the island run four times weekdays, three times weekends.

OTHER ISLANDS

Central Lau
Aside from Lakemba, other islands of Central Lau include Nayau, Vanua Vatu, Aiwa, and Oneata. **Oneata** is famous for its mosquitos and tapa cloth. In 1830 two Tahitian teachers from the London Missionary Society arrived on Oneata and were adopted by a local chief who had previously visited Tonga and Tahiti. The men spent the rest of their lives on the island and there's a monument to them at Ndakuloa village.

In a pool on **Vanua Vatu** are red prawns similar to those of Vatulele and Vanua Levu. Here too the locals can summon the prawns with a certain chant.

Southern Lau
Mothe is known for its tapa cloth, which is also made on Namuka, Vatoa, and Ono-i-Lau. **Komo** is known for its beautiful girls and dances (meke), which are performed whenever a ship arrives. Mothe, Komo, and Olorua are unique in that they are volcanic islands without uplifted limestone terraces.

The **Yangasa Cluster** is owned by the people of Mothe, who visit it occasionally to make copra. Fiji's best tanoa are carved from vesi wood at **Kambara**, the largest island in southern Lau. The surfing is also said to be good at Kambara, if you can get there.

Fulanga is known for its woodcarving; large outrigger canoes are still built on Fulanga, as well as **Ongea**. Over 100 tiny islands in the Fulanga lagoon have been undercut into incredible mushroom shapes. The water around them is tinged with striking colors by the dissolved limestone.

Ono-i-Lau, far to the south, is closer to Tonga than to the main islands of Fiji. It consists of three small volcanic islands, rem-

staghorn fire coral *(Millepora alcicornis)*

acropora

CORALS OF THE PACIFIC

table coral

mushroom coral
(Fungia fungites)

elkhorn fire coral
(Millepora platyphylla)

honeycomb coral *(Favia matthaii)*

brain coral *(Meandrina)*

nants of a single crater, in an oval lagoon. A few tiny coral islets sit on the barrier reef. The people of Ono-i-Lau make the best *mangi mangi* (sennit rope) and *tambu kaisi* mats in the country. Only high chiefs may sit on these mats. Ono-i-Lau formerly had air service from Nausori but this has been suspended.

The Moala Group

Structurally, geographically, and historically, the high volcanic islands of Moala, Totoya, and Matuku have more to do with Viti Levu than with the rest of Lau. In the mid-19th century they were conquered by the Tongan warlord Enele Ma'afu and today they're still administered as part of the Lau Group. All three islands have varied scenery with dark green rainforests above grassy slopes, good anchorage, many villages, and abundant food. Their unexplored nature yet relative proximity to Suva by boat make them an ideal escape for adventurers. No tourist facilities of any kind exist in the Moala Group.

Triangular **Moala** is an intriguing 68-square-km island, the 9th largest in Fiji. Two small crater lakes on the summit of Delai Moala (467 meters) are covered with matted sedges which will support a person's weight. Though the main island is volcanic an extensive system of reefs flanks the shores. Ships call at the small government station of Naroi, also the site of an airstrip which receives weekly Fiji Air flights.

Totoya is a horseshoe-shaped high island enclosing a deep bay on the south. The bay, actually the island's sunken crater, can only be entered through a narrow channel known as The Gullet and the southeast trades send high waves across the reefs at the mouth of the bay making this a dangerous place. Better anchorage is found off the southwest arm of the island. Five Fijian villages are found on Totoya, while neighboring **Matuku** has seven. The anchorage in a submerged crater on the west side of Matuku is one of the best in Fiji.

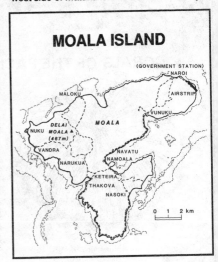

MOALA ISLAND

(GOVERNMENT STATION)
NAROI
MALOKU
AIRSTRIP
VUNUKU
DELAI
MOALA
NUKU MOALA ▲
(467m)
VANDRA
NAVATU
NAMOALA
NARUKUA
KETEIRA
THAKOVA
NASOKI

0   1   2 km

ROTUMA

This isolated, volcanic, six- by 14km island, 500 km north of Viti Levu, is surrounded on all sides by more than 322 km of open sea. There's a saying in Fiji that if you can find Rotuma on a map it's a fairly good map. In the beginning Raho, the Samoan folk hero, dumped two basketloads of earth here to create the twin islands joined by the Motusa Isthmus and installed Sauiftonga as king. Tongans from Niuafo'ou conquered Rotuma in the 17th C. and ruled from Noa'tau until they were overthrown.

The first recorded European visit was by Capt. Edwards of HMS *Pandora* in 1791, while searching for the *Bounty* mutineers. Christianity was introduced in 1842 by Tongan Wesleyan missionaries, followed in 1847 by Marist Roman Catholics. Their followers fought pitched battles in the religious wars of 1871 and 1878, with the Wesleyans emerging victorious. Escaped convicts and beachcombers also flooded in but mostly succeeded in killing each other off. Tiring of strife, the chiefs asked Britain to annex the island in 1881 and it has been part of Fiji ever since.

European planters ran the copra trade from their settlement at Motusa until local cooperatives took over.

Rotuma is run like a colony of Fiji with the administration in the hands of a district officer responsible to the district commissioner at Levuka. Decisions of the appointed Rotuma island council are subject to veto by the national government. The island wasn't directly represented in the old house of representatives, being lumped into the Lau Group constituencies, although it did have an appointed senator. In early 1988 Rotuma attempted to secede from Fiji, citing human rights violations by the military-backed republican regime. The Fijian district officer on the island promptly demonstrated his disgust by blasting the flag of the new Republic of Rotuma with a shotgun. Soon after a "peacekeeping force" of 13 Rotuman soldiers arrived and the protesters were taken to Suva and charged with sedition.

Some 2,800 Rotumans presently inhabit the island, and another 4,600 of their number live in Suva. The light-skinned Polynesian

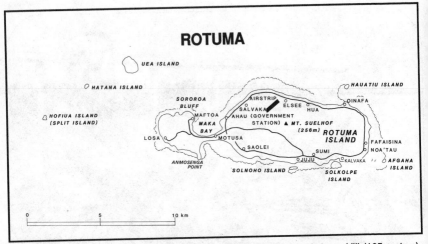

ROTUMA

Rotumans are easily distinguished from Fijians. The climate is damp. Rotuma kava is noted for its strength and the women weave fine white mats. Fiji's best oranges are grown here.

Sights Of Rotuma

Shipping arrives at a wharf on the edge of the reef, connected to Oinafa Point by a 200-meter coral causeway which acts as a break-water. There's a lovely white beach at **Oinafa**. The airstrip is to the west, between Oinafa and Ahau, the government station. At **Noa'tau** southeast of Oinafa is a co-op store; nearby, at **Sililo**, a hill with large stone slabs and old cannon scattered about mark the burial place of the kings of yore. Fine stained-glass windows are in the Catholic church at **Sumi** on the south coast. Inland near the center of the island is Mount Suelhof (256 meters), the highest peak. Climb it for the view.

Maftoa across the Motusa Isthmus has a cave with a freshwater pool. In the graveyard at Maftoa are huge stones brought here long ago. It's said four men could go into a trance and carry the stones with their fingers. **Soro-roa Bluff** (218 meters) above Maftoa should be climbed for the view. Deserted **Vovoe Beach** on the west side of Sororoa is one of the finest in the Pacific. A kilometer south-

west of Sororoa is Solmea Hill (165 meters), with an inactive crater on its north slope. On the coast at the northwest corner of Rotuma is a natural **stone bridge** over the water.

Hatana, a tiny islet off the west end of Rotuma, is said to be the final resting place of Raho, the demigod who created Rotuma. A pair of volcanic rocks before a stone altar surrounded by a coral ring are said to be the King and Queen stones. Today Hatana is a refuge for seabirds. *Hofiua* or Split Island looks like it was cut in two with a knife. A circular boulder bridges the gap.

Getting There

Fiji Air flies to Rotuma from Nausori twice a week (F$133). The monthly government boats (F$45 cabin, F$22 deck) carry mixed cargo out, copra back. Unless you really want to spend a month on Rotuma book your return flight before leaving Suva.

As yet there are no organized accommodations on Rotuma. Many Rotumans live in Suva, however, and if you have a friend he/she may be willing to send word to his/her family to expect you. Ask your Rotuman friend what you could take along as a gift. Tourism is discouraged, so flying to Rotuma without knowing anyone isn't a good idea; if you go by ship you'll probably have made some local friends by the time you get there.

BOOKLIST

GUIDEBOOKS

Bruce, Erroll. *Deep Sea Sailing.* London: Stanley Paul, 1953. The classic text on ocean cruising. Study it beforehand if you're thinking of working as crew on a yacht.

Douglas, Norman and Ngaire. *Fiji Handbook: Business and Travel Guide.* Sydney, Pacific Publications, 1987. Though heavily burdened with rather dry accounts of administrative structures, official statistics, and economic data, this encyclopedic overview does provide useful background reading. If you want a *serious* guide to Fiji, this is it.

Gravelle, Kim. *Fiji Explorer's Handbook.* Suva: Pacific Graphics, 1985. A thorough guide to the roads of Viti Levu and Ovalau with excellent highway maps.

Hatt, John. *The Tropical Traveler.* Pan Books, 1985. Over a thousand tips covering every aspect of tropical travel.

Hinz, Earl R. *Landfalls of Paradise: The Guide to Pacific Islands.* Western Marine Enterprises, 4051 Glencoe Ave., Suite 14, Marina del Rey, CA 90292-5607; $39.95. The only genuine cruising guide to all 32 island groups of Oceania. Beware of *A Cruising Guide to the South Pacific* "by" Terry Harper, which is only a brazen reprint of the D.M.A. *Sailing Directions.* Also avoid *Charlie's Charts of Polynesia.*

Lucas, Allan. *Cruising in Tropical Waters and Coral.* International Marine Publishing, Box 220, Camden, ME 04843. A how-to book for sailors in paradise.

Schutz, Albert J. *Suva: A History and Guide.* Sydney: Pacific Publications, 1978. This slim volume is all you need to *really* get to know the city.

Stanley, David. *South Pacific Handbook.* Chico, CA: Moon Publications. Covers the whole South Pacific in the same manner as the book you're reading. There's also a *Micronesia Handbook.*

Street, Donald. *The Ocean Sailing Yacht.* New York: Norton, 1973. A complete handbook on the operation of a cruising yacht.

DESCRIPTION AND TRAVEL

Siers, James. *Fiji Celebration.* New York: St. Martin's Press, 1985. Primarily a color-photo, coffee table book, Siers also provides a good summary of the history of Fiji.

Stewart, Robert A.C., ed. *Pacific Profiles.* Suva: Extension Services, University of the South Pacific, 1982. A hundred heartwarming tales of island life. Probably no other book will bring you closer to the Pacific peoples than this.

Wibberley, Leonard. *Fiji: Islands of The Dawn.* New York: Ives Washburn, Inc., 1964. A masterful mixture of history and travel.

Wright, Ronald. *On Fiji Islands.* New York: Penguin Books, 1986. Wright relates his travels to Fijian history and tradition in a most pleasing and informative way.

GEOGRAPHY

Derrick, R.A. *The Fiji Islands: Geographical Handbook.* Suva: Government Printing Office, 1965. Along with the 140 maps and diagrams this handbook contains a complete list of all of the islands of Fiji.

Freeman, Otis W., ed. *Geography of the Pacific.* New York: John Wiley, 1951. Although somewhat dated, this book does provide a wealth of background information on the islands.

NATURAL SCIENCE

DeLuca, Charles J., and Diana MacIntyre DeLuca. *Pacific Marine Life: A Survey of Pacific Ocean Invertebrates*. Rutland, VT: Charles E. Tuttle Co., 1976. An informative 82-page pamphlet.

Hargreaves, Bob, and Dorothy Hargreaves. *Tropical Blossoms of the Pacific*. Hargreaves Company, Inc., Box 895, Kailua, HI 96734. A handy 64-page booklet with color photos to assist in identification; a matching volume is titled *Tropical Trees of the Pacific*.

Martini, Frederic. *Exploring Tropical Isles and Seas*. Englewood Cliffs, New Jersey: Prentice-Hall, 1984. A fine introduction to the natural environment of the islands.

Mayr, Ernst. *Birds of the Southwest Pacific*. Rutland, VT: Charles E. Tuttle Co., 1978. Though poor on illustrations, this paperback reprint of the 1945 edition is an essential reference list for birders.

Merrill, Elmer D. *Plant Life of the Pacific World*. Rutland, VT: Charles E. Tuttle Co., 1981. First published in 1945, this handy volume is a useful first reference.

Pratt, Douglas. *A Field Guide to the Birds of Hawaii and the Tropical Pacific*. New Jersey: Princeton University Press, 1986. The best of a poorly covered field.

Tinker, Spencer Wilkie. *Fishes of Hawaii: A Handbook of the Marine Fishes of Hawaii and the Central Pacific Ocean*. Hawaiian Service, Inc., Box 2835, Honolulu, HI 96803; $25. A comprehensive, indexed reference work.

HISTORY

Bellwood, Peter. *Man's Conquest of the Pacific*. New York: Oxford University Press, 1979. One of the most extensive studies of the prehistory of Southeast Asia and Oceania ever published.

Brewster, A.B. *The Hill Tribes of Fiji*. London: Seely, Service & Co., 1922. Reprinted in 1967 by the Johnson Reprint Corp., New York. A record of 40 years' intimate connection with the tribes of the mountainous interior of Fiji with a description of their way of life.

Davis Wallis, Mary. *Five Years Among the Cannibals*. Parnassus Books, 1967. First published in 1851, this book is the account of a New England missionary in Fiji.

Derrick, R.A. *A History of Fiji*. Suva: Government Press, 1950. This classic work by a former director of the Fiji Museum deals with the period up to 1874 only.

Garrett, John. *To Live Among the Stars: Christian Origins in Oceania*. Suva: Institute of Pacific Studies, 1982. The first complete history of Christianity in the Pacific.

Gravelle, Kim. *Fiji's Times: A History of Fiji*. Suva: Fiji Times and Herald, 1979. An anthology of stories from *The Fiji Times*.

Howe, K.R. *Where the Waves Fall*. Honolulu: University of Hawaii Press, 1984. This South Seas history from first settlement to colonial rule maintains a steady and sympathetic focus on the islanders themselves.

Oliver, Douglas L. *The Pacific Islands*. Honolulu: University of Hawaii Press, 1989. A new edition of the classic 1951 study of the history and economies of the entire Pacific area.

Scarr, Deryck. *Fiji: A Short History*. Hawaii: Institute for Polynesian Studies, 1984. An academic look at Fijian history from first settlement to 1982.

PACIFIC ISSUES

Bulletin of Concerned Asian Scholars. 3239 9th St., Boulder, CO 80302-2112, USA. The Volume 19, Number Four, 1987, issue contains several excellent articles on Fiji.

Crocombe, Ron, ed. *Land Tenure in the Pacific*. Suva: Institute of Pacific Studies, 1987. Eighteen specialists contributed to this basic study.

Crocombe, Ron, and Freda Rajotte, eds. *Pacific Tourism As Islanders See It*. Suva: Institute of Pacific Studies, 1980. A collection of 24 essays and studies in which island residents give their impressions of island tourism.

Dean, Eddie, and Stan Ritova. *Rabuka: No Other Way*. Australia: Doubleday, 1988. An "as told to" biography of the self-styled general in which he outlines his motives for overthrowing the elected government of Fiji.

Fairbairn, Te'o I.J. *Island Economies*. Suva: Institute of Pacific Studies, 1985. A comprehensive study of economics and economic policy in the South Pacific written for the layman.

Lal, Brij V., ed. *Politics in Fiji: Studies in Contemporary History*. Hawaii: Institute for Polynesian Studies, 1986. The five essays in this book provide a summary of the political situation in Fiji prior to the emergence of the Labor Party. A more recent Lal book, *Power and Prejudice,* published by the Institute of Pacific Affairs, Wellington, deals with the 1987 military coups.

Norton, Robert. *Race and Politics in Fiji*. New York: St. Martin's Press, 1977.

Robertson, Robert T., and Akosita Tamanisau. *Fiji—Shattered Coups*. Australia: Pluto Press, 1988. The first detailed analysis to emerge from Fiji of events which shook the South Pacific. Robertson, a history lecturer at the University of the South Pacific until expelled by Rabuka, and his wife Tamanisau, a reporter with the *Fiji Sun* until Rabuka closed the paper down, wrote the book secretly in Fiji and smuggled out the manuscript chapter by chapter. A military raid on their Suva home failed to uncover the book in preparation.

Winkler, James E. *Losing Control*. Suva: Lotu Pasifika Productions, 1982. This summary of the impact of transnational corporations affords a surprising revelation of who gains most from current development in the Pacific.

SOCIAL SCIENCE

Bayliss-Smith, Tim, Richard Bedford, Harold Brookfield, and Marc Latham. *Islands, Islanders and the World*. Cambridge: Cambridge University Press, 1988. The colonial and post-colonial experience of Eastern Fiji. Written shortly before the Rabuka coups, the authors freely admit in their introduction that "the reader will seek in vain for any real premonition of this disaster for Fijian democracy, social harmony and economic progress." Like almost all outside observers they failed to recognize the "complex and changing play of contradictions, in which allegiance and rebellion, ethnic confrontation and cordial interdependence, traditionalism and modernity, clan and class, east and west with the nation, all had their parts." This admission adds a second focus of interest to their work.

Belshaw, Cyril S. *Under the Ivi Tree*. Berkeley: University of California Press, 1964. Society and economic growth in rural Fiji.

Bigay, John, Mason Green, Dr. Freda Rajotte, and others. *Beqa: Island of Firewalkers*. Suva: Institute of Pacific Studies, 1981. Focuses on the interaction between the people and their environment, plus the transition from traditional to modern life.

Lifuka, Neli, edited and introduced by Klaus-Friedrich Koch. *Logs in the Current of the Sea: Neli Lifuka's Story of Kioa and the Vaitupu Colonists*. Canberra: Australian National University, 1978. The troubled story of the purchase in 1946 and subsequent settlement of Kioa Island off Vanua Levu by Polynesians from Tuvalu, as told by one of the participants.

Norton, Robert. *Race and Politics in Fiji.* New York: St. Martin's Press, 1977. The impact of race on the political life of Fiji.

Oliver, Douglas L. *Native Cultures of the Pacific Islands.* Honolulu: University of Hawaii Press, 1988. Intended primarily for college-level courses on precontact anthropology, history, economy, and politics of the entire region; an abridged version of Oliver's *Oceania* listed above.
Oceania: The Native Cultures of Australia and the Pacific Islands. Honolulu: University of Hawaii Press, 1988. A massive, two-volume, 1,264-page anthropological survey.

Prasad, Shiu. *Indian Indentured Workers in Fiji.* Suva: South Pacific Social Studies Association, 1974.

Ravavu, Asesela. *The Fijian Way of Life.* Suva: Institute of Pacific Studies, 1983. Contributes to an understanding of the organization of Fijian society and its effects on attitudes and behavior.

Roth, G. Kingsley. *Fijian Way of Life.* 2nd ed. Melbourne: Oxford University Press, 1973. A standard reference on Fijian culture.

Sahlins, Marshall D. *Moala: Culture and Nature on a Fijian Island.* Ann Arbor: University of Michigan Press, 1962. The results of a thorough study carried out in 1954 and 1955.

LANGUAGE AND LITERATURE

Hall, James Norman, and Charles Bernard Nordhoff. *The Bounty Trilogy.* New York: Grosset and Dunlap, 1945. Retells in fictional form the famous mutiny, Bligh's escape to Timor, and the mutineers' fate on Pitcairn.

Kikau, Eci. *The Wisdom of Fiji.* Suva: Institute of Pacific Studies, 1981. This extensive collection of Fijian proverbs opens a window to understanding Fijian society, culture, and philosophy.

Schutz, Albert J. *Say It In Fijian.* Sydney: Pacific Publications, 1979. An entertaining introduction to the language. Another text by Schutz, *The Fijian Language,* is published by the University of Hawaii Press.

Subramani. *South Pacific Literature.* Suva: Institute of Pacific Studies, 1985. The most comprehensive survey of Pacific Islands writers to date.

REFERENCE BOOKS

Carter, John, ed. *Pacific Islands Yearbook.* Sydney: Pacific Publications; US$29.95. Despite the name, a new edition of this authoritative sourcebook has come out about every three years since 1932. The information is heavily slanted toward official bureaucratic structures and overseas trade statistics, but the history sections are quite good.

Dickson, Diane, and Carol Dossor. *World Catalogue of Theses on the Pacific Islands.* Honolulu: University of Hawaii Press, 1970.

Snow, Philip A., ed. *A Bibliography of Fiji, Tonga, and Rotuma.* Coral Gables, FL: University of Miami Press, 1969.

Taylor, Clyde R. *A Pacific Bibliography: Printed Matter Relating to the Native Peoples of Polynesia, Melanesia and Micronesia.* Oxford: Clarendon Press, 1965. Extensive.

PERIODICALS

Commodores' Bulletin. Seven Seas Cruising Assn., Box 1256, Stuart, FL 34995, USA. This monthly bulletin is chock-full of useful information for anyone wishing to tour the South Pacific by sailing boat. All Pacific yachties and friends should be Seven Seas members!

Fiji Voice. Box 106, Roseville, NSW 2069, Australia (US$40 a year to North America). Published by the Fiji Independent News Service, this monthly newsletter is perhaps the best way of keeping up with political developments in Fiji. Also excellent is *Davui* (Box R500, Royal Exchange, NSW 2000, Australia; A$12 a year worldwide), put out by the Movement for Democracy in Fiji.

Islands Business. Box 12718, Suva, Fiji Islands (annual airmailed subscription US$38 to North America, US$50 to Europe, A$32 to Australia, NZ$40 to New Zealand). A monthly news magazine with the emphasis on political, economic, and business trends in the South Pacific.

Journal of Pacific History. Australian National University, GPO Box 4, Canberra, ACT 2601 (twice annual subscription US$30). Since 1966 this publication has provided reliable scholarly information on the area. The volume XXI 3-4 1986 issue includes several scholarly articles on recent events in the South Pacific. Outstanding.

Journal of the Polynesian Society. Department of Anthropology, University of Auckland, Private Bag, Auckland, New Zealand. Established in 1892, this quarterly journal contains a wealth of specialized material on Polynesian culture.

Mana. Box 5083, Raiwaqa, Suva, Fiji Islands. A South Pacific literary journal with poems, short stories, and articles by island writers.

Pacific Islands Monthly. Box 22250, Honolulu, HI 96822 (annual subscription A$24 to Australia, US$45 to North America, and A$63 to Europe). Founded in Sydney by R.W. Robson in 1930, PIM is the granddaddy of regional magazines. Since being absorbed into the media empire of Rupert Murdoch in 1987, however, it has gained in gloss and lost in substance.

Pacific Magazine. Box 25488, Honolulu, HI 96825 (every other month; US$12 annual subscription). This business-oriented magazine keeps you up to date on what's happening in the American territories in the Pacific. An excellent means of keeping in touch with the region.

Pacific News Bulletin. Box A391, Sydney South, NSW 2000, Australia (monthly; A$7.50 a year in Australia, A$13.50 a year elsewhere).

Pacific Perspective. Box 5083, Raiwaqa, Suva, Fiji Islands. Published twice a year, with articles of economic, social, and related fields in the South Pacific.

Pacific Report Box 25, Monaro Cres. P.O., ACT, 2603, Australia. Helen Fraser's fortnightly newsletter providing up-to-the-moment coverage of political and business affairs in the South and Central Pacific region. Airmail subscriptions are A$110 in Australia, A$120 elsewhere for six months.

Pacific Viewpoint. Information and Publications Section, Victoria University of Wellington, Private Bag, Wellington, New Zealand. Twice a year; annual subscription US$24 worldwide. A scholarly journal with in-depth articles on regional social issues.

Tok Blong SPPF. South Pacific Peoples Foundation of Canada, 409-620 View St., Victoria, BC V8W 1J6, Canada ($10 a year). A quarterly of news and views of the Pacific islands.

FREE CATALOGS

Books from the Pacific Islands. The Institute of Pacific Studies, University of the South Pacific, Box 1168, Suva, Fiji. The largest publisher of books by Pacific island writers.

Books, Maps & Prints of Pacific Islands. Colin Hinchcliffe, 12 Queens Staith Mews, York, Y01 1HH, England. An excellent source of antique books, maps, and engravings.

Books & Series in Print. Bishop Museum Press, Box 19000-A, Honolulu, HI 96817-0916 USA. An indexed list of publications on the Pacific available from the Bishop Museum.

Defense Mapping Agency Catalog of Maps, Charts, and Related Products: Part 2—Hydrographic Products, Volume VIII, Oceania.

Defense Mapping Agency Combat Support Center, ATTN: DDCP, Washington, DC 20315-0010 USA. This complete index and order form for nautical charts of Polynesia is the only catalog listed here which is not free (send US$2.50).

Hawaii and Pacific Islands. The Book Bin, 2305 NW Monroe, Corvallis, OR 97330 USA. A complete mail-order catalog of hundreds of rare books on the Pacific. If there's a book about the Pacific you want but can't manage to locate this is the place to try (tel. 503-752-0045).

AN IMPORTANT MESSAGE

Authors, editors, and publishers wishing to see their publications listed here should send review copies to:

David Stanley
722 Wall St.,
Chico, CA 95928, USA

GLOSSARY

Andi—the female equivalent of Ratu

ANZUS Treaty—a mutual-defense pact signed in 1951 between Australia, New Zealand, and the U.S.

archipelago—a group of islands

atoll—a low-lying, ring-shaped coral reef enclosing a lagoon

bareboat charter—chartering a yacht without crew or provisions

barrier reef—a coral reef separated from the adjacent shore by a lagoon

beche-de-mer—sea cucumber, trepang; an edible sea slug;

blackbirder—a European recruiter of island labor in the South Seas during the 19th century

breadfruit—a large round fruit with starchy flesh grown on a tree *(Artocarpus altilis)*

caldera—a wide crater formed through the collapse or explosion of a volcano

cassava—manioc; the starchy edible root of the tapioca plant

ciguatera—a form of fish poisoning caused by microscopic algae

coir—coconut-husk sennit used to make rope, etc.

confirmation—A confirmed reservation exists when a supplier acknowledges, either orally or in writing, that a booking has been accepted.

copra—dried coconut meat used in the manufacture of coconut oil, cosmetics, soap, and margarine

coral—a hard calcareous substance of various shapes comprised of the skeletons of tiny marine animals called polyps

coral bank—a coral formation over 150 meters long

coral head—a coral formation a few meters across

coral patch—a coral formation up to 150 meters long

custom owner—traditional tribal or customary owner based on usage

cyclone—Also known as a hurricane (in the Caribbean) or typhoon (in the Pacific). A tropical storm which rotates around a center of low atmospheric pressure; it becomes a cyclone when its winds reach 64 knots. In the Northern Hemisphere cyclones spin counterclockwise, while south of the equator they move clockwise. The winds of cyclonic storms are deflected toward a low-pressure area at the center, although the "eye" of the cyclone may be calm.

direct flight—a through flight with one or more stops but no change of aircraft, as opposed to a nonstop flight

dugong—a large plant-eating marine mammal; called a manatee in the Caribbean

EEZ—Exclusive Economic Zone; a 200-nautical-mile offshore belt of an island nation or seacoast state which controls the mineral exploitation and fishing rights

FAD—fish aggregation device

filaria—parasitic worms transmitted by biting insects to the blood or tissues of mammals. The obstruction of the lymphatic glands by the worms can cause an enlargement of the legs or other parts, a disease known as elephantiasis.

FIT—foreign independent travel; a customdesigned, prepaid tour composed of many individualized arrangements

fringing reef—a reef along the shore of an island

guano—manure of sea birds, used as a fertilizer

ivi—the Polynesian chestnut tree *(Inocarpus edulis)*

jug—a cross between a ceramic kettle and a pitcher used to heat water for tea or coffee in Australian-style hotels

kai—freshwater mussel

kaisi—a commoner

kava—a Polynesian word for the drink known in the Fijian language as *yanggona*. This traditional beverage is made by squeezing a mixture of the grated root of the pepper shrub *(Piper methysticum)* and cold water through a strainer of hibiscus bark fiber.

kokonda—chopped raw fish and sea urchins with onions and lemon

koro—village

kumala—sweet potato

kumi—stencilled tapa cloth

lagoon—an expanse of water bounded by a reef

lali—hollow log drum

lapita pottery—pottery made by the ancient Polynesians from 1600 to 500 B.C.

leeward—downwind; the shore (or side) sheltered from the wind, as opposed to "windward"

LMS—London Missionary Society, a Protestant group which spread Christianity from Tahiti (1797) across the Pacific

lolo—coconut cream

lovo—an earth oven; *umu*

mana—authority, prestige, virtue, "face," psychic power, a positive force

mangiti—feast

mangrove—a tropical shrub with branches that send down roots forming dense thickets along tidal shores

manioc—cassava, tapioca, a starchy root crop

masi—*see* tapa

masa kesa—freehand painted tapa

mata ni vanua—an orator who speaks for a high chief

matanggali—basic Fijian landowning group

matrilineal—a system of descent through the mother

mbalawa—pandanus, screw pine

mbalolo—a reef worm *(Eunice viridis)*

mbete—a traditional priest

mbilimbili—a bamboo raft

mbilo—a kava cup

Mbose vaka-Turanga—Great Council of Chiefs

Mbose vaka-Yasana—Provincial Council

mbuli—Fijian administrative officer in charge of a *tikina;* subordinate of the *Roko Tui*

Melanesia—the high island groups of the western Pacific (Fiji, New Caledonia, Vanuatu, Solomon Islands, Papua New Guinea)

mbure—a village house

meke—traditional song and dance

Micronesia—chains of high and low islands mostly north of the Equator (Carolines, Gilberts, Marianas, Marshalls)

mynah—an Indian starling-like bird *(Gracula)*

ndalo—see "taro"

Ndengei—the greatest of the pre-Christian Fijian gods

ndrua—an ancient Fijian double canoe

overbooking—the practice of confirming more seats, cabins, or rooms than are actually available to insure against no-shows

Pacific rim—the continental land masses and large countries around the fringe of the Pacific

PADI—Professional Association of Dive Instructors

palusami—a Samoan specialty of young taro leaves wrapped around coconut cream and baked

pandanus—screw pine with slender stem and prop roots. The sword-shaped leaves are used for plaiting mats and hats.

pass—a channel through a barrier reef, usually with an outward flow of water

passage—an inside passage between an island and a barrier reef

patrilineal—a system of descent through the father

pelagic—relating to the open sea, away from land

Polynesia—divided into Western Polynesia (Tonga and Samoa) and Eastern Polynesia (Tahiti-Polynesia, Cook Islands, Hawaii, Easter Island, and New Zealand)

punt—a flat-bottomed boat

rain shadow—the dry side of a mountain sheltered from the windward side *rara*—a grassy village square

Ratu—a title for male Fijian chiefs, prefixed to their names

reef—a coral ridge near the ocean surface

Roko Tui—senior Fijian administrative officer

salusalu—garland, lei

scuba—self-contained underwater breathing apparatus

self-contained—This may mean that a hotel room has cooking facilities or it may simply refer to private facilities (a toilet and shower not shared with other guests); we use the term in the former sense.

sennit—braided coconut-fiber rope

sevu sevu—a presentation of *yanggona*

shareboat charter—a yacht tour for individuals or couples who join a small group on a fixed itinerary

shifting cultivation—a wasteful method of farming involving the rotation of fields instead of crops

shoal—a shallow sand bar or mud bank

shoulder season—a travel period between high/peak and low/off-peak

SPARTECA—South Pacific Regional Trade and Economic Cooperation Agreement; an agreement which allows certain manufactured goods from Pacific countries duty-free entry to Australia and New Zealand

subduction—the action of one tectonic plate wedging under another

subsidence—geological sinking or settling

sulu—a sarong-like wraparound skirt, kilt, or loincloth

takia—a small sailing canoe

tambu—taboo, forbidden, sacred, set apart, a negative force

tambua—a whale's tooth, a ceremonial object

tanoa—a special, wide wooden bowl in which *yanggona* (kava) is mixed; used in ceremonies in Fiji, Tonga, and Samoa

tapa—a cloth made from the pounded bark of the paper mulberry tree (*Broussonetia papyrifera*). It's soaked and beaten with a mallet to flatten and intertwine the fibers then painted with geometric designs; called *masi* in Fijian.

taro—a starchy elephant-eared tuber (*Colocasia esculenta*), a staple food of the Pacific islanders; called ndalo in Fijian

tavioka—tapioca, cassava, manioc, arrowroot

teitei—a garden

tikina—a group of Fijian villages administered by a *mbuli*

TNC—transnational corporation (formerly referred to as a "multinational" corporation)

toddy—The spathe of a coconut tree is bent to a horizontal position and tightly bound before it begins to flower. The end of the spathe is then split and the sap drips down a twig or leaf into a bottle. Fresh or fermented, toddy *(tuba)* makes an excellent drink.

tradewind—a steady wind blowing toward the equator from either northeast or southeast, depending on the season

trench—the section at the bottom of the ocean where one tectonic plate wedges under another

tridacna clam—eaten everywhere in the Pacific, its size varies between 10 cm and one meter

tropical storm—a cyclonic storm with winds of 35 to 64 knots

tsunami—a fast-moving wave caused by an undersea earthquake

tui—king

turanga—chief

turanga-ni-koro—village mayor

umara—see *kumala*

lovo—an underground, earthen oven; After A.D. 500 the Polynesians had lost the art of making pottery, so they were compelled to bake their food rather than boil it.

vakaviti—in the Fijian way

vigia—a mark on a nautical chart indicating a dangerous rock or shoal

volcanic bomb—lumps of lava blown out of a volcano, which take a bomb-like shape as they cool in the air

windward—the point or side from which the wind blows, as opposed to "leeward"

yam—the starchy, tuberous root of a climbing plant

yanggona—see *kava*

zories—rubber shower sandals, thongs, flip-flops

CAPSULE FIJIAN VOCABULARY

Although most people in Fiji speak English fluently, their mother tongue may be Fijian, Hindi, or another Pacific language. Knowledge of a few words of Fijian, especially slang words, will make your stay more exciting and enriching. Fijian has no pure *b, c,* or *d* sounds, as they are known in English. When the first missionaries arrived they invented a system of spelling with one letter for each Fijian sound. To avoid confusion, all Fijian words and place names in this book are rendered phonetically, but the reader should be aware that, locally, "mb" is written "b," "nd" is "d," "ng" is "g," "ngg" is "q," and "th" is "c."

au lako mai Kenada—I come from Canada
au sa lako ki vei?—Where are you going?
au la o—Vanua Levu version of *mbarewa*
au lili—affirmative response to *au la o* (also *la o mai*)
au ni lako mai vei?—Where do you come from?

dua tale—once more
duo oo—said by males when they meet a chief or enter a Fijian *mbure*

e rewa—a positive response to *mbarewa*

io—yes

kambawangga—prostitute
kana—eat
kiavalangi—foreigner
kothei na yathamu?—What's your name?

lailai—small
lako mai eke—come here

levu—big, much
loloma yani—please pass my regards

maleka—delicious
mbarewa—a provocative greeting for the opposite sex
mbula—a Fijian greeting
mothe—goodbye

ndaru lako!—Let's go!
nggara—cave
nice mbola—You're looking good
ni sa mbula—Yello, how are you? (can also say *sa mbula* or *mbula vinaka*; the answer is *an sa mbula vinaka*)
ni sa mothe—good night
ni sa yandra—good morning

phufter—a gay male (a disrespectful term)

rewa sese—an affirmative response to *mbarewa*

senga—no, none

talatala—reverend
tambu rewa—a negative response to *mbarewa*
tilou—excuse me

vaka lailai—a little
vinaka—thank you
vinaka vaka levu—thank you very much
vu—an ancestral spirit

wai—water

yalo vinaka—please
yanggona—kava, grog

CAPSULE HINDI VOCABULARY

accha—good
bhaahut julum—very beautiful (slang)
dhanyabaad—thank you
hum jauo—I go (slang)
jalebi—an Indian sweet
kaise hai?—how are you?
khana—food
kitna?—how much?

namaste—hello, goodbye
pani—water
rait—okay
ram ram—same as *namaste*
roti—a flat Indian bread
seedhe jauo—go straight
thik hai—I'm fine.

CAPSULE HINDI VOCABULARY

INDEX

Numbers in **boldface** indicate the primary reference;
numbers in *italics* indicate information in captions, maps, charts, and photos.

ABOUT THE AUTHOR

During the late '60s David Stanley got involved in Mexican culture by spending a year
in several small towns near Guanajuato. Later
he studied at the universities of Barcelona
(Spain) and Florence (Italy), before settling
down to get an honors degree (with distinc-
tion) in Spanish literature from the University
of Guelph (Canada). Since then he's back-
packed through 123 countries, including a
three-year journey from Tokyo to Kabul. Although Dr. Livingston proved elusive, Stanley
managed to link up with "Gypsy Bill" Dalton in
1977 and together they wrote the first edition
of the *South Pacific Handbook*. Since then
David has mixed island hopping with com-
puter printouts, while Bill settled into the sed-
entary world of publishing. (The name "Moon"
originated on a moonlit Goa beach in 1973,
when Dalton had a vision which inspired him
to become a publisher/author.) Stanley lives
like a hermit crab, shedding one shell for the
next. His only home still fits on his back.

Travel books by David Stanley:

Alaska-Yukon Handbook
Eastern Europe on a Shoestring
Fiji Islands Handbook
Micronesia Handbook
South Pacific Handbook
Tahiti-Polynesia Handbook

YOUR CAT CAN SAVE A DROWNING DOLPHIN WITHOUT EVEN GETTING HER PAWS WET.

Both cats and humans are faced with a choice.

We can keep buying tuna fish and tuna-flavored products.

Or we can save the dolphins.

Hundreds of thousands of dolphins are being intentionally slaughtered by the Pacific tuna fleet. They set their nets on dolphin families to catch tuna swimming below.

Baby dolphins, pregnant dolphins, and mothers nursing their young are most vulnerable. Because dolphins breathe air just like the rest of us.

Trapped in the nets, unable to surface, they drown.

Millions of Americans are joining a national boycott of all canned tuna products.

We'd like your cat to join the boycott, too.

After all, millions of pounds of tuna are sold to cat food makers. And they need to feel the pressure along with the other big canners.

Together, we can force the tuna fleets to change their fishing methods. So they catch as many fish. But stop killing the dolphins.

In fact, you can help us apply all kinds of pressure.

We're working very hard to strengthen the federal law that's supposed to protect the dolphins. This law is now being violated by the tuna fleets.

Videotapes taken undercover and shown on national news confirm that hundreds of thousands of dolphins are being massacred off the Pacific coast.

It's the biggest kill of marine mammals in the world today. And only your cat — and you — can stop it.

Of course, not every cat will *volunteer* to rescue dolphins from drowning.

In that case, just explain that you're the one who buys the food.

And a hundred thousand dead dolphins is too high a price to pay.

Please boycott all brands of tuna cat food.

Robert Mosbacher
Secretary of Commerce
Commerce Building
14th Street NW
Washington, DC 20230

We can't allow the massacre of dolphins to go on. It's time to enforce the federal Marine Mammal Protection Act and bring the dolphin kill down to zero. Future generations won't forgive inaction.

NAME _____

ADDRESS _____

CITY _____ STATE ____ ZIP ____

(we'll forward this portion to Sec. Mosbacher)

I've joined the tuna boycott as of today. Here's my contribution to your fight to rescue the 75,000 to 150,000 dolphins now killed each year. [ ] $10 [ ] $15 [ ] $25 [ ] $50 [ ] $150 [ ] more. Keep me posted.

EARTH ISLAND INSTITUTE
DOLPHIN PROJECT
300 Broadway, Suite 28
San Francisco, CA 94133
ATTN: David Brower
(415) 788-3666

Produced by Public Media Center

Did You Enjoy This Book?

Then you may want to order other MOON PUBLICATIONS guides.

Like the guide you're holding in your hands, you'll find the same high standard of quality in all of our other titles, with informative introductions, up-to-date travel information, clear and concise maps, beautiful illustrations, a comprehensive subject/place-name index, and many other useful features. All Moon Publications guides come in this compact, portable size, with a tough Smyth-sewn binding that'll hold up through years of hard traveling.

The Pacific/Asia Series

FIJI ISLANDS HANDBOOK   by **David Stanley**
Fiji, everyone's favorite South Pacific country, is now easily accessible either as a stopover/or as a whole Pacific experience in itself. This guide covers it all—the amazing variety of land and seascapes, customs and climates, sightseeing attractions, hikes, and beaches, even how to board a copra boat to the outer islands. Packed with practical tips, everything you need to know in one portable volume. 12 color pages, 44 b/w photos, 24 illustrations, 34 maps, 8 charts, Fijian glossary, index.
200 pages.   **$8.95**

SOUTH PACIFIC HANDBOOK   by **David Stanley**
Here is paradise explored, photographed, and mapped—the original comprehensive guide to the history, geography, climate, cultures, and customs of the 16 territories in the South Pacific. A finalist for the prestigious Thomas Cook Travel Guide Award in 1986, no other travel book covers such a phenomenal expanse of the Earth's surface, and no other traveler knows the South Pacific like David Stanley. 20 color pages, 195 b/w photos, 121 illustrations, 35 charts, 138 maps, booklist, glossary, index.
750 pages. **$15.95**

TAHITI-POLYNESIA HANDBOOK   by David Stanley

Legendary Tahiti, isle of love, has long been the vision of "La Nouvelle Cythere," the earthly paradise. All five French Polynesian archipelagoes are covered in this comprehensive new guidebook by Oceania's best-known travel writer. Leap from the lush, jagged peaks of Moorea and Bora Bora to the exotic reefs of Rangiroa and Paul Gauguin's lonely grave on Hiva Oa. Rub elbows with the local elite at the finest French restaurants and save francs by sleeping in a lagoonside tent, then take in the floor show at a luxury resort for the price of a drink. This handy book shows you how to see Polynesia in style for under $50 a day. 12 color and 45 b/w photos, 64 illustrations, 33 maps, 7 charts, booklist, glossary, index.
250 pages. **$9.95**

MICRONESIA HANDBOOK:
Guide to the Caroline, Gilbert, Mariana, and Marshall Islands
by David Stanley

Midway, Wake, Saipan, Tinian, Guam—household words for Americans during WWII, yet the seven North Pacific territories between Hawaii and the Philippines have received little attention since. Enjoy the world's finest scuba diving in Belau, or get lost on the far-flung atolls of the Gilberts. With insight into island culture, leads on the best diving locales and other recreation, and creative accommodation and dining suggestions, *Micronesia Handbook* cuts across the plastic path of packaged tourism and guides you on a real Pacific adventure all your own. 8 color pages, 77 b/w photos, 68 illustrations, 69 maps, 18 tables and charts, index.
300 pages. **$9.95**

INDONESIA HANDBOOK   by Bill Dalton

This one-volume encyclopedia explores island-by-island Indonesia's history and geography, her people, languages, crafts and artforms, her flora and fauna, ancient ruins, dances, and folk theater. It's a gypsy's manual packed with money-saving tips, pointing the way to Indonesia's best-value eating and accommodations, and guiding you through the cities, mountains, beaches, and villages of this sprawling, kaleidoscopic island nation. The *Sunday Times* of London called this "one of the best practical guides ever written about any country." 30 b/w photos, 143 illustrations, 250 maps, 17 charts, booklist, extensive Indonesian vocabulary, index.
1,050 pages. **$17.95**

BALI HANDBOOK   by Bill Dalton

Since the early 20th century, foreigners have been drawn to Bali, an island so lovely that Neh called it "the morning of the world." They're seldom disappointed, for Bali's theater-stage scene its spectacular music and dance, its highly developed handicrafts, its baroque temples, its tro cal climate, glorious beaches, and colorful religious festivals have no equal. This comprehensive, w informed guide has detailed travel information on bargain accommodations, outstanding dining, volca climbing, surfing and diving locales, performing arts, and advice on exploring beyond the crowded sou ern beach resorts.12 color and 29 b/w photos, 68 illustrations, 35 maps, glossary, booklist, index.
428 pages. **$12.95**

HAWAII HANDBOOK by **J.D. Bisignani**

This definitive travelers' resource to the magnificent archipelago takes you beyond the glitz and high-priced hype and leads you to a genuine Hawaiian experience. It offers a comprehensive introduction to the islands' geography, history, and culture, as well as inside tips on the best sights, entertainment, services, food, lodging, and shopping. This is also the guide for the outdoor enthusiast, with extensive listings for land and water sports of every sort. 12 color pages, 318 b/w photos, 132 illustrations, 74 maps, 43 graphs and charts, Hawaiian and pidgin glossaries, appendix, booklist, index. 788 pages. **$15.95**

MAUI HANDBOOK: Including Molokai and Lanai by **J.D. Bisignani**

Maui is one of the most enchanting and popular islands in all of Oceania. Luxuriate on glistening beaches, swim and snorkel in reef-protected waters, dive into the mysteries of a submerged volcanic crater, or challenge the surf at world-famous beaches. Discover unspoiled Molokai, where ethnic Hawaiians still work the land, and sail the "Lahaina Roads" to Lanai for beauty and solitude. Bisignani offers "no fool-'round" advice on these islands' full range of accommodations, eateries, rental cars, shopping, tours, and transport, plus a comprehensive introduction to island ways, geography, and history. 8 color pages, 60 b/w photos, 72 illustrations, 34 maps, 19 charts, booklist, glossary, index. 350 pages. **$10.95**

KAUAI HANDBOOK by **J.D. Bisignani**

From its dazzling chain of uncrowded beaches to its highest peak, Hawaii's "Garden Island" bows to no other for stunning scenery. Kauai is where Hawaiians come when they want to get away from it all. *Kauai Handbook* introduces you to the island's history, culture, and natural features, and takes you into a world away from the hustle and crowds of Waikiki. With up-to-date facts on accommodations, dining, shopping, entertainment, and services, plus detailed coverage of outdoor recreation, *Kauai Handbook* is the perfect antidote to the workaday world. 8 color and 36 b/w photos, 21 maps, 11 tables and charts, 54 illustrations, Hawaiian and pidgin glossaries, booklist, index. 225 pages. **$9.95**

BLUEPRINT FOR PARADISE: How to Live on a Tropic Island
by **Ross Norgrove**

This one-of-a-kind guide has everything you need to know about moving to and living comfortably on a tropical island. Derived from personal experiences, Norgrove concisely explains: choosing an island, designing a house for tropical living, transportation, installing electrical and water systems, adapting to the island lifestyle, successfully facing the elements, and much more. Norgrove also addresses the special concerns of "snowbirds"—those Northerners who escape to an island getaway each year to leave winter far behind. Whether you're an armchair Robinson Crusoe dreaming of faraway beaches, or your gear is packed and you're ready to leave the mainland behind, you'll find *Blueprint for Paradise* as entertaining as it is practical. 8 color pages, 40 b/w photos, 3 maps, 14 charts, appendices, index. 212 pages. **$14.95**

The Americas Series

NEVADA HANDBOOK   by **Deke Castleman**

Nevada—born of Comstock silver, and prospering from casino gold. Fastest-growing and second-most-visited, Nevada is also the wildest state in the Union, indoors and out. You can get married on a whim and divorced in a flash, freely partake of the world's oldest profession, protest nuclear testing and dumping, and turn your hands black feeding one-armed bandits. Basque ranchers and cowboy poets, tuxedoed high-rollers and topless showgirls, nine residents per square mile and 30 million visitors—Nevada has it all, and then some. *Nevada Handbook* puts it all into perspective and makes it manageable and affordable. 34 b/w photos, 43 illustrations, 40 maps, charts, booklist, index. 300 pages.   **$10.95**

NEW MEXICO HANDBOOK   by **Stephen Metzger**

New Mexico is a haunting and magical land of gorgeous mountains, fertile river valleys, broad expanses of high desert, and breathtakingly beautiful skies. This guide takes you from prehistoric Indian ruins to 16th-century Spanish settlements, to ghost towns and 20th-century artists' colonies. Explore the badlands where Billy the Kid roamed, wander through the stark redrock plains of Navajo country, ski the high peaks of the southern Rockies. *New Mexico Handbook* offers a close-up and complete look at every aspect of this wondrous state, including its geology, history, culture, and recreation. 8 color and 85 b/w photos, 63 illustrations, 40 maps, charts, booklist, index. 400 pages.   **$11.95**

ARIZONA TRAVELER'S HANDBOOK   by **Bill Weir**

Arizona, the sunniest state in the Union, is a land of dazzling contrasts, packed with as much history and natural beauty as one state can hold: giant saguaro cactus and shimmering aspen, ancient pueblos and sophisticated cities, the lofty peaks of the San Francisco Range, and of course, the magnificent Grand Canyon. This meticulously researched guide contains a comprehensive introduction, motel, restaurant, and campground listings, trail maps and descriptions, and travel and recreation tips —everything necessary to make Arizona accessible and enjoyable. 8 color pages, 250 b/w photos, 81 illustrations, 53 maps, 4 charts, booklist, index. 448 pages.   **$13.95**

UTAH HANDBOOK by Bill Weir

Three states rolled into one, Utah has the pristine alpine country of the Rockies, the awesome canyons of the Colorado Plateau, and the remote mountains of the Great Basin. Take in cosmopolitan Salt Lake City, ski Utah's "greatest snow on earth," and explore the spectacular rock formations in Zion, Bryce, Capitol Reef, Canyonlands, and Arches national parks. Or choose among the many national monuments and other special areas for outstanding scenery, geology, Indian lore, and pioneer history. Weir gives you all the carefully researched facts and background to make your visit a success. 8 color pages, 102 b/w photos, 61 illustrations, 30 maps, 9 charts, booklist, index. 468 pages. **$11.95**

BRITISH COLUMBIA HANDBOOK by Jane King

British Columbia is snowcapped mountains and shimmering glaciers, dense green forests and abundant wildlife, mirror-perfect lakes and mighty rivers teeming with salmon and trout, thriving cosmopolitan cities and fun-filled resorts. *British Columbia Handbook* introduces you to the province's colorful history, geography, flora and fauna, and more. With an emphasis on outdoor adventures, this guide covers mainland British Columbia, Vancouver Island, the Queen Charlotte Islands, and the Canadian Rockies, and includes attractions, good-value restaurants, entertainment, transportation, and accommodations from tentsites to luxury hotels. 8 color and 56 b/w photos, 45 illustrations, 60 maps, 4 charts, booklist, index. 396 pages. **$11.95**

WASHINGTON HANDBOOK by Dianne J. Boulerice Lyons

Few states are as geographically diverse and rich in recreational opportunities as Washington. Volcanos, deserts, rainforests, islands, glaciers, lakes, rivers, and seashore offer outdoor diversions from mountain climbing to clam digging, cycling to sun worshipping. Seattle and other cities offer such urban delights as award-winning restaurants, world-class shopping, and myriad cultural and historical attractions. *Washington Handbook* covers sights, shopping, services, and transportation, hot spots for hiking, boating, fishing, windsurfing, birdwatching, and other outdoor recreation, and has complete listings for restaurants and accommodations. 8 color and 92 b/w photos, 24 illustrations, 81 maps, charts, booklist, index. 425 pages. **$11.95**

ALASKA-YUKON HANDBOOK by Deke Castleman, Don Pitcher, and David Stanley

Alaska occupies a special place in the geography of the imagination; its mystery and m netism have compelled adventurers northward for over a hundred years. *Alaska-Yuk Handbook* guides you to North America's tallest mountains, wildest rivers, greatest glaci largest wilderness parks, and most abundant wildlife. The authors provide the inside story, v plenty of well-seasoned advice to help you cover more miles on less money, tips on work in Alaska, plus what the Alaskans themselves do for recreation and where they take visitors fun. 8 color pages, 26 b/w photos, 92 illustrations, 90 maps, 6 charts, booklist, glossary, ind 375 pages. **$11.95**

GUIDE TO CATALINA: and California's Channel Islands
by **Chicki Mallan**

Twenty-six miles across the sea from Los Angeles, Santa Catalina Island offers a world of vacation opportunities right in Southern California's back yard. A complete guide to these remarkable islands, from the windy solitude of the Channel Islands National Marine Sanctuary to bustling Avalon, *Guide to Catalina* covers hiking and birdwatching; the best locations for scuba diving and snorkeling, fishing, swimming, and tidepooling; and activities for children. Boaters will especially appreciate the comprehensive listing of marinas and other boating facilities in the area. 8 color pages, 105 b/w photos, 65 illustrations, 40 maps, 32 charts, booklist, index. 262 pages. **$9.95**

GUIDE TO THE YUCATAN PENINSULA: Including Belize
by **Chicki Mallan**

Explore the mysterious ruins of the Maya, plunge into the color and bustle of the village marketplace, relax on unspoiled beaches, or jostle with the jet set in modern Cancun. Mallan has gathered all the information you'll need: accommodations and dining for every budget, detailed transportation tips, plans of archaeological sites, and accurate maps to guide you into every corner of this exotic land. The new section on Belize helps open up this delightful, little-known Caribbean getaway just over the border from Mexico. 8 color pages, 154 b/w photos, 55 illustrations, 57 maps, 70 charts, appendix, booklist, Mayan and Spanish glossaries, index. 400 pages. **$11.95**

The International Series

EGYPT HANDBOOK   by **Kathy Hansen**

Land of ancient civilizations, diverse cultures, and sharp contrasts, Egypt presents a 5,000-year-old challenge to all comers. *Egypt Handbook* leads you through the labyrinth of sprawling Cairo, along the verdant Nile, across the desert, and into the far oases. With a deeper appreciation for Egypt's profound cultural legacy than any other guidebook, *Egypt Handbook* helps the traveler to unravel the complexities of the "Gift of the Nile," from prehistory to the present. An invaluable companion for intelligent travel in Egypt. 8 color and 20 b/w photos, 150 illustrations, over 80 detailed maps and site plans to museums and archaeological sites, Arabic glossary, booklist, index. 500 pages. **$14.95**

IMPORTANT ORDERING INFORMATION

PRICES: All prices are subject to change. We always ship the most current edition. We will let you know if there is a price increase on the book you ordered.

SHIPPING & HANDLING OPTIONS:
1) Domestic UPS or USPS 1st class (allow 10 working days for delivery): $3.00 for the 1st item, 50¢ for each additional item.

Exceptions:
- **Indonesia Handbook** shipping is $4.00 for the 1st item, $1.00 for each additional copy.
- **Moonbelts** are $1.50 for one, 50¢ for each additional belt.
- Add $2.00 for same-day handling.
2) UPS 2nd Day Air or Printed Airmail requires a special quote.
3) International Surface Bookrate (8-12 weeks delivery): $3.00 for the 1st item, $1.00 for each additional item.

FOREIGN ORDERS: All orders which originate outside the U.S.A. **must** be paid for with either an International Money Order or a check in U.S. currency drawn on a major U.S. bank based in the U.S.A.

TELEPHONE ORDERS: We accept Visa or Mastercard payments. **Minimum Order is U.S. $15.00.** Call in your order: (916) 345-5473. 9:00 a.m.—5:00 p.m. Pacific Standard Time.

How did you hear about Moon guides?_____

Are Moon guides available at your local bookstore?_____

If not, please list name of store and we will follow up:_____

_____

_____

ORDER FORM
(See important ordering information on opposite page)

Name: _____ Date: _____
Street: _____
City: _____
State or Country: _____ Zip Code: _____
Daytime Phone: _____

Quantity	Title	Price

Taxable Total	
Sales Tax (6%) for California Residents	
Shipping & Handling	
TOTAL	

Ship to: ❏ address above ❏ other _____

_____

_____

Make checks payable to:
Moon Publications, Inc., 722 Wall Street, Chico, California 95928, USA
We accept Visa and MasterCard
To order: Call in your Visa or MasterCard number, or send a written order with your Visa or
MasterCard number and expiration date clearly written.

Card Number: ❏ Visa ❏ MasterCard
❏❏❏❏ ❏❏❏❏ ❏❏❏❏ ❏❏❏❏

Expiration date: _____

Card Name:
  ❏ same as above ❏ other _____

Signature_____

45-X

THE METRIC SYSTEM

Since this book is used by people from all around the world, the metric system is employed throughout. Here are the equivalents:

1 inch = 2.54 centimeters (cm)
1 foot = .304 meters (m)
1 mile = 1.6093 kilometers (km)
1 km = .6214 miles
1 fathom = 1.8288 m
1 chain = 20.1168 m
1 furlong = 201.168
1 acre = .4047 hectares (ha)
1 sq km = 100 ha
1 sq mile = 59 sq km
1 ounce = 28.35 grams
1 pound = .4536 kilograms (kg)
1 short ton = .90718 metric ton
1 short ton = 2000 pounds
1 long ton = 1.016 metric tons
1 long ton = 2240 pounds
1 metric ton = 1000 kg
1 quart = .94635 liters
1 US gallon = 3.7854 liters
1 Imperial gallon = 4.5459 liters
1 nautical mile = 1.852 km

To avoid confusion, all clock times follow the 24-hour airline timetable system, i.e., 0100 is 1:00 a.m., 1300 is 1:00 p.m., 2330 is 11:30 p.m. From noon to midnight, merely add 12 onto regular time to derive airline time. Islanders operate on "coconut time": the coconut will fall when it's ripe.

To compute Centigrade temperatures, subtract 32 from Fahrenheit and divide by 1.8. To go the otherway, multiply Centigrade by 1.8 and add 32. Unless otherwise indicated, north is at the top of all maps in this book. When using official topographic maps you can determine the scale by taking the representative fraction (RF) and dividing by 100. This will give the number of meters represented by one centimeter. For example, a map with a RF of 1:10,000 would represent 100 m for every cm on the map.

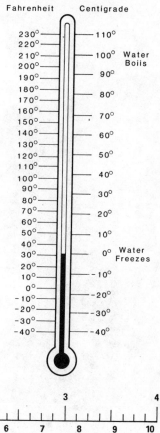